GAYDAR CULTURE

Gaydar Culture
Gay Men, Technology and Embodiment in the Digital Age

SHARIF MOWLABOCUS
University of Sussex, UK

ASHGATE

Published by
Ashgate Publishing Limited
Wey Court East
Union Road
Farnham
Surrey, GU9 7PT
England

Ashgate Publishing Company
Suite 420
101 Cherry Street
Burlington
VT 05401-4405
USA

www.ashgate.com

British Library Cataloguing in Publication Data
Mowlabocus, Sharif.
Gaydar culture : gay men, technology and embodiment in the digital age.
1. Internet and gay men. 2. Gay culture--Great Britain.
3. Gay culture. 4. Digital media--Social aspects--Great Britain. 5. Digital media--Social aspects.
I. Title
303.4'833'086642-dc22

Library of Congress Cataloging-in-Publication Data
Mowlabocus, Sharif.
Gaydar culture : gay men, technology and embodiment in the Digital Age / by Sharif Mowlabocus.
p. cm.
Includes bibliographical references and index.
ISBN 978-0-7546-7535-8 -- ISBN 978-1-4094-1044-7 1. Gay men--Great Britain. 2. Digital media--Great Britain. I. Title.
HQ76.2.G7M69 2010
302.23'108664--dc22

2010016291

ISBN 9780754675358 (hbk)
ISBN 9781409410447 (ebk)

Mixed Sources
Product group from well-managed forests and other controlled sources
www.fsc.org Cert no. SA-COC-1565
© 1996 Forest Stewardship Council
FSC

Printed and bound in Great Britain by
MPG Books Group, UK

Contents

List of Figures and Tables

Figures

Tables

Acknowledgements

There are many of people who, in different ways, have played a role in helping to get this book researched and written. This project started life as a DPhil in media and cultural studies at the University of Sussex and I am grateful to all those in the department of media and film who have leant support to this project, in whatever form that may have been. I was luck enough to study in a department that had a thriving and 'busy' postgraduate community and this had a tremendous impact on both me and my work. Special thanks to my (at one time or another) fellow students David Berry, Martin Dines, Craig Haslop, Melanie Hoyes, Ian Huffer, Steve Jones, Ewan Kirkland, Shamira Meghani, Lucy Robinson and Mike Riley – and to the members of the Sussexualities – all of whom have provided advice, support and suggestions during the course of this project. I would also like to acknowledge the support I received, in the form of funding and other research resources from the University of Sussex, without which I could not have even begun, let alone finished my thesis. My thanks to Sue Thornham for her leadership and for encouraging doctoral students to see themselves as active members of the research community and to Alun Halkins for developing and sustaining a genuine research culture within the Humanities GRC.

Among the many supportive colleagues who have helped me complete this book there are a couple of people who I must identify and thank individually. To my supervisor, colleague, mentor and friend Andy Medhurst, thank you for continually pushing me, for agreeing to supervise a thesis on digital media (despite your ambivalence of all that newfangled technology), and for doing so with compassion, professionalism and genuine intellectual interest. Academics are not paid to deal with hissy-fits and tantrums, but you nevertheless put up with mine … repeatedly. I lose count of the times you have calmed me down, stopped me from doing something rash, and fought the corner of DPhil students in general – and for me in particular. Whatever I have achieved here is in no small way down to your faith in my abilities. Thank you Andy. To Caroline Bassett, thank you for your ongoing support, for making my Viva experience a surprisingly enjoyable one, and for reading through my messy, poorly referenced drafts. The suggestions and advice you've given me over the years regarding this project – and my career – have been indispensible.

I would also like to thank those who have acted as an audience when I have presented elements of this research at conferences, symposia and seminars. I hope I have managed to reflect and incorporate at least some of your feedback here. Thanks in particular to AoIR, MeCCSA and IAMCR for allowing me to present elements of this book at their annual conferences. Thanks to the staff at the Elton

John Unit for inviting me to speak way back when, and for your openness and frankness in discussions.

My gratitude to Neil Jordan at Ashgate, for his initial and ongoing interest in the project and for asking 'how is it going?' and 'are you finished yet?' in ways that didn't fill me with dread and terror. I am also very grateful to the reviewers of my initial proposal, the advice of whom, I have tried to take on board – for the most part.

I am indebted to all the research participants who shared their adventures and stories with me. Your input has been key to the success of this project and I am eternally grateful to you for taking the time to be a part of it. A special thanks to Sam Milford and Real Brighton for advertising the research. I am very grateful to all those who responded to email requests including QSoft Consulting, the Terrence Higgins Trust, George House Trust, Lifeormeth.com and BarebackJack.com and for permission to use images from some of these organisations.

To all the Brighton Boys, past and present, cheers! I miss you a lot and some of you are no longer around, but your thoughts and ideas have been really helpful and I am immensely grateful. Special thanks must go to Mark Daly, my PB, for keeping my spirits up when the going got tough, for the weekly coffees and the drunken nights in bars and clubs that shall remain nameless. I suddenly realised that I've been working on this project for almost as long as you've been in this country – HVDY/I! To my ever-supportive and loving family – Mum, Dad, Minou, Auntie Ying, Uncle Med, Rosie and Feiz – thank you for being you and for allowing me to be me. Mum and Dad, your unwavering belief in me is the best gift a son could ever ask for. I could never have done this without you.

Finally, to my boyfriend Andrew, thank you for going through all of this with me. You've been there for the highs and the lows, and held my paw through it all. I am so grateful for the love and support you've given me, for knowing when to leave me to get on with it, and for knowing when and how to help me get away from it. Thank you.

Sharif Mowlabocus

Chapter 1
Introductions: The Personal, the Political and the Perverse

This book begins with the story of a man who is bored and horny. He comes home after a dissatisfying evening out with some friends, strides purposefully through his loft apartment and sits in front of his computer. A dial-up modem springs to life, with its familiar crackle of white noise and atonal bleeping, and the man clicks on a browser icon before selecting 'Gaymanchestersex' from a drop-down list. Soon he is gazing at the screen in front of him, scrutinising thumbnail images as he scrolls down a webpage. He clicks on the hyperlink for 'Goodfuk'... the screen slowly displays an image of a naked man (head cropped from the photo) as it downloads via the modem. 'Oh yes!' the man purrs to himself, smiling as he gazes at the body appearing on his monitor. He types 'Apartment 16 Mariner's Court' into the chat programme that fills the rest of the screen. 'On my way:-)' comes the reply a few moments later. It is Britain, 1999. The man's name is Stuart, and this is Russell T. Davies' landmark television series, *Queer As Folk*.

I begin with this story for several reasons but not because this story represents some kind of genesis moment for the project that has since become this book. To my mind, no such origin story exists for this research and I am sorry to say that I cannot remember the point at which investigating gay men's digital culture first became a concrete idea for me. Instead, I start with this story because it resonates with my object of study on a number of levels. Firstly, *Queer As Folk* (the original series) is British, and while it speaks to, and holds an appeal for, international audiences, the British-ness of Davies' series cannot be underplayed. In an area of research that often stumbles over concepts such as 'cultural specificity' and 'national identity' (though this has started the change over the last five years) the nationality of this project is similarly important. Much of what I write about in what follows, and many of the conclusions I draw, undoubtedly resonate far beyond the borders of this sceptred isle. The gay male subculture portrayed in the TV series is inflected with international tones (be it the red ribbon of AIDS awareness, the music, the references to international travel and non-British gay male characters), and the case studies that inform this research are similarly coloured with, and shaped by, an increasingly global understanding of gay male subculture. But the roots of each project are bound up with the social, political and cultural history of British gay male subculture. This will become more evident in Chapter 2, when I chart the specific historical context in which gay men in Britain first encountered the Internet.

The second similarity between the TV series and this book lies in their shared recognition of gay male subculture as being something that is both physical and 'virtual'. Furthermore, both projects acknowledge that these two concepts are not discrete but pervade one another, with digital communications often structuring physical practices, identities and experiences. When I began thinking about gay men's digital culture, around 2001, much of the academic discourse on 'cyberculture' or 'new media' posited online worlds as being an escape from, or a response to, offline contexts, problems and obstacles. This is perhaps best exemplified in what Campbell (2004: 10) describes as the 'disembodiment thesis'. Like Campbell, I found myself reading the work of Bruckman (1993), Rheingold (1994), Jones (1995) and Turkle (1995) but struggled to see how their conclusions regarding disembodiment, gender play and virtual life married with what my friends and I were getting up to online – and, just as importantly – offline. I shall return to Campbell's work shortly but I mention it here in order to support my argument that gay men's digital culture has always had an intense relationship with other spheres of gay male life, and that this has often stood in opposition to assumptions and ideas of cyberculture propagated within mainstream academic commentary.

Finally, and leading on from this point, I would argue that both Davies and I see gay male digital culture as being an embodied – and erotic – experience. The image that downloads onto the computer screen in the story above is of the guy who turns up at Stuart's door later in the episode. The image that downloads is a *naked* image of that guy and Stuart's sole purpose for going online is to find someone to have sex with. I am not suggesting that gay men only use digital ICTs for sex, and I am not suggesting that this is Davies' opinion either. But a discourse of sex permeates gay male digital culture and serves to frame our experiences of digital spaces in very particular ways, and with particular consequences. This is a theme I return to in detail later, in Chapter 3 and in many ways this assertion structures much of what is to come.

This book explores gay male digital culture from a British perspective and, in doing so, it offers a series of case studies that highlight how issues of identity, sexual practice, politics, sexual health and space are being addressed, explored and reconfigured via a range of digital platforms, texts and acts. The challenge of investigating gay male digital culture, and its relationship to contemporary British gay male subculture, appears at first sight to be unmanageable. The forms and spaces of this culture, for instance, are too numerous to identify beyond the most cursory of categorisations (lifestyle, pornographic, health, financial, legal, political etc.). Even then, such categorisations become unstable almost immediately as health websites adopt pornographic vernaculars and lifestyle websites include financial information or involve a discussion of economic factors. Alongside this question of how to tackle such an investigation is the question of how to undertake such research within the context of wider material gay male subculture.

My aim is not to provide a taxonomy of gay men's digital culture. Instead, I have chosen to explore specific instances of this digital culture, in order to illustrate what I perceive to be some of the key themes that pervade gay men's digital lives. These themes have only recently received coverage in academic writing on digital culture, and as such, this book seeks to make a critical intervention within this field. When I began researching this area of digital culture there was only a small amount of literature dedicated to this subject. I shall provide a brief overview of some of this shortly, but for now, I turn to one of the first articles that I came across, and which, for many years, has provided the motivation for my research and continuing line of enquiry.

Back in 2000, when digital culture was still in its infancy – a time when bandwidths were narrow and domestic internet connections in the UK were most commonly made through dial-up modems – Schwartz and Southern (2000) published an article in a special edition of the *Journal of Sexual Addiction and Compulsivity*. Their paper discussed the use of computer-mediated communication (CMC) technologies by (amongst others) men who have sex with men. In line with the journal editor's own research, this study suggested a queering of these new forms of communication:

> Cybersex has much in common with the tea-room. Anonymous persons engage in easily accessible ritualized behaviour that leads to impersonal, detached sexual outlet. (128)

Judging by the title of the journal, it is perhaps unsurprising to learn that 'tea-room trade'[1] and cybersex were coded by both the editor and the contributors as deviant behaviour. It is also unsurprising that the link between gay male sexuality and sexual compulsion was re-enforced and maintained throughout the journal. This is, of course, not to suggest that the articles in this special edition were methodologically flawed. Reading the journal, one is left in little doubt that gay men are indeed using the CMC for sexual purposes in disproportionate numbers compared to other social groups.

Yet it must also be recognised that in identifying the gay men of their study as sexually abnormal, studies such as this one continue to measure such abnormality in relation to heteronormative standards. It has been one of the successes of the international gay rights movement to have homosexuality removed from the World Health Organisation's register of mental illness (*Mind*, online)[2] and the journal does not posit homosexual sex, per se, as deviant. However, the removal of homosexual sex from the register has not precipitated a qualitative re-evaluation of homosexuality. It may no longer be acceptable to label homosexuality a

---

1 *Tearoom Trade* is the title of Humphries' (1970) study of male homosexual public sex, a 'tearoom' being a North-American euphemism for a public toilet.

2 It was not until 1992 that the WHO de-classified homosexuality as a mental illness.

perversion, but the practices, cultures and identities that are constructed around same-sex desire continue to be considered contrary to a 'regular' heterosexuality, which itself is regarded as fixed; a central point around which all other sexualities orbit.

To illustrate this point, consider the following incident, which happened in the same year that Schwartz and Southern published their article. A 32-year-old man, let's call him David, a regular on his local gay scene, went out one Friday evening to a club in the gay village. Towards the end of the night, David plucked up the courage to speak to someone (we'll call him Anthony) he'd previously made eye contact with on the dance floor. They began to make small talk. Sadly their night could not continue into the small hours as David had an early start the following morning. It was already late and, contrary to his desires, he could not pursue the evening any further. Not wanting to seem uninterested, he asked for Anthony's phone number, to which Anthony replied with a single word. Seeing the puzzled look on David's face, he added 'its my username, you know, on Gaydar. Look me up and message me if you want to get together'. The next morning, at work, David looked up Anthony's profile. He learned about his likes and dislikes, about what he enjoyed doing, and why he was living in Britain (Anthony was originally from Greece). He then messaged Anthony and suggested they meet up. They dated for six passionate months before Anthony's visa ran out and he returned home.

This anecdote (one of the many I have been lucky enough to collect over the last ten years) exemplifies gay men's investment in digital media technologies, and as such it lends further credence to the claims made by the psychologists mentioned above. But it also reveals the hegemonic processes at work within the conclusions of the cybersex studies and identifies the cultural assumptions inherent in such work. Schwartz and Southern saw gay men's use of the Internet as negative, labelling it anti-social, disruptive to (monogamous) relationships and hindering the user's ability to form new (lasting) relationships. By contrast, David's experience identifies gay men's use of the Internet as positive, helping to bring gay men together, allowing them to negotiate issues of (safer) sex and sexual preferences and providing a space outside of a bar or club in which they can get to know one another better. Lastly, and within the context of this book, perhaps most importantly, these two differing perspectives serve to demonstrate the failure of the psychologists to contemplate the relationship that exists between physical space and digital space. The anecdote, I believe, underscores the importance of examining gay men's digital culture within the wider contexts of contemporary gay male subculture as it is experienced, challenged and conceptualised today.

Addressing such discrepancies between popular understandings of gay male digital culture and (normative) academic discourse on new media is one of the primary incentives for writing this book, and manifests itself as a central tension throughout. Considering the fact that a fair percentage of those writing about the Internet have forged their academic identities in a melting pot of disciplines including cultural studies, media studies, sociology, anthropology, performance studies, cultural geography, history and fine art, it is somewhat surprising to find that the new discipline of 'Internet Studies' (just one of its *nom de plumes*) has often suffered from an impaired awareness of its own cultural position, its own cultural *privilege*. This impairment is now being acknowledged and addressed by some of those working within the field, yet it remains the case that the vast majority of papers, chapters, books and conferences dedicated to digital culture and people's use of CMC lack a sense of self-reflexivity, remaining unaware of the specific cultural position(s) from which they speak.

Negotiating this discrepancy is therefore one of the central motivations behind this book and underpinning the research documented in the following chapters is a desire to marry the abstract with the material: academic discussion with lived reality. This is reflected in the case studies, all of which are rooted within specific social, economic and cultural environments. It is apparent in the second chapter, which spends relatively little time talking about computing and a lot of time talking about the history of British gay male subculture. It also influences the research methodology, which draws from a wide variety of disciplines, employs numerous (and sometimes conflicting) theoretical frameworks, and relies on rigorous academic analysis but not at the expense of personal and cultural experience.

This last point warrants expansion, not least to allay the fears of those who, reading this, are already wondering whether this book is anything more than a series of anecdotes, rumours, stories and gossip. While I consider such informal forms and networks of knowledge as being every bit as important as the critical theory that I employ to discuss and interrogate them, they are by no means the book's methodological mainstay. However, it is necessary to position my own subjectivity within this body of work, not least because it is the other motivation behind my research. Living in what is often referred to as Britain's 'gay capital', Brighton, for over ten years, I experienced first-hand the changes brought about by new forms of communication, especially those that operated via the World Wide Web. Where once cruising for sex in the 'rainbow city' meant standing on a freezing cold seafront for hours, by the 2000s this term had expanded to include sitting at home, logging on to a website, chatting to someone on IRC and then (depending on who was more eager) either jumping on a bus to get to their flat or waiting around for them to turn up at yours. Despite gloomy predictions that the Web would eradicate traditional cruising grounds, the briefest of walks along Hove Lawns or down to Duke's Mound on a summer's evening will illustrate that these are by no means redundant spaces, and have not been vacated by men seeking sex with other men. However, the introduction of firstly domestic and then mobile Internet access, has served to build upon traditional notions of cruising, and similar changes have occurred across gay male subculture as a result of digital ICTs.

Having witnessed these changes first-hand, together with the burgeoning wealth of popular cultural references to gay men's relationship to digital media, I was surprised to find a comparative dearth of academic comment about the intersection between gay/queer culture and cyberspace. The literature that did exist when I began my research bore little relationship to the spaces that my friends and acquaintances, indeed that I, inhabited online. While television series such as *Sex in the City* and *Queer As Folk*[3] referenced gay male web spaces similar to those popular in British gay male subculture, queer studies of the Internet were exploring MUDs, homo-themed chat rooms and queer diasporic websites. None of these studies were wrong, indeed, their findings are useful, not least because they made in-roads into what was a heterosexually dominated discipline. But rarely did any of them discuss 'popular' websites, and rarely did their authors analyse websites that have become a part of British gay culture. Wakeford (1997: 26) commented that 'in recent years the World Wide Web has become the most prominent focus of many cyberqueer activities' yet there remained a disparity between the popularity of the web amongst gay male consumers and academic discussion of the spaces, activities, identities and practices that make it so popular. Furthermore, much of the first-wave of cyberstudies that I came across did not seem to grasp the fact that the web has always been used by gay men as a means by which physical interaction could be sought, negotiated and organised. Gay men's digital spaces have historically provided an environment in which offline intimacies can be facilitated.

The word 'I' runs through this book, since to try and remove myself from this analysis would not only be difficult, it would mar the structure of the research. Without the 'I', without my own subjectivity present in this research, many of the oscillations between opposing ideas, many of the arguments over gay men's use of digital media, and many of the conclusions that I draw from the case studies would not have been possible. When people learn of my research they generally react in one of two ways. They either smirk, 'clarify' my statement for me by saying 'so you're 'researching' gay porn then?' and go on to tell me their own stories of digitally-enhanced love, sex and infidelity, or they ask me the question that I hate answering: 'so is it doing us any good or not?' I hate this question not because I think it is invalid, or too simplistic or flippant. In many ways it is *the* question that studies such as this one seek to explore and, in some small way, answer. No, I abhor this question, not because of its content but because I never have the time to answer it properly.

The context in which the question is proffered is rarely conducive to a response that incorporates feminist psychoanalysis and Foucauldian discourse theory. Or one that utilises Kappeler's work on pornographic representation and Barthes' discussion of photography. My questioner would likely walk away long before I completed the review of existing cyberqueer literature and a contextual discussion of gay male culture, which I would need to give to in order to frame my response. By the time I got to discussing various practices and spaces that exist within gay male digital culture, not only would my unwitting discussant have made his

3 Both series have used gay Internet dating sites as plot devices. In the 'La Doleur Exquise' episode of *Sex and the City*, series 2 for instance, gay talent agent, Stanford Blatch similarly arranges blind dates under the pseudonym 'rick9plus' via an online dating service.

exit, doubtless the majority of people nearby would have also vacated the room. Alongside the 'political' motivation identified above, then, the opportunity to consider the implications of this kind of question before offering some form of reasoned and informed answer forms the personal motivation behind this book, and perhaps also goes some way to explaining my own position in relation to my research.

Mapping the terrain: Writing (on) gay men's digital culture

This book offers a critical discussion of gay men's digital culture and in doing so it builds on, extends and responds to existing work focused at the intersection of sexual dissidence and cyberculture. Writing on gay/queer men's use of new media technologies has grown steadily over the last fifteen years and as early as 1997, Shaw was examining the text-based world of gay Internet Relay Chat (IRC). Even at this point, there was clear evidence that gay men were adept at, and active in using, digital media to search for, chat to, and meet other men. Shaw refers to a 1994 list, published in *Wired* magazine, which lists three gay channels within the top ten most populated chat rooms on *AOL*. He goes on to conclude that:

> For some, IRC is mere entertainment, For others it has been an integral part of their coming-out process and the formulation of a gay identity … Most of the men in the online gay community found IRC through another member and all had introduced at least one other friend to the community. They all want to meet other gay men, and most posit CMC as the only alternative to a gay bar. Thus, for the gay men participating in CMC, the virtual experiences of IRC and real-life experience share a symbiotic relationship; that is, relationships formed within the exterior gay community lead the users to the interior CMC gay community, where they, in turn, develop new relationships which are nurtured and developed outside the bounds of CMC. (143)

Shaw's work on gay CMC is arguably the first to directly focus on gay men's digital culture and in many ways this book can be seen as both an extension of, and a response to, his 1997 article. Perhaps one of the most interesting observations to be made of here is the awareness Shaw demonstrates of the relationship existing between 'offline' gay culture and 'online' gay life. He posits a 'symbiotic' relationship between the physical and virtual and identifies the fact that gay men interact and form relationships across both. In other words, from the very beginning, at least some of the work on gay men's digital culture has recognised the fact that the digital is not separate from other spheres of gay life, but in fact grows out of, while remaining rooted in, local, national and international gay male subculture.

In 1997, the acknowledgement of this slippage between online and offline worlds challenged understandings of digital life and complicated existing debates regarding the relationship between digital and physical communities and spaces. For much of the 1990s such debates privileged definitions of both concepts that were arguably heteronormative, and which drew on understandings formulated around 'mainstream' culture. Many commentators of the period envisaged the migration of traditional forms of community into cyberspace at a time when such forms were said to be being lost through the increasing privatisation of our daily lives. Rheingold (1993: 6) went so far as to suggest that:

> One of the explanations for this phenomenon is the hunger for community that grows in the breasts of people around the world as more and more informal public spaces disappear from our real lives.

Ignoring the Westernised assumption that *all* societies and cultures are suffering the same loss of public space, this statement serves to essentialise the concept of 'community', suggesting that there is a standardised notion of what it is, and that 'we' all seek this same community out; that it is something which 'grows' inside us as a natural state of communion. Later in this book, I directly challenge this assertion and demonstrate how digital technologies provide for acts of queer communion that often respond to 'heteronormative' (Warner, 1991: 3) codes of community and public life. For now I wish to point out the fact that non-heterosexual people rarely experience community as either naturally occurring or something which they are implicitly a part of. A sense of non-belonging and of 'placelessness' (Knopp, 2004) characterises the life narratives (especially the early life narratives) of many queer people. Such non-belonging stems from these same fixed notions of community, which often rely on patterns of heterosexual kinship and family.

Of course Rheingold's early work was regularly criticised for its utopianism by opponents of the term 'online community', and for many the digital worlds being created were poor imitations of 'the real thing'. Interestingly, these criticisms also relied on a rhetoric of essentialism within their argument. For example, Sadar (1995: 788) drew on Lockard's (1995) assertion in claiming that 'cyberspace is to community what Rubber Rita is to woman' owing to the fact that real communities 'are shaped by a sense of belonging to a place, a geographical location, by shared values, by common struggles' (787). Kitchin (1998) similarly questioned the depth, bond and strength of virtual communities, and in doing so implied that community in the real world was experienced in the same way by all. Meanwhile, Jones (1997: 16) raised concerns that interaction was being mistaken for community. In doing so he referred to a similar configuration of place and belonging that Rheingold used:

> … community relies on what I previously referred to as 'inhabitance' as being not just in the same place at the same time in interaction with others but as being a part of that place, as if one is a part of the landscape.

Arguably the kind of 'inhabitance' mentioned here is predicated on the displacement of queer men and women who do not 'fit' in to this landscape. As Hillis (2009: 234) recently commented, queer people are most often seen as existing 'outside' or 'over there' rather than ever fully 'here'. This 'here' is arguably the community alluded to by Jones, Kitchin, Sadar and others, and it is an avowedly heterosexual 'here', which at best, leaves queer people clinging on to the margins of community and at worse, forcefully positions them outside of it and perceives them as a threat to the established order. Campbell (2004: 109) acknowledges heteronormative conceptions of (virtual) community, and brings their contingency to the fore when he writes that 'in addition to communities of affirmation and solidarity, these are communities of self-discovery' and that 'in opening up avenues for erotic exploration, which, in turn, can lead to a significant reconceptualisation of an individual's offline sexual identity, these virtual gay bars become loci for communities of material consequence'. Wilbur (1997: 8) also responds to normative understandings of community when he suggests that 'community has achieved a remarkable flexibility in its career as a political term'.

I do not seek to criticise these earlier works, nor do I question their wholesale validity, but I call attention to them in order to demonstrate how critical commentary on digital media and cyberculture often falls foul of the same cultural blind spots, which, in other spheres of life, render queer people invisible and unrecognised. Shaw draws parallels between online and offline gay cultures, identifying both types as 'word-of-mouth' communities' (ibid: 137). There has been an ongoing debate regarding the validity and use of the term 'gay community' (see Moon, 1995; Peacock *et al*., 2001 and Fraser, 2008), not least because 'gay' is often perceived as failing to adequately represent all LGBT identities, (though often assumed to do so), as well as different racial and ethnic identities (Ridge *et al.* 1999). The term has also been accused of concealing tensions and conflicts that exist between gay men and lesbians (Humphrey, 2000), and hiding practices of exclusion based on class difference (Valocchi, 1999). Inevitably, it also serves to maintain illusory binaries based on sexual difference (Sedgwick, 1991). What concerns us here, however, is the fact that while 'community' is a multifaceted concept, open to contestation, change and re-articulation, only one manifestation of it has been validated through the mainstream discourse on cyberculture. Conversely, such questioning often pervades queer scholarly work. Weeks (1990: 216) for example, identifies the 'virtual' community created by technology in his discussion of Icebreakers, the first les/bi/gay telephone support service to be set up in Britain in 1973. He writes that:

> [w]hat most callers had in common was a sense of isolation – either physical or in their inability to speak of their problems with family or friends. An on-going contact with Icebreakers provided a lifeline out of this loneliness.

This statement contrasts and responds to the heteronormative assumptions identified above and demonstrates how media technologies, long before the advent of the Internet, provided a sense of community that represented the individual's struggles, values *and* interests far more accurately than the physical community in which those individuals lived. That Icebreakers subsequently formed social spaces for gay men and women, and that these events were 'enormously successful' (ibid) highlights the historical relationship between physical and non-physical spaces of interaction and community within gay people's lives. While the original objective of Icebreakers, and other telephone services was to support the 'breakdown of rigid gender division' in order to liberate gay men and women and establish 'a new society' (ibid: 217)[4] their lasting achievement was the constitution and development of 'a gay community growing up within the confines of the dominant culture' (ibid). Thirty years after Icebreakers, Campbell (2004: 101) was to find the web providing a similar sense of community and togetherness.

Wilbur's (1997: 8) discussion of early cyberspaces echoes Weeks' comments above, and provides for a more robust framework through which we can understand communities:

> Community seems to refer primarily to relations of commonality between persons and objects, and only rather imprecisely to the site of such community. What is important is a holding-in-common of qualities, properties, identities or ideas. The roots of community are sunk deep into rather abstract terrain.

Identifying the malleability of the term 'community' is central to any understanding of digital cultures that operate outside of the mainstream. Gross's (2003: 226) discussion of Internet use by young gay men and lesbians emphasises this and argues that gay and lesbian youth are using networked communications in order to bridge the queer diaspora and connect with others. He continues by remarking that:

> It isn't only teenagers for whom the Internet can provide a lifeline and a bridge. Moving beyond the highly developed and fully furnished gay subcultures found in most western and westernized countries, emerging gay communities in many parts of the world have found the Internet a venue for solidarity and support.

Gross's assertion is validated in the work of Tsang (1996), McLelland (2001), Berry *et al.* (2003), Campbell (2004), Nip (2004), O'Riordan (2007) and Gray (2009), to name just a few, all of whom identify digital media technologies (especially the Internet) as providing ways in which both emerging and established communities of LGBT people can connect with one another, for a variety of reasons, and within a variety of contexts.

---

4 A philosophy that echoed the political ambitions of the Gay Liberation Front.

Wakeford (2001: 410) asserts that the term cyberqueer, 'an uneasy amalgam of two words … each of which has already been overloaded with the definitions it has been required to contain', is important because it demands that sexuality – all sexuality – becomes an integral concern within the mapping and discussion of those spaces created by new media technologies. She defines 'cyberqueer' as 'an act of resistance' to discourses that focus on the *form* of cyberspace at the expense of the methods of *representation* that operate within it and states that 'cyberspace is a multifaceted, multilayered, and very segmented place' and that 'this is as true for queer spaces as for electronic online places which are not primarily defined as queer' (ibid: 405).

It is here that we begin to see the parallels between cyberspace and les/bi/gay/queer space emerging. The latter are often conceptualised as unstable and contested sites of power in much the same way as cyberspaces are. Wakeford's comment that cyberspace possesses a 'multifaceted, multilayered' nature, could just as easily be applied to discussions of gay pride marches, lesbian social spaces, bars, nightclubs, health centres, or cruising grounds. All of these sites represent and articulate multiple relations of power, relations that serve to constitute space as subjectively experienced and never fixed or natural. Wakeford's assertion echoes Dishman's (1995: 3) argument that, just as queer space is a visible space within real life, so queer space in cyberspace is real. Dishman sees similarities between these two spaces, and these similarities spring from a shared understanding of queer peoples' relationship to spaces:

> For many queers, just as with the child's fixation on the body in space, there is comfort derived from being near 'family'. At the same time that we are repulsed by the non-queer communities, we are attracted to and by the existing queer community. We are drawn closer to spaces where queers are known to safely and comfortably congregate.

Queer space, for Dishman, offers safety, care and validation to individuals who are elsewhere 'cut adrift for most of the time in a world drenched in straightness' (Dyer, 1992: 135). Unlike heteronormative configurations, queer articulations of community are flexible, transient and in some sense always virtual. They also highlight the unstable and shifting nature of all space, including that occupied by community.

Gross's reference above to queer Internet use in non-Western contexts also finds relevance within much scholarly work on 'cyberqueer' culture and particular attention has been paid to the Internet use of LGBTQ people in cultures and contexts that are non-Western, 'diasporic' or do not have 'established' and politically visible queer communities. For example, while arguing that 'the electronic environment does not screen out racist sentiments', Tsang (1996: 312) does identify an opening up of spaces for racially and sexually dissident individuals and communities. His discussion of Bulletin Board (BBS) usage by queer men of East-Asian heritage suggests that text-based representations of the self allow cultural specificities to come to the fore, bypassing the essentialising category of 'Asian-American' and providing users with a greater sense of cultural identity.

Outside of the USA, McLelland (2001) has identified the growing importance of the Internet within Japanese gay men's lives. McLelland acknowledges the difficult cultural choice that these men face, namely the choice between adopting a visibly 'out' Western gay identity and adhering to Japanese cultural norms of uniformity and non-confrontation. He also identifies the high cost of living in urban Japan citing this as a reason why many men in their twenties and even thirties continue to live at home. With these cultural and economic contexts in mind, McLelland argues that the Internet provides a safer and more private method of communicating with other men than other mediums:

> Given the difficulties of even holding a telephone conversation in one's own home, it is easy to appreciate the advantages that the Internet has brought to gay men who want to keep in regular contact with their friends as well as make contact with sexual partners. (210)

Other studies, such as Berry and Martin's (2003) discussion of Taiwanese and Korean Net use, have explored tensions and connections between 'local' and 'global' (often meaning Western) digital spaces and the configurations of queer sexual identity that are embedded within them. Meanwhile, Kuntsman's (2007) analysis of 'flaming' as a performative practice within the LGBTQ Russian migrant community of Israel demonstrates how notions of community, inclusion and identity can be articulated in ways that, at first sight, appear hostile, violent and anti-communitarian (and counter to the normative concept of community identified above). The study of queer cyberculture has included work as wide-ranging as blogging within the Indian diaspora (Mitra and Gajjala, 2008), the use of the Internet within Singaporean queer activism (Offord, 2003), the performance of 'sissyness' within Taiwanese cyberspaces (Lin, 2006) and the relationship between offline and online queer communities in Hong Kong (Nip, 2004) (to name just a few examples). Throughout much of this work, the relationships between the centre and margin, the individual and society and the local and global and have been exposed and interrogated as a means of understanding and elaborating upon the complex and often tense relationships that exist between physical and digital queer life. Where mainstream Internet scholarship began with the binary offline/online, work on queer cyberculture has, it seems, always been invested in dismantling such a binary, in seeing the porosity of such boundaries and the slippage between such worlds.

Of course while much attention has been paid to exploring how non-Western LGBTQ people are using the Internet, there has also been a growing amount of literature published regarding 'homonormative' (Duggan, 2003) digital spaces, technologies and practices. Indeed, many of the studies mentioned above tacitly critique such homonormativity by focusing on contexts that either seek to escape the dominant Western conception of 'gayness', or are actively marginalised on account of race, gender performance, class, body shape or cultural heritage. Woodland (2001) for example, identifies the tendency towards Western ideals of gayness within many gay male cyberspaces in his discussion of ModemBoy, a text-based cyberspace modelled on an American high school. He suggests that while the 'textual play' found in this space 'allows for an appropriation and redemption of negative high school experiences' (418) the use of 'images common in gay male subculture … potentially disenfranchises more diverse expressions of queer identity (419–420). ModemBoy thus offers a digital articulation of what Sinfield (1998: 6) terms 'metropolitan' gay male culture and in doing so, ascribes to the same sub-cultural hierarchies, taste preferences and practices of exclusion as can be found within urban gay male culture in the West today. I shall return to Sinfield's term in the following chapter as it provides a useful framework for understanding the digital spaces I encounter elsewhere in this book.

The 'digitalisation' of Western gay male subculture (by which I mean the embedding of digital practices, technologies and spaces within that subculture), has been most extensively discussed by Campbell (2004). In *Getting it On Online*, the author examines what are primarily text-based virtual environments dedicated to gay men and to date, this has been the largest and most in-depth discussion of Western gay male digital culture. Campbell's central assertion is that, unlike the 'disembodiment thesis' (5) of much cyberculture work, gay male culture relies on the body of the user as a point of reference within its digital interactions and virtual spaces. In this respect he follows in the same footsteps as Shaw, challenging dominant understandings of digital life and arguing for cultural specificity when examining digital forms. However, Campbell goes further than Shaw and explores how and why the gay body is (re)produced in digital contexts suggesting that cyberspace offers 'not only an affirming space for erotic exploration but also an alternative means for speaking of the body' (17).

While unwilling to subscribe to utopian rhetoric that posits cyberspace as liberating the body, the author does see scope for the formation of new and alternative discourses of embodiment and beauty in online interactions. His study of gay male IRC focuses on three specific channels, #gaymuscle, #gaymusclebears and #gaychub, all of which support the (re)validation of body types that might otherwise be considered as 'failing' according to homonormative regimes of beauty. For example, in both #gaymuscle and #gaychub, the author identifies the promotion of 'big' or 'huge' bodies, where muscle 'freaks' and fat 'gainers' find appreciative audiences, support, advice and a sense of camaraderie. In both of these channels the legitimacy of these bodies is restored, countering, Campbell argues, 'the idealised image of the erotic male body' (161) found within gay male subculture, together with the hierarchies of beauty that often devalue these 'freakish' bodies. Reflecting upon his three case studies, the author suggests that:

> Far from being a means of escaping the body, online interaction constitutes a mode of rearticulating our relationship to the physical body and, at least for these interactants, resisting dominant models of beauty and the erotic. (191)

Campbell does temper this assertion by acknowledging the formation of new regimes of beauty, 'a proliferation of competing beauty myths' (157) within these channels, and he is also quick to note that issues of masculinity, gender performance and race are also far from absent in these spaces, and treated in highly judgemental ways:

> Far from being spaces of experimentation, exploration, and play in regard to gender, these online collectives maintain many of the dominant and oppressive notions of how individuals should act based on their biological sex. (68)

However, while acknowledging the problematic way in which gender performances are policed in these online environments, Campbell ultimately celebrates the freedom that he sees gay IRC providing its users, and positions this freedom as an *a priori* political endeavour when occurring in contexts and against backdrops that privilege heterosexuality and discriminate against queer identities.

Campbell's work makes an important intervention into the study of gay male digital culture and I refer to it regularly throughout this book. It would be a misnomer to see his discussion of IRC as being 'historical' and therefore irrelevant to contemporary digital life. The fetishistic manner in which many studies (and scholars) of digital media celebrate new technologies largely based on their 'newness' serves to obfuscate the fact that such artefacts have material histories, lineages, forebears and politics. Campbell acknowledges this fact in his reference to Winner's (1986) work and I would argue that for many scholars of digital culture who write from, about or to marginalised constituencies, identifying the political contexts in which the 'technological' takes place has been both a key concern and a motivating force.

Campbell's work, which draws on the fields of gender studies, cultural studies, sociology and anthropology, remains culturally relevant and many of the findings contained within this book echo those identified in *Getting It On Online*. My discussion of Gaydar, for example, similarly finds regimes of beauty being established online. While Gaydar operates according to a far more homonormative definition of male beauty than those found in the channels discussed by Campbell, both contexts draw upon historical understandings of the gay male body and perpetuate certain ideals regarding that body.

Likewise, the policing of masculinity and of gender performance found in #gaymuscle is also apparent in the cybercottage, the user profile and the bareback web forums – all spaces that get discussed in the following chapters. Such performances take different forms and are more or less explicitly policed depending on context, but they are nevertheless apparent. Both of these findings, which this book shares in common with Campbell's work, also support the notion that the physical and digital spheres of gay men's lives are far from discrete and in fact permeate one another. Campbell argues against using terms such 'online' and 'real life' or 'RL' and while I do use the terms 'online' and 'offline' to demarcate digital and non-digital environments, I agree with Campbell's criticism that such demarcations can run the risk of suggesting that digital life is 'less real of meaningful than experiences offline' (20).

One of the central arguments that I make in this book is that gay male subculture (offline) and gay men's digital culture (online) are part and parcel of the same thing. While a bar or a club might be considered a physical gay space and a website a digital one, such boundaries are at best, difficult to maintain, and at worse, fabrications that conceal the truth of gay male subculture; that it is now *both* digitally and physically manifested, and that these multiple manifestations occur simultaneously and shape one another continuously. I explore this in more detail in Chapter 7, when I investigate new trends in cruising practice. I mention it here, however, firstly to identify another intellectual connection between Campbell's work and my own, and secondly to demonstrate that, while I feel that both of us argue the same point, we do so from slightly different positions.

I would suggest that Campbell is concerned that we do not see IRC as being separate from the physical world that its users inhabit because such a perspective could in fact be maintained quite easily. This is due to the location of users, dispersed as they are across the United States (and further afield) and the lack of interaction that appears to take place between users, in physical contexts. Campbell acknowledges the fact that users do use IRC to arrange meetings (whether that be for friendship, working out, sex or a combination of these). However, much of the book focuses on interactions that both take place online and which *revolve* around online life. This is perhaps best illustrated in Campbell's notion of IRC being a 'virtual gay bar' (57). I understand how and why he invokes the gay bar as a means of describing the channels under investigation. At relevant points in the ensuing chapters I also allude to physical spaces, though the implied meaning behind my use is, I feel, markedly different.

For, unlike IRC, the digital spaces I am interested in here are either 'embedded' in physical spaces (as in the case of the cybercottage and of digital cruising), have a specific relationship to physical spaces (such as the bars, clubs and events promoted under the Gaydar brand) or otherwise suggest that physical interaction between users is the primary motivation behind the space (as in the case of the barebacking websites). Additionally, many of the spaces that I discuss may in fact be accessed by users while in the 'physical' space of a gay bar or club. Hence Grindr (an Internet application for mobile phones) may well be accessed by a man while in a bar, in order to assess the compatibility of other gay men nearby. Indeed, as revealed by David's story at the beginning of this chapter, the digital permeates the physical even when no Internet connection is present.

Leading on from this, there are other important points of difference between Campbell's work and this book, which should be acknowledged in order to better understand how and why some themes pervade otherwise divergent digital forms and others appear to be more specifically located. Alongside the issue of slippage between physical and digital, there is the issue of visual culture. Campbell makes specific reference to several images he obtains via IRC, but acknowledges that such images are relatively rare on the channels under investigation. By contrast, even where the primary mode of interaction is textual, all of the case studies in this book rely on digital images to maintain and bolster communication. Such an (over)investment in the visual may lead us to assume that the kind of online deception Campbell reports[5] is now a thing of the past. As I demonstrate, however, even in spaces that privilege the visual, anxieties regarding the authenticity and validity of users – and their intentions – persist.

There is also the issue of who 'owns' the space and for what purpose. Campbell's work focuses on spaces that are 'neither maintained nor moderated by private companies' and, in line with many studies of IRC around this time, he identifies the 'communal effort' involved in maintaining the channel and the fact that they are often 'moderated by a group of interactants who volunteer their time to do so' (57). By comparison, the websites and other digital spaces under investigation here are owned by private companies, some of which are very large, and all of which are driven by profit motives. Gaydar has a multimillion-pound turnover and BarebackJack.com is supported through the sale of pornographic video. The cybercottage of Chapter 5 may well be free to access and cost its users nothing, but the hosting company gains revenue from advertising, which features at the bottom of every posting to the group forum. Campbell's later work (2005) explores the uneasy relationship being formed between corporate and community values online and coins the term 'Janus-faced' to describe the political-economy of many gay commercial websites. Arguably the spaces under discussion in this book can also be considered Janus-faced, to different extents, though I hope to demonstrate how the relationship between capitalism and gay subculture operates way beyond the 'confines' of a single website.

Methodology: Of (computer) mice and (critical) magpies

Finally, there is the issue of methodology, which inevitably shapes the findings of any research study. Intellectually, *Getting It On Online* and *Gaydar Culture* draw from similar wells of theory and critique. Both employ work that spans the fields of cultural studies, queer theory, gender studies, sociology, media studies and anthropology, though to different degrees and in different ways. While the intellectual hinterland is similar, the methods of data capture do vary. Campbell relies on ethnography, employing participant-observation and interviews in a context that lends itself to these methodological styles. IRC is renowned for offering a wealth of text – and not much more. This is not to suggest that the poverty of the bandwidth results in either a poverty of experience or of research data, far from it. But a website, for instance, offers a wealth of detail that may

5 Campbell reports that during his research, one of his online friends, and research participants, 'younghung' confessed that the digital body he had created in IRC bore no significant relationship to the body he inhabited offline.

otherwise be missed by interviewing the participants who use it, or the creator who maintains it.

I have been acutely aware throughout my research of the methodological minefield posed by the study of digital media. By and large, the research that I refer to in this book falls into one of two camps. Firstly, and by far the most favoured if we believe the publishing traditions that are being created, is the social science approach. This approach focuses on the web as a place, as a form of living laboratory perhaps, and methodologies that unfold by viewing digital culture from this perspective are informed according to this belief. Meanwhile the humanities approach offers researchers the opportunity to negotiate new relationships with digital artefacts and practices and draw on a range of critical frameworks that find their origins in other disciplines. This is in part due to the humanities' understanding of digital culture as a series of *texts*, similar to an art gallery, a place where people display the texts they have created. By positing websites, homepages, postings and other virtual spaces as texts in the same way that films, poems, popular songs or soap operas are texts, the humanities researcher can engage with the web from critical perspectives and use critical tools that have been successfully applied to other cultural artefacts. In focusing on the digital as text, the humanities approach allows the researcher to foreground the inhabited space as opposed to the interaction encapsulated within it.

Beyond the humanities/social sciences binary that I have crudely drawn, there are other traditions of analysis, not least those coming from the already hybrid field of media studies. The Internet is a medium in and of itself but it is also linked to an entire history of different media and, as such, is one the latest points of media convergence, drawing in elements more commonly associated with film, television, telephony and print. This convergence can be seen in the language we use to talk about digital culture. We use *screens* to view *pages*. For many people in the 1990s and early 2000s, their first contact with the Internet was via a *dial-up* connection, and the phone line remains central to many people's experiences of the Internet. In terms of content, web-design often resembles the storyboarding of other narrative-driven mediums such as film and digital media are intimately tied to these older forms of communication. As such, a study that seeks to examine elements of this new media needs to also recognise a process of methodological convergence.

Throughout my research I have referred to my approach as 'magpie methodology'. Like its namesake, this methodology shamelessly appropriates the glittering highlights of theory from a diverse range of disciplines. I am indebted to Andy Medhurst for both coining the term 'magpie methodology' in order to describe the theoretical thrust of this project, and for providing a typically eloquent and barbed remark with which to undermine the supremacy and pretensions of 'high' theory, abstract thought and rigid methods, within media and cultural studies:

> What are rigorous methodologies other than laughably vain attempts to glue a sense of order on to the emotional complexities that cultural experiences summon up? (Medhurst, 2000: 25)

This magpie methodology permeates the case studies and critical analyses that form much of this book. Following a discussion of recent gay history in Chapter 2, I begin my exploration of gay men's digital culture by weaving together two critical strands in order to form a new theoretical framework for the ensuing analyses. While I refer to scholarly work on digital media, it is to the feminist work of Kappeler (1986), writing on the subject of pornography, and the critical theory of Foucault (1977 [1995], 1976 [1990]) that I turn in this critical-theoretical chapter. These writers provide a framework for exploring key tropes that operate across gay men's digital culture, and also provide a means for identifying the increasing slippage between physical and virtual spaces within gay male subculture.

From here, I begin my detailed exploration of gay digital life by exploring *representations of the self*, articulated through user profiles (Chapter 4). Again, it is not digital theory that informs my analysis here, but critical approaches developed within the fields of film studies and photography. In my discussion of the user profile, I develop a psychoanalytic approach that draws from feminist film theory before re-orienting my focus through the work of Barthes (1980), employing his theory of the *Punctum* in order to complicate the previous psychoanalytic reading. A combination of these two theoretical lenses results in a new understanding of the profile, which for many gay men is an integral facet of their online identities, and which operates in a variety of ways, serving several different purposes.

In Chapter 5, I utilise Morton's (1995, 1999) critiques on (cyber)queer culture and thought in order to engage with *a digital space in which gay men perform straight masculinities* in response to a perceived homonormativity within metropolitan gay male subculture. Throughout this analysis, I continue to contextualise the members of this 'cybercottage' within the gay male spaces that they inhabit in other spheres of their lives. In Chapter 6, I construct a critical framework using the work Rofes (1998), Watney (1996, 2000), Adam (2005) and other commentators on the HIV/AIDS crisis in order to interrogate the official and unofficial discourses of barebacking websites – *controversial spaces that promote unprotected gay male sex*. Once again, 'offline' theory (here originating from cultural studies, sociology and media studies) is employed in order to understand both the motivations and the implications bound up in such online spaces.

Finally, in Chapter 7, I bring together the work of De Souza (2006) and Miller (2009), together with readings of Malinowski (1923) and Bauman (2001) in order to form a critical response to *the emergence of new forms and practices engendered by digital culture's increasing mobility*. Key works from these four scholars are subjected to a queering process, whereby the conceptions of communion, individuation, sociality and space that they propose are rearticulated and responded to through a reading of mobile digital culture that operates from a non-normative and non-heterosexual reading of public life.

A final few words before getting started

I mentioned above the need to recognise the continuing relevance of Campbell's work in spite of the fact that gay men's digital culture – and by extension *all* digital culture – has moved on a great deal since 2004, the year that *Getting It On Online* was first published. I maintain this point of view, while also acknowledging that I am perhaps asking for the same consideration to be taken in relation to this book. Campbell published his book some three years after I had first begun researching online gay male subculture in Britain. *Gaydar Culture* started its life as a doctoral thesis (at the University of Sussex), which was completed in 2006. As such, and while every attempt has been made to keep the commentary, analysis and discussion contemporary, the following chapters might be best thought of as a series of snapshots, taken over a ten-year period during which an initial research question became a series of analyses, leading to a fully-formed doctoral thesis, and finally, this book. These snapshots attempt to convey a multi-faceted sense of how and why gay male subculture in Britain has been engaging with digital media technologies over the last decade. At the same time, they seek to identify the tensions, anxieties, pleasures and politics that have structured these digital 'immersions' during this period. At the time of writing, all of the websites and digital spaces that are discussed in this book remain 'live' and online. Inevitably this will not be the case in the future and already some of the sites have been redesigned, reorganised and refocused. This is the 'nature' of digital platforms and is but one of the challenges that scholars working with these technologies must overcome, or at the very least, acknowledge.

However, while framing this book within the first decade of the 21st century, and recognising the historical specificity of the case studies employed, I would argue against claims that the ensuing discussions are already 'out of date' or, worse still, irrelevant. The arguments I form in the next six chapters extend well beyond the limits of any one website or forum or mobile application and I am confident that the themes and perspectives that I bring in to play in my analyses will remain relevant to future discussions of gay men's digital practice. This confidence stems largely from the fact that such themes and perspectives are not new at the time of publication, and were not new in 2001, when I first engaged with them in the context of this project. Rather, they pervade, and have pervaded, the subcultures, identities, politics, spaces and practices that gay men have constructed over the last 40 years (and beyond). This is, in part, why the next chapter begins in the 1980s, in a time when the Internet was not available to domestic consumers in Britain – or indeed anywhere. What I hope to provide in the following pages is an examination of the relationship between the digital and physical aspects of gay male subculture; one that identifies the continuing legacies of recent material history, and the experiences of gay men living in the UK. It is through such legacies that I believe we can begin to critically engage with, and better understand, some of the recent and contemporary forms, practices and spaces that make up gay male digital subculture in Britain today. And it is to such legacies and experiences that I now turn my attention.

Chapter 2
Contexts and Frameworks: British Gay Male Subculture – 1984 and Beyond

If we are to fully understand gay male digital culture – to comprehend the methods by which gay men are representing themselves online, the reasons behind their manifold digital interactions and the subculture's interest in new forms of communication – then we need to begin by stepping outside of digital culture and engaging with the wider contexts, discourses and structures that frame gay male subculture in Britain. Arguably this act of distancing and surveying is a prerequisite for any study seeking to investigate cultural manifestations as they operate across digital platforms. It would be naïve, for instance, to conceive of studying gay dating profiles without any understanding of the broader political landscape that has helped shape the identities contained in such profiles. Similarly, if we are to fully comprehend the rise of online bareback subculture, we must recognise the social, sexual and political dimensions of gay subculture, which have led to some men actively rejecting conventional safer sex advice.

In the four case studies that make up the analyses chapters of this book, specific references to wider socio-political contexts are continually made in order that direct links between the 'offline' and 'online' can be maintained. In many of these cases, the argument isn't simply one of (offline) cause and (online) effect and, where possible, I try to characterise the interaction between offline and online (such terms themselves becoming increasingly empty) as being one of dialogue; a sub-cultural conversation that moves across spaces, and through identities, be they digital, corporeal, physical or virtual. Indeed, my final case study moves towards a hybrid understanding of gay male life, whereby digital technologies simultaneously reconfigure and rely on the physical spaces through which gay men move. But while each analysis ties digital phenomena to wider themes and tensions in gay male subculture, there is also a need to acknowledge the broader social and political conditions in which British gay men have engaged with, and become immersed in, digital forms. Thus my aim in this chapter is to provide a brief overview of some of the cultural and legal frameworks that shadowed, and continue to shape gay male subculture's involvement with digital technologies of communication.

Within the context of this book, this chapter serves two functions. Firstly, for anyone unfamiliar with the recent history of British gay male subculture, it offers a thumbnail sketch of the legal, political and cultural climate in gay Britain since 1984. While much of this book will resonate with the experiences of gay men across the West, particularly those who participate in urban gay male subcultures, and while this is intentional, I would argue that there does remain a need to identify the cultural specificity of both my analysis, and various aspects of those forms I am interrogating here. Hopefully what follows in this chapter will be illuminating for anyone operating outside of a British context, or for those who have a limited knowledge of British gay male subculture and the forces that have shaped it.

Of course I am unable to provide anything even remotely approaching a totalising history of British gay male subculture and in this chapter I am grateful to be able to draw on some of those scholars who have undertaken extended and detailed analyses of gay and lesbian subcultures in the recent past. This includes the work of Babuscio, 1988; Lumsden, 1988; Weeks, 1990; Jeffrey-Poulter, 1991; Grey, 1992, 1997; Garfield, 1994; Power, 1995; Hugh, 1997; Engel, 2001 and Lent, 2003. I rely on many of these authors here and would encourage anyone interested in gaining a richer and deeper history of homosexuality in Britain to explore the work of those I mention in this chapter. In comparison to these more expansive historical accounts, the outline I provide here is humble, primarily serving the interests of this book as opposed to offering an independent discourse on Britain's queer past. To the hitherto uninformed, however, I hope to provide a flavour of British gay subculture – both the challenges it faced and the battles it had won – as it existed immediately before and during the first decade of mass digital integration in Britain.

This leads into the second reason for writing this chapter, which is evidenced in the tripartite focus I have chosen to adopt. By tracing three key elements that have influenced the development of British gay male subculture to different degrees – gay political activism, the gay press, and HIV/AIDS – my aim is to identify the cultural, social and political milieu gay men in Britain found themselves in at the point at which they began to use digital media in significant numbers. By adopting such an approach, the intellectual and critical links between this chapter and the ensuing discussions of gay men's digital culture should become apparent.

In spotlighting these three elements it should of course be clear that I am not suggesting that every gay man has experienced HIV/AIDS in the same way, or that all gay men read gay magazines, or that all gay men are (a)political. Likewise, in focusing on gay male digital culture I am acutely aware that some gay men do not use digital technologies for anything that could be considered 'gay' and some may not use digital technologies at all. But, in choosing these themes I am suggesting that these three elements are integral to an understanding of gay male subculture in the 1980s, 1990s and the 2000s and while individual relationships to viruses, newspapers or political organisations may vary greatly, the impact of these three elements on this subculture can nevertheless be charted. These impacts must therefore be recognised and understood if we are to develop a holistic appreciation of gay male subculture's bond with digital technologies and practices.

It should hopefully become apparent as to why I have chosen these three distinct foci, but to précis my discussion, my decision to explore these elements can be summed up as follows. I begin by briefly exploring the political (and therefore also the legal) history of male homosexuality in Britain, not least because, qua Foucault (1976), such institutional discourses (and responses to them) serve to construct the homosexual, as a subject, at the point at which they seek to identify, describe, locate and exert power over him. Since 1967, British gay men have moved from being illegal non-citizens to legally recognised subjects within UK society. Where they were once the victims of judicial and disciplinary forces, they are now increasingly protected by such institutions, and the servants of such institutions. In less than half a century the gay male couple have gone from being outlaws to having 'in-laws' and gay rights as a political issue has migrated from the fringes to the centre with every major political party today having a gay and lesbian group affiliated to its national committee. This trajectory, however has been neither smooth, nor without setbacks and, as shall be discussed, gay political activism is neither homogenous or without its own internal tensions and dynamics. The recent history of gay politics and the tectonic shifts that have occurred in the legal status and legal rights of gay men inevitably mark and influence gay male subculture, even when many critics decry the apolitical nature of 'the scene' and the political apathy of younger gay men. In choosing this first theme, I want to highlight this influence not least because it throws up some interesting contradictions and peculiar resonances within the digital facet of this subculture.

My second area of focus, the gay press, has been chosen because in many ways the gay press was the precursor to the Internet within gay male subculture. Whether it be contact adverts, bar listings, soft porn, lifestyle features, sexual health material, or 'gay news', the gay press was for a long time *the* medium for disseminating information within gay male subculture, and, as I shall argue, served to construct that subculture at the same time that it spoke to it. I do not have the opportunity here for an extended discussion of the history of gay print media, but in choosing to reflect on the establishment of, and shifts within this industry, I want to identify both the relationship between the press and more recent forms of communication and, in turn, suggest why some gay men have turned away from the gay press having found their voices censored and unacknowledged in the pages of magazines and newspapers.

For anyone who grew up and came of (gay) age in the 1980s or 1990s, the decision behind my third focus, HIV/AIDS, should be self-explanatory. At the time of writing this, it is World Aids Day (completely co-incidental and nevertheless true). I have just received a tweet from a commercial gay organisation that I follow on the microblogging service, Twitter. The post responded to a brief news article appearing in *The Metro*, a free 'commuter' newspaper distributed in major towns and cities in England. In today's edition (1st Dec 2009: 14) the paper juxtaposed reports of candlelit vigils in London with claims of complacency regarding viral transmission in Britain and across Europe. Gay men were the only social group to be singled out in the article. Almost thirty years after the first confirmed AIDS deaths in Britain, it is a disappointing reality that within the mainstream British press gay men continue to be aligned with HIV/AIDS more than any other demographic, an alignment ushered in on waves of unspoken blame and finger-pointing. Indeed, for much of the period I am going to be discussing in this chapter, homosexuality could only be spoken about under the aegis of disease and disease prevention if the speaker was funded through a Local Authority. HIV/AIDS has left an indelible mark on gay male subcultures across the world but that mark is not necessarily the same and the British experience of the virus – and the concomitant narratives of fear, prejudice, death and activism – is arguably different to (for example) the North American experience or the Australian experience. Focusing on how the virus permeated gay male subculture on different levels (physical, psychological, culturally, politically) within Britain is imperative if we are to fully understand how and why some of the practices (most notably barebacking) covered in this book have come about. Again, and risking repetition once more, I cannot and shall not attempt to provide a detailed history of the virus in Britain, but instead, with broad strokes, what I offer is an overview of the British HIV narrative in order to highlight how the virus has contributed to the development of gay cultures, identities and practices as they have manifested themselves via digital platforms.

Collectively, these three themes help to sustain one of the central principles of this book, that principle being that British gay men have integrated platforms such as the Internet into their everyday lives as a direct *consequence* of the immediate history of gay male subculture. This subculture's characteristic shape needs to be considered briefly here, before I go on to detail its historical evolution.

In 1998 Sinfield employed the term 'metropolitan' in identifying a contemporaneous urban-centric gay male subculture. This 'metropolitan model' encapsulated the dominant expression of male homosexuality in the West at the end of the 20th century (an expression which continues to dominate global gay male subculture at the time of writing this). The metropolitan model suggests a particular geographical preference (large cities and urban conurbations), a particular lifestyle (imbued with the rhetoric of compulsory consumption and late capitalism) and an (over)investment in forms of (white, middle-class, Eurocentric) masculinity. Sinfield reflected on this upwardly-mobile and confident metropolitan model stating that:

> In North America and North-western Europe, the years since Stonewall have afforded good opportunity to those who have wanted to be what we have come to recognise as gay or lesbian. We have developed significant institutions and the beginnings of a climate where we may express ourselves without too many restraints. (6)

Two points contained within this statement warrant further expansion here. Firstly, in mentioning 'Stonewall', and thus alluding to the Greenwich Village riots, Sinfield identifies the 1969 riots as the birthplace of contemporary gay culture in the West and acknowledges the influence of the USA on British gay subculture. This influence inevitably has repercussions when we encounter spaces and bodies that are not bounded by physical, geographical or political borders, and the migration and circulation of a global metropolitan gay subculture (its ideas, aesthetics, identities and practices) has witnessed a marked increase in velocity through digital media technologies. Secondly, in identifying the genesis of the metropolitan model Sinfield acknowledges the contingency of gay culture, writing that:

> A second leading idea is that we have to entertain the thought that 'gay' as we have produced it and lived it, and perhaps 'lesbian' also, are historical phenomena and may now be hindering us more than they help us. (5)

It is this notion of 'gay' being a historical phenomenon that I am most interested in here. 'Gay' signifies the formation of a sub-cultural identity based around certain desires at a point in history when the capacity for such an identity to be constructed and maintained as valid, has become a reality. 'Gay men' have not always existed – we are a relatively new species, much younger than the 'homosexual' or the 'homophile' or other same-sex desiring subjects (although we undoubtedly share some things in common with these earlier identities), and we would do well to remember the 'newness' of the 'gay man'. We would also do well to acknowledge the fact that this recent identity is but one of many and, while it is the most widely recognised form of male homosexuality, it by no means speaks for all same-sex desiring men. Nor is it an identity that is open to all.

That said, 'gay' does signify the most visible and arguably the most powerful expression of homosexuality to have existed in the last two thousand years. Metropolitan gay subculture spans continents in a way that no other queer subculture has done previously. It is visible in cities as geographically diverse as Sydney, Sao Paulo, Madrid, and Cape Town and it is visible within mainstream Western media output, including television, film and print media. Of course to say that this form of gay culture is 'global' is not to suggest that it is international. Metropolitan gay culture ignores (and is ignored by) vast swathes of the world including many developing countries, rural and poverty-stricken areas, and nations where religious and/or political hegemonies explicitly discourage homosexuality. This exclusion is largely due to two linked factors. Firstly, economic freedom is not available in many parts of the world and as a result, subcultures that rely on economic independence (that is, the freedom of being able to live outside of the family unit) are unable to establish themselves. This is as true for some developed nations, as it is for developing countries.[1] Secondly, the perceived sexual permissiveness of Western cultures and the consumer-driven element of metropolitan gay subculture does not always fit with the existing social, legal and moral order of specific nation states. These two factors mean that while gay subculture expands across the globe,

1 See McLelland (2000), for instance, for a discussion of how economics and urban living costs impact on Japanese gay male subculture.

societies that do not subscribe to Western ideologies, or who do not provide the necessary economic conditions are left off the map, 'switched off' as it were.[2]

For those who do have the opportunity to become 'plugged in' – those who can afford it, are able to access to it, can choose to engage with it, and are young enough, pretty enough or rich enough to be a part of it – metropolitan gay male subculture provides recognition, validity, identity and lifestyle. It demarcates the physical spaces of gay men's lives, offering an array of pleasure zones that span continents, and which appear to be simultaneously unique and uncannily similar to one another. As Simpson (1999: 7) comments '[i]n the gay world, everything is reassuringly similar, wherever you go. Gays are better at franchising than McDonalds'. It outlines subcultural practices of consumption and aspiration (whether that be buying a loft-apartment in New York's Chelsea district or this season's Aussiebum underwear) and offers a never-ending catalogue of practices and products to purchase. It manufactures desires – for specific bodies, particular sexual practices and erotic experiences – and then caters to those desires through taxonomies of pornography, niche club-nights, commercial sex environments, bars, websites, gyms, holidays and parties. It tells the gay man who he is and what he is. It invites him to conform while celebrating the distinctiveness of gay subculture. And all the time it compels him to spend, spend, spend, like there's no tomorrow.

Futurity has never been gay male subculture's strong point – indeed we have all too often been denied a past, a present or a future. We have been erased from histories, we have been outlawed from civil society, we have been analysed into redundancy and we have risked being wiped out altogether. 'The family tree ends here' proclaimed one T-shirt I saw at a San Francisco Gay Pride parade, and we have not only embraced this end-point, we have turned it into a lifestyle. Civil partnerships, gay marriage, HIV medication, joint mortgages, life insurance, gay adoption, gay parenting, pension rights. The legal, medical and economic frameworks seem to be leading gay men towards a bright and happy future, but the message that resonates through metropolitan gay male subculture, like a bass line that just won't quit, continues to be 'why bother with tomorrow? The party is here tonight!'

This may sound overly pessimistic, and of course I am not saying that all gay men live this life, or indeed that metropolitan gay subculture is wrong. It might sound as though I am criticising this lifestyle-oriented subculture, but I find it hard to do so without sounding like a hypocrite. Living in Brighton and then London, socialising in Soho, holidaying in gay-friendly destinations and even wearing the (currently) de rigour Aussiebums, I have to concede that, to a degree, I am 'plugged in' to this culture – I am the gay man I referred to a moment ago. I identify this metropolitan scene here not because I want to chastise it but because I believe that it is from within that scene that British (and Western) gay

2 I use the term 'switched off' with direct reference to Castells' discussion of the emerging 'fourth world' of the information poor. See Castells, 1999: 409.

men's digital culture grows, whether it be an extension of metropolitan life or a radical response to it and rejection of it. Like it or not, the global phenomena of a metropolitan gay subculture is the most visible and most powerful articulation of male homosexuality today. In what follows I hope to explore why and how it has achieved such prominence in order to then understand how it informs the digital culture that I interrogate later in this book.

From the GLF to *OutRage!*: The recent politics of homosexuality in Britain

The partial decriminalisation of homosexual activities between consenting males in the UK (and in private) occurred in 1967 and from this moment on gay men in Britain were not only legal, they were able to organise themselves politically without having to remain in the closet. There had been homosexual-oriented organisations in Britain prior to decriminalisation, most notably the Homosexual Law Reform Society (HLRS)[3], but members of such groups could not publicly acknowledge their homosexuality, since to do so would not only run the risk of prosecution, but could also damage the legitimacy of the organisation.[4] Only after their legal status was changed were homosexual men offered the *potential* to campaign in their own name and speak through their minority status.

The Gay Liberation Front (GLF), established in 1970, defined itself as a 'revolutionary organisation' and this meant a 'consequential stress on homosexuality as a political issue' (Weeks, 1991: 186). Though it only lasted four years, the impact that the GLF had on gay culture – and society at large – would be felt throughout the rest of the twentieth century. Power (1995: 283) describes the GLF as such:

> If you see GLF as a dandelion which grew, flowered and then degenerated into a fluffy but insubstantial head full of seeds which were then blown by several gusts into new areas of the meadow, it is easy to understand the way in which it is connected to a whole host of major lesbian and gay initiatives of the 1970s, 1980s and even 1990s.

Identifying the concrete triumphs of the GLF is somewhat difficult. As a political organisation it achieved little in terms legal change, but the GLF did not want to

---

3 Set up in 1958 following the publication of the Wolfenden report, the society campaigned for the recommendations of the report to be implemented, most notably the decriminalisation of homosexuality. The Albany Trust was a charity set up by the HLRS in order to raise funds for the society (see Jeffrey-Poulter, 1991: 38).

4 For how could the society be tolerated if it was known that it comprised of individuals who engaged in criminal activities? See Jeffrey-Poulter (1991) and Grey (1992) for further information on the organisational and financial details of the HLRS.

change the existing law, nor did it seek to work within the contemporary political system. As Lent (2003: 38) comments:

> The revolutionary ideals of the earlier mobilisation undoubtedly had a high degree of empirical credibility in the early 1970s. Many young activists of this era genuinely believed that radical social transformation was close at hand. Although this, of course, proved wrong, events of the time seemed to bear out such a view.

Alongside its ardent belief in imminent social upheaval, the GLF encouraged its supporters to look inward via 'consciousness-raising' or 'CR' (Power, 1995: 45)[5], the development of a self-awareness in relation to one's own homosexuality, and one's own internalised homophobia. For the first time gay men and women were asked to recognise the hatred and shame they had for themselves and acknowledge the methods by which society had created such self-loathing. Power (ibid) describes CR meetings as allowing people to 'explore what their true feelings were as opposed to those which society had imposed upon them' and such self-exploration continues to be a key part of many gay peoples' experiences of coming out.

CR was integral to the GLF ideology and is one of the most visible aspects of the GLF legacy in contemporary gay culture. 'Being true to yourself' is, on the surface at least, a prerequisite for being an out gay man. Coming out (another tenet of the GLF philosophy) has become the cornerstone of Western gay male culture and implies a process of self-awareness, of realising who one really is. Rahman (2000: 51) writes that 'gay liberation provided a positive social identity around which homosexuals could organise and with which they could identify' and it was through the act of CR, at an individual and group level, that this positive identity was firstly constructed and secondly disseminated. Following the feminist dictum that the personal was political, CR also sought to abolish any distinction between self and society.

Other seeds from the GLF dandelion included the establishment of the Lesbian and Gay Switchboard, the foundation of a self-identifying gay press, and the mobilisation of nascent gay culture around specific political goals (Power, 1995). This political mobilisation is surprising considering that the GLF never saw itself as a single-issue group. Just as it had grown out of the women's movement, black civil rights, anti-war demonstrations and trade union battles, so it regarded itself as supporting these organisations. Power (1995: 79) records the mixed reactions the GLF received on a demonstration for jailed dockers but identifies the effect that such allegiances had for the GLF:

5 Consciousness raising was not an activity unique to the GLF. As with much of its ideology and its methodology, the Front appropriated CR from second-wave feminism.

> The involvement of GLF in activities in support of other causes often also provided a useful vehicle for bringing gay issues to the notice of other rights movements.

By contrast, gay politics in the 1980s focused on single-issue campaigning as the links between feminism and gay politics, so deeply binding in the early 1970s, were eroded in the following decade. As gay male subculture fetishised the performance of hyper-masculinity, feminists such as McKinnon and Dworkin alienated many through their anti-porn campaigns that positioned men, straight or gay, as sexual oppressors (Dyer, 1989: 198–212).

It is more than a little ironic that the actions of the GLF created the right environment for the development of openly (proudly) gay commercial spaces, which cashed in on the emerging gay consciousness. Prior to the 1967 repeal, there had been a history of underground drinking dens and queer pubs in Britain (see Weeks, 1990; Norton, 1992 and Houlbrook, 2005), but the aftermath of both the legal reform and the GLF provided the correct atmosphere for the development of a fully-fledged gay scene. Hugh (1997: 231) labels the period 1967 to 1982 a 'fifteen-year Indian summer', and the GLF were central to the establishment of spaces in which 'it was possible for men to meet up and talk about "the gay community"'. As the 'scene' emerged as a visible entity, so the need to go to political meetings to meet other gay men diminished. In comparing the differences between the GLF and *OutRage!* Lent (2003: 44) identifies one of the major advantages that the GLF had over subsequent organisations and movements:

> Prior to the GLF's launch, no route existed for gay men and lesbians to express their sexuality in an open and free manner. Thus, when the Front did come about it attracted support as much for the personal liberation it offered to gay men and lesbians as to its grander vision of social transformation.

The establishment of commercial gay venues removed this incentive and while Lent sees the links between the Left and the gay and lesbian movement growing during the early eighties, there was no single national organisation devoted to the type of direct action employed by the GLF until 1988.[6] This absence has been directly linked to the commercial scene by Edwards (1994), who identifies tensions between the scene and gay political structures, tensions that ultimately undermined gay political endeavours by the end of the decade. Inevitably there was also a level of campaign fatigue and disillusionment with the radical politics of the 1970s. Margaret Thatcher's election victory in 1979 signalled a seismic shift in the British political climate, and the Left-wing political agenda of the 1970s was crushed under the weight of the Tory government's free market philosophy (see McIntosh, 1993).

---

6 Though the Campaign for Homosexual Equality (formerly the HLRS) continued to undertake political lobbying work during this period.

The loss of a gay organisation dedicated to direct action is characteristic of a period in which the emphasis in gay politics shifted from social revolution to political assimilation. Reform and acceptance became the favoured mode of engagement as Labour-controlled local councils began to recognise their gay and lesbian constituents. Cooper (1994: 2) charts the emerging relationships between local government and gay communities during the 1980s and in the introduction to her analysis of gay and lesbian politics during this period she considers the reasons for these new relationships between the State and the gay community:

> Municipal lesbian and gay work emerged at the intersection of several different processes: the growing size and confidence of Britain's lesbian and gay communities; the institutionalisation of the new urban left; identity politics; and the developing influence of feminism within local politics.

Calls to overthrow the State were substituted for rhetoric rooted in identity politics, defined by Cooper (1994: 25) as being grounded in campaigning for 'reforms that would defend and protect social identities such as homosexuality'. Gay men and lesbians carved out lifestyles within the State based on their sexuality and 'identity *affirmation* rather than sexual deconstruction became the priority' (ibid). Councils such as Haringey, Southampton, Manchester and the Greater London Council (GLC) were attacked by the reactionary mainstream press during this period for supporting gay – and lesbian – centred initiatives. These initiatives included the 'Changing The World' charter, published by the GLC (1985), which focused on promoting lesbian and gay rights and the Camden Lesbian and Gay Unit, founded in 1987. The national Labour party may have oscillated between 'radical' interventions and a more centralist campaign, but lesbians and gay men – if they were involved in politics – found a degree of power when arguing for public funding, space and protection at more local levels government. Given the Conservative government in power at the time, the localised nature of these campaigns was perhaps inevitable, but localisation inevitably ran the risk of fragmentation and atomisation, leaving lesbian and gay men living outside of the catchment area of more progressive Labour councils out in the cold. It was not until the Government of the day proposed a piece of legislation so shockingly homophobic in content and so directly targeted at gay people, that Britain saw a national LGB political organisation again.

Clause 28[7], hit the headlines of *Gay News* in December 1987 and over the course of the next six months dominated the gay press, encountering an unprecedented response from the British gay community before finally being passed into law and coming into force in May 1988[8]. Since her election in 1979, Margaret Thatcher

---

7 Which until being passed into law was known as firstly Clause 27, before the Bill it was attached to was renumbered and it became Clause 28.

8 Jeffrey-Poulter (1991) provides a comprehensive account of the Clause's passage into law and I would refer interested readers to this detailed narrative for further

and her government had undertaken a campaign to combat the permissive society, which they believed was responsible for the moral decline of society and the breakdown of the nuclear family. This campaign included a clampdown on gay and lesbian lifestyles and in October 1987, the Prime Minister was quoted as saying that 'children who need to be taught to respect traditional moral values are being taught that they had an inalienable right to be gay' (Weeks, 1990: 231). This followed an election campaign earlier that year in which the Conservatives criticised the Labour party for its imputed pro-gay sympathies. In particular, as Jeffrey-Poulter (1991: 165) notes, the Tory campaign demonised Labour as at threat to the moral safety of Britain's children:

> An election poster [for the Conservative party] appeared featuring the book *Young Gay and Proud* under the headline 'IS THIS LABOUR'S IDEA OF COMPREHENSIVE EDUCATION?'

Just as they had been in the 1950s (see Hugh, 1997), gay men and women became targets in the Conservative government's propaganda war and this time their political allegiances with 'rogue' councils such as the GLC added another dimension to their pariah status. The third consecutive Tory win in 1987 signalled that the time was right to launch Clause 28, a piece of legislation wholly antithetical to both Labour's and the Liberal Party's election promises at the time, to protect the rights of homosexuals[9].

Put simply, the Clause sought to restrict the public funding of gay and lesbian organisations. Most importantly it stated that:

> [1] A local authority shall not
> [a] intentionally promote homosexuality or publish material with the intention of promoting homosexuality;
> [b] promote the teaching in any maintained school of the acceptability of homosexuality as a pretended family relationship.
> (Pringle *et al.*, 1991: 4)

Within the context of the unfolding AIDS crisis the second point stated that the Clause should not 'prohibit the doing of anything for the purpose of treating or preventing the spread of disease' (ibid). Finally, the Clause stated that:

> [3] In any proceedings in connection with the application of this section a court shall draw such inferences as to the intention of the local authority as may reasonably be drawn from the evidence before it. (ibid)

---

information.

9 Jeffrey-Poulter (1991) outlines these campaigns and readers are referred to this detailed account of the political campaigning that took place in 1987.

The wording of the first point, twinned with the threat of court proceedings in the third meant that Clause 28 could potentially be cited as a reason to refuse funding to any publicly-funded organisation, publication or event that so much as *mentioned* homosexuality. While homosexual sex could be discussed in schools (for instance) within the context of disease, infection and transmission control, any discussion of homosexuality outside of this was open to legal repercussions. Grey (1997: 56) comments on the wording of the Clause stating that:

> despite repeated complaints that no one really knew just what 'promoting homosexuality' actually meant, Government spokesmen persisted throughout adhering to this cloudy formula, and even resisted amendments designed to exclude from it activities intended to discourage discrimination against or to protect the civil rights of anyone.

In spite of the vagueness of the wording, the Conservative government was able to send out a clear message to (Labour-led) councils and gays and lesbians alike: homosexuality may be legal but it was definitely second-class. Gay and lesbian families were not 'real' and gay and lesbian lives were socially inferior. Rayside (1998: 19) identifies the legislation as stemming from '[a] postwar pattern of legal regulation that had tolerated homosexuality in private but had secured heterosexual public space'. Homosexuality per se was not the problem; it was the challenge it seemed to pose to heterosexuality (namely that of being a viable alternative lifestyle) that was proving too much for the State. This separation of the public and the private was a direct contrast to the earlier attempts by civil rights activists (including the GLF) to collapse these two spheres.

Within a matter of weeks of the government's announcement, 'Stop The Clause' campaigns were launched nationwide, and at two marches in Manchester and London gay men, lesbians and their friends joined ranks in their thousands to protest against the proposed legislation. Unlike the raiding of New York's Stonewall bar in 1969, Clause 28 was British in origin and was tangible in terms of its aims, effects and prejudices. It was this tangibility, twinned with the ramifications of the legislation, which motivated gays and lesbians to take to the streets and protest. Weeks (1990: 242) reports 20,000 people gathering in Manchester in February 1988 to fight the Clause while Jeffrey-Poulter (1991: 32) cites a figure of 30,000 for the London rally in April that same year. Section 28 eventually passed into law on 9th March 1988 and came into effect two months later. But while it proved to be a somewhat ineffectual and hollow piece of legislation, the course of its passage into law provided the impetus for the next decade of gay rights campaigning. Rayside, (1998: 43) notes that:

> [a] number of those who campaigned against the Local government Bill recognized not only the potential of a new wave of activism, but also the importance of more substantial and skilful engagement with mainstream political processes.

Similarly, Engel (2001: 93) writes that:

> Section 28 not only backfired in that it became a rather ineffective law, but it also unintentionally produced what it was attempting to legislate away: gay visibility in the public sphere.

Palmer (1995: 35) suggests that Section 28 was 'a defining moment' within British lesbian and gay history that 'helped to politicize a new generation of lesbians and gay men'. By the end of the decade two groups emerged from the ashes of the 'Stop the Clause' campaigning and continued the political battle for equality in the shadow of Section 28. These two organisations have come to define the two poles of gay political activism in Britain at the beginning of the 21st century and are Stonewall and *OutRage!*

Gay politics in contemporary Britain – Stonewall and *OutRage!*

Section 28 was a wake-up call to the gay community and served to highlight the continued lack of equality afforded gay men and lesbians in Britain. Yet its consequences for gay urban subculture, comprising mainly of private commercial interests, were minimal. If anything the commercial scene grew in the early 1990s, often accommodating the growing focus on identity politics (if the price was right).

For example, Hearn (1991) identifies the evolution of LANGUID (Lesbians And Gays United In Disabilities) and gay disability rights during this period, while Nevins (1991) discusses how Clause 28 campaigning helped to mobilise black gay men and gay people of colour. While the first black lesbian and gay organisations were set up as early as 1980,[10] black lesbian and gay identity politics came to the fore during and immediately after the 'Stop the Clause' campaign (see also Cole and Allen, 1994). Such groups demanded recognition and the commercial scene was willing to cater for them, so long as they were spending money in their venues.

Stonewall, the campaigning group that pursues a gradualist and assimilationist route towards LGB equality, was founded in 1989 in the aftermath of the 'Stop the Clause' protests. It promotes the notion that gay people should be provided with the same rights as their heterosexual counterparts, and be protected by anti-discriminatory law in the same way that other minority groups are. Originally conceived by those who had been active within the Clause 28 campaigns, Stonewall identifies itself as 'a professional lobbying group' (Stonewall – overview and remit, online) that aims to prevent 'attacks on lesbians, gay men and bisexuals ever occurring again' (ibid). It also aims 'to put the case for equality on the mainstream

10 The London Black Lesbian and Gay Centre was subsequently formed in 1985. (Knitting Circle, online).

political agenda by winning support within all the political parties' (ibid). The organisation has since expanded its remit, taking test cases to court, forging links with other anti-discriminatory groups across the cultural spectrum and working in partnership with NGOs and private businesses to promote the needs of lesbian gay and bisexual people.

The organisation's structure differs from previous gay political organisations with a self-elected committee and paid workers, and to many outsiders Stonewall's composition and methods may seem as though the organisation defers to the machinations of mainstream government. However as Lent (2003: 43) points out, there are clear reasons for this:

> Stonewall … has adopted the classic movement organisation response to loss of mass support by replacing the free but part-time and amateur labour of highly committed activists with the waged but full-time and professional labour of a small number of officers. This approach has even extended as far as maintaining a hierarchical structure with no significant input from a base of supporters.

Such a structure has been necessary in order to maintain momentum, ensure professional standards and cope with the shifts in both the political climate and gay culture. As mentioned above, contemporary organisations can no longer rely on the social incentives that drove many to get involved with the GLF.

Stonewall has had significant success in its campaigning. The organisation was central to the processes by which the gay age of consent was lowered in 2001 and Section 28 was finally repealed in 2003. It's most recent success came in the form of the government's 2004 Civil Partnership Bill, which Stonewall heavily promoted through lobbying work. This success, which grants (almost) equal rights to gay and lesbian couples as to married couples, highlights not only the relationship between gay and mainstream politics today, but also the primacy of assimilationist rhetoric within contemporary gay politics. In it's campaigning, Stonewall summarised the Bill as follows:

> The scheme would be for adult same-sex couples who are not in an existing registered partnership or marriage and are not closely related. Couples who register would have a new legal status as 'registered civil partners', and would acquire a package of rights and responsibilities. (Stonewall, Civil Partnership Bill, online)

Dissolution of the partnership runs parallel to existing divorce law and pension and inheritance claims are legally recognised subsequent to the registration of the partnership. While this is arguably a much better position than the current situation of gay men and lesbians in the United States (for example), the Civil Partnership Act does carry with it certain restrictions; it only recognises and protects the material rights of couples who enter into a State-recognised civil partnership and the organisation of that protection is dictated by the State, not by the individual. This may be acceptable to many, and I do not intend to suggest that it is not. Instead, I want to draw attention to the massive gulf that exists between the promotion of civil union rights by Stonewall in the 2000s and the GLF's opinion on *all* state-recognised unions back in the 1970s. Indeed, according to Power (1995: 110) all forms of 'coupledom' were a 'sin' for the GLF, who saw it as stifling the ability to form balanced relationships. By 2005 such 'coupledom' was being legally recognised by the British government, and that recognition was pushed for by Stonewall.

OutRage! was similarly born in the wake of the Clause 28 rallies and its remit continues to be founded on 'challeng[ing] anti-gay discrimination, confront[ing] the perpetrators of homophobia face to face' and 'promot[ing] the public visibility and media debate of queer issues' (*OutRage!*, online). In contrast to Stonewall[11], it favours direct action over lobbying tactics and its highest-profile figure, Peter Tatchell, has attracted considerable publicity and notoriety in a succession of spectacular protest events.

OutRage! is also more encompassing in its remit than the GLF, though undoubtedly it owes much to its ancestor, Tatchell's previous experience of GLF zaps having 'informed the tactics and targets of *OutRage!*' (Power, 1995: 288). Conversant with the queer project of the 1990s gay and lesbian academy, the organisation campaigns against anti-gay discourse irrespective of the target of such discourse. It also seeks to promote an understanding of queer identities both within and external to the metropolitan model tacitly promoted by Stonewall. This is reflected in Tatchell's self-identification as both a gay rights *and* human rights activist. This identity consciously articulates the concerns that many raised in the 1990s regarding the exclusions that the term 'gay' implied, the continued investment in identity politics and the process of assimilation that this identity came to represent for many.

During the 1990s academics, activists and sexually dissident individuals who found themselves marginalised by the metropolitan model of gay subculture began to appropriate the previously derogatory term 'queer' in order to create a space in which those who did not conform to the metropolitan image of homosexuality could find a political voice. Since then, queer theory has become by turn, a lifestyle, a political position, a fashion accessory, and a commodity. Some, such as Morton (1996: 21) criticise the queer project for its focus on desire (as opposed to need). Contrasting the new project to the Left-wing radicalism of the 1970s he positions queer theory as:

> playing a pivotal role in the transition to a new bourgeois morality and state of consciousness that is desperately needed by late multinational capitalism to maintain its exploitative and oppressive regime of class relations [.]

---

11 *OutRage!* officially recognise Stonewall on their website, stating that they appreciate all groups who work towards the promotion of homoequality (*OutRage!* online).

There isn't space here for a totalising discussion of queer theory but it is a significant aspect of the current political climate within gay culture in the early part of the 21st century. *OutRage!* identifies itself as a queer issues organisation and in form, structure and action it represents a major part of the queer project in Britain today. Its awareness of the media, and manipulation of it, is in keeping with the rhetoric of queer appropriation, while its refusal to promote the metropolitan model over other configurations of non-normative sexualities echoes the criticisms that queer theorists, activists and commentators have levelled at 'mainstream' gay culture and gay identity politics (see Butler, 1990; Bersani, 1995; Simpson, 1999). Identifying as queer as opposed to gay, *OutRage!* differs from Stonewall in that it does not seek to promote one version of homosexuality. Tatchell describes its remit as 'articulat[ing] a new model of queer politics that [is] critical and sceptical of both mainstream society and orthodox gay culture' (Tatchell Rights Fund, online). The tension that exists between the 'gay' (mainstream) politics of Stonewall and *OutRage!*'s (radical) 'queer' politics echoes a political debate that has pervaded the gay movement since the 1967 Sexual Offences Act. Rimmerman (2000: 54) sums up the two sides of this debate as 'the assimilationists, who typically embrace "insider" political strategies and liberationists, who are often associated with "outsider" and grassroots political strategies'.

The proposed 'Unmarried Partners Act' authored by Tatchell exemplifies radical queer politics' opposition to both anti-gay legislation *and* the promotion of a singular model of gay identity. In this version of the Civil Partnership Act partners of 12 months or longer would be able to choose from a list of rights and responsibilities without having to get married in a State-approved ceremony (Tatchell, online). The key differences between the *OutRage!* model and the Stonewall proposal lie in the State's level of involvement in gay partnership rights and the emphasis on emulating the heterosexual (not to mention patriarchal) institution of marriage; an institution that has previously been criticised for turning bodies into property and re-inscribing contrived gender relations (see Greer, 1970; Firestone, 1970). Urging caution, Tatchell (online) questions Stonewall's campaign:

> Why should getting married be the only way that couples can secure legal rights? Plenty of unmarried partners have relationships that are as loving and long-lasting as those of their wedded counterparts.

It is not the idea of gay 'marriage' that affronts *OutRage!* but the notion that in order to receive full rights, gay men would *have* to enter into such a union. It is within this tension that the differences between the assimilationist rhetoric of Stonewall and the more radical activist discourse of *OutRage!* can be identified. Stonewall wants gay men and lesbians to be recognised within the existing structures of the State. By contrast, *OutRage!* seeks the re-invention of legal, religious and State structures so that *all* identities, relationships and lifestyles, homosexual or otherwise may be identified.

Stonewall and *OutRage!* may exemplify opposite poles of contemporary gay politics, but both share an awareness that politics is far from a priority in the lives of many gay people. By and large both organisations have resigned themselves to the fact that the grass roots support for gay politics that the GLF enjoyed in the early 1970s or that the 'Stop the Clause' campaign motivated in the 1980s cannot be reasonably imagined in the near future. Engel (2001: 95) finds comparisons between the British and American gay movements and remarks that:

> The two decades since the decline of British gay liberation have witnessed a fluctuating pattern of support for the British gay and lesbian movement extraordinarily similar to the circumstances experienced by the American counterpart.

The splintering of gay politics into 'assmimilation versus radicalism' has resulted in a dilution of political discourse. Meanwhile many gay men who align themselves with the metropolitan identity and lifestyle identified by Sinfield find that they are able to lead comfortable, happy gay lives within Britain with relatively little difficulty. Civil partnerships have, I suspect, been viewed by many as the end point for gay politics, and many gay men feel comfortable with the level of rights bestowed upon them, perhaps even relishing the freedom that their sexual identity affords them. While projects such as *Out On My Own* (Cull *et al.*, 2006) and *Count Me In Too* (Browne *et al.*, 2007) continue to identify immense disparities in the quality of life experienced by marginalised LGBT people, the middle-class, urban-centric metropolitan gay subculture now visible in major towns and cities across Britain appears to be less interested in fighting for the rights and safety of marginal identities and more interested in partying.

This movement away from political action to lifestyle and fun can be charted in the history of the gay press, which has functioned as a mouthpiece for LGBT Britain, serving to construct the community it speaks to. In doing so it has furnished queer folk with information on relevant political and legal changes, details of gay venues and spaces and gay interest stories. As the next section details, more recently it has also been unwavering in its endorsement of the metropolitan model and of assimilationist agendas, often at the expense of alternative views and opinions.

Mouthpiece or marketplace? The evolution of the British gay press

The gay press has been central to the political and social formation of gay male subculture in Britain and its birth coincided with the founding of the first homosexual political organisations. As such, it is not difficult to understand how and why the structural, economic and cultural changes that have occurred within the press over the last twenty-five years echo the shift in dominant strategies of LGBT political campaigning and activism that have occurred in Britain since the 1980s. The Campaign For Homosexual Equality (CHE) published *Lunch* in order to raise awareness of its activities and it's campaigning (Weeks, 1990: 219). Likewise, the GLF's sporadically published *Come Together* provided a vehicle for the dissemination of the GLF manifesto, details of social and political events, information on gay organisations and relevant news (Power, 1995). In the late 70s *Gay Left* was a short-lived Marxist journal written mostly by GLF veterans, while *Rouge* in the 1980s, had links with the campaigns in around the Labour party. *Square Peg* employed the emerging intellectual tools of critical theory and second-wave feminist discourse in order to problematise both heteronormative society and the misogyny of the commercial gay scene.

These politicised titles, however, were by no means the only gay titles available. Others shunned political matters in favour of lifestyle features, coded gossip and soft porn. Magazines of this type, such as *Jeremy* and *Timm*, infuriated the GLF who berated them for being '"a load of absolute bullshit and an outright insult to gay people."' (Power, 1995: 33–34). It was the covert nature of such titles that offended the GLF, who saw such magazines as politically disengaged, contrary to the politics of 'coming out' and commercial enterprises that made money off gay people while doing little to improve their self-esteem or self-identity. Ultimately it was not the magazines' politics but their 'pornography' that so often proved to be their downfall. The charging of John Stamford (publisher of *Spartacus*) in 1971 for 'sending indecent material through the post' (Jeffrey-Poulter, 1991: 105) demonstrates that while a homosexual media industry did exist, it was subject to legal intervention, police harassment and custom and excise confiscation. Other gay publications did not fare much better. Lumsden (1988: 201) mentions the trial of Denis Lemon, editor of *Gay News*, during the late seventies who was 'charged and found guilty of publishing a blasphemous libel' after the newspaper printed a 'gay' poem about the crucifixion. Raids by police vice squads on the editorial offices of *HIM/Gay Times*[12] and *Capital Gay*, were not uncommon and gay media outlets such as *Gays the Word* and *Zipper*, continued to face police harassment throughout the 1980s.[13]

Despite police intimidation and the risk of legal prosecution, by 1984 the gay press had established itself within a rapidly growing market, though market forces meant that many publications were short-lived. Weeks (1990: 220) reports that despite *Gay News*, (first published in 1972), becoming the 'world's largest circulation newspaper for homosexuals' in 1976, by 1983 it had collapsed due to financial instability. Although the paper was resurrected later that same year, its readership had already been tempted away by *Him Monthly* which, 'having established itself as the heir to the newspaper, duly renamed itself *Gay Times*' (Jeffrey-Poulter, 1991: 167). The real impact of *Gay News* was that it succeeded in creating *and* speaking to a community of gay people. In 1983 it became a victim

12 Issue 73 of *Gay Times*, (Sept. 1984) reported on the 'porn squad' raid on its offices the previous month.

13 The offices of *Capital Gay* also became the site of an arson attack during the height of the 'Stop The Clause' campaign.

of such success and the community it had helped to identify was happy to decamp to the newer, more polished and aesthetically pleasing formula of the monthly lifestyle magazine.

Archives at the University of Sussex and the London School of Economics reveal a surprising number of gay news magazines published during the 1980s. *Gay Noise* began publishing in 1980 and was joined by *Gay Youth* in 1981. These were later joined by *Gay East Midlands*, *Gay Star*, *Gay Scotland* and *Gay Life*, all of whom enjoyed publishing runs that lasted at least two years. Many ultimately succumbed to economic difficulties despite being published on cheap stock with skeleton staff, voluntary contributions and little or no colour printing. During the 1990s production values increased as titles including *Midlands Zone*, *Uncover*, *Man*, and *The British Pride* began to feature better quality stock and a more professional layout (thanks largely to the advent of personal DTP software). Many of these were regionally based, reporting and appealing to local gay communities, with the occasional mention of national events and more often than not sound bites on political activism and law reform.

Financial crises and power-wrangling aside, the links between the gay press and the gay community/market continued to grow during the 1980s and 1990s. Or rather, as Weeks (1990: 222) states, 'papers such as *Gay News* did not just reflect passively an emerging gay community, they also helped to mould it'. However, the term 'community' soon became another way in which to talk about 'consumers', and Weeks goes on to remark that '*Gay News* was no longer just speaking to a community; it was speaking to, and helping to create, a market' (ibid).

By 1984 *Capital Gay* and *Gay Times* were producing comparatively professional publications filled with a combination of gay-related news items, information on holiday destinations, adverts for new clothing stores and bars, celebrity news and interviews and of course, contact adverts. Back issues of *Gay Times*, around this period reveal a tension between the shadow of Left-wing radicalism and the increasingly commercial attitude taken towards content by editors, but by the mid-eighties the call for revolution had become nothing more than a whisper. The affluent hedonism celebrated in the increasingly glossy pages of the 1980s gay press did, however, have to negotiate two unavoidably politicised issues during this decade, namely the crisis of HIV/AIDS and the scandal of Clause 28.

In June 1983 *HIM Monthly* ran its first front cover AIDS story, entitled 'A.I.D.S. Gay Death-Plot Panic – Fact or Science Fiction?' At the time the article was dubbed 'the most comprehensive study to be published in Britain' and aimed at combating the 'muddled, beside the point and downright inaccurate' coverage of the disease within the mainstream media. In its discussion of the virus the magazine stressed the need for the gay community to educate itself:

> What should we do? In the absence of firm medical evidence common sense alone would indicate that we should take some form of evasive action, in particular if living in or near a large city. Whatever way the disease is developed

> or transmitted, the following could decrease your chances of becoming a victim. (*Him Monthly*, no. 58, June 1983: 35)

The article went on to list nine points of advice regarding sexual habits and lifestyle including the avoidance of 'known drug users', 'all types of heavy dirty sex', 'excessive use of drugs (including nitrates)' and 'promiscuous partners'. Point five – 'try using a sheath when engaging in rectal intercourse' – subsequently became the foundation of HIV/AIDS awareness campaigning within the gay community long before the government promoted such behaviour.

Gay Times started providing monthly updates on the killer disease sweeping through communities in New York and San Francisco, whilst recognising the importance of providing gay men with the right information in the face of the sensational reportage found elsewhere:

> In the last issue we printed a letter from someone who was in a panic over hearing that someone he knew had AIDS. From other letters that we have received it is clear that, besides rational fears about AIDS, there is also a lot of ignorance about the illness amongst members of the gay community. If you are frightened about AIDS and want some information or simply want to talk to someone about your fears then ring the AIDS Helpline … run by the Terrence Higgins Trust. (*Gay Times*, September 1984: 59)

Letters pages throughout the 1980s became a site for education and advice on the disease. Long before the government released funding to educate those most at risk from the virus, the gay press became the link between organisations such as the Terrence Higgins Trust and the wider gay population. By 1986, *Gay Times* was carrying a list of local and national AIDS help lines every month and by 1988 Simon Watney was regularly contributing to the title with his AIDS-watch column.

As one of the most consistent reporters on the AIDS crisis within the gay press, Watney is uniquely qualified to comment on the industry's handling of the epidemic. Reflecting on this period, he stated that, at the time 'in the absence of other, reliable sources of information for lesbians and gay men, the gay press ha[d] particular duties' (Watney, 2000: 111). Although he retrospectively finds the early coverage of the epidemic in *Gay Times* and *Capital Gay* too inconsistent, he later identifies the power of the gay press, and in turn, its responsibilities:

> I believe that the gay press has certain clear responsibilities in the AIDS crisis. First, it has to continue to do its best to undo and correct the mischief and malice that dominates the rest of the mass media coverage of the epidemic … We must also be able to help people make sense of the epidemic as it affects us as individuals, and as groups of friends. (113)

By 1987 the gay press not only spoke directly to gay men, it began to criticise the government's handling of the burgeoning crisis. Jeffrey-Poulter (1991: 285) records that *Capital Gay* published a 'blistering editorial' following the Government's belated reaction to AIDS entitled 'FOUR WASTED YEARS' and demanded that 'the Department of Health answer charges of gross negligence over its handling of the epidemic'. *Gay Times* also reported on the Health Department's awareness campaign, airing criticisms made about the 'cautious language' of the adverts and calling for 'ads directed at gay men, drug users and ads which confront fear of Aids in the workplace' (*Gay Times*, April 1986: 6).

Back issues of gay magazines and newspapers published during this period demonstrate that while AIDS stories were present throughout most of the decade, they rarely made front cover news; reporting of the crisis was consistent but relatively low-key. By contrast, Clause 28 burst out of the pages of *Gay Times* in January 1987 and continued to dominate the first five pages of the magazine every month for almost a year. This focus within the gay press reflected the sudden political mobilisation within lesbian and gay communities across Britain. As the headlines of *Capital Gay* shouted in December 1987, the Clause was positioned as the 'Challenge of the Century' (*Capital Gay*, December 1987: 1). The gay press was at the forefront of the anti-clause campaign, reporting on but also publicising the London and Manchester rallies, the initiatives of local LGB groups, celebrity support and the international response to the proposed legislation. The weekly publishing cycle, twinned with its location, meant that *Capital Gay* was well positioned to provide almost immediate reporting on the progression of what it called 'the most serious legal attack on our rights since male homosexuality was outlawed more than 100 years ago' (ibid). *Capital Gay* was joined by the weekly freesheet, *The Pink Paper*, which came into existence shortly before the 'Stop the Clause' campaign in 1988. From the start *The Pink Paper* saw itself as 'the authoritative voice of the gay community', aiming to combine 'up-to date news reporting with extensive analysis and opinion' on 'important issues like partnership rights or Section 28' (*Pink Paper* – remit, online). Its headline on 5th May 1988 read 'Out and Proud' and stated that:

> If the lesbian and gay movement came of age on the first Stop the Clause march back in January, it matured beyond all expectations on Saturday when mile upon mile of dykes, faggots and friends paraded through the streets of London to show their anger at Section 28 of the Local Government Bill. (1)

Where *Capital Gay* focused on the London gay community, *The Pink Paper*, 'Britain's only national newspaper for lesbians and gays' (ibid) in the late eighties, addressed the national community mobilising political groups across Britain and pulling them together for national demonstrations such as those mentioned above.

Thus, whilst the gay press of the 1980s became more professional and commercially-oriented, it was also charged with political and politicised discussion by two seismic events that shook gay male subculture (indeed all LGBT subcultures) during this decade. As of 2010, HIV/AIDS continues to remain a key topic of concern within gay male subculture and the British government continue to drag their feet in granting lesbian and gay men full rights and protection under law. But the contemporary gay press looks, reads and feels very different to its earlier incarnations and while advertising for HIV medication and testing continues to pepper the pages of the gay weeklies and monthlies, much of the political campaigning and debate has been evacuated from its' pages, replaced by a focus on lifestyle that renders many gay male titles all but indistinguishable from their heterosexual counterparts in terms of structure, aesthetics and form.

A change in *Attitude*: The rise of the gay lifestyle magazine

Gay Times remains consistent in its inclusion of national and international gay-related news stories, together with 'media-watch' and regular articles on homophobia, discrimination and HIV. However, the launch of the gay fashion monthly *Attitude*, in 1994, signalled a decisive new turn in the history of the gay press. After the calls for revolution in the 1970s and the political clashes of the 1980s, the gay press metamorphosed into its latest incarnation in the 1990s. Slickly edited, advertising-heavy lifestyle publications have become the norm and the primary focus has firmly shifted from campaigning to consuming. Lip-service is occasionally paid to political issues, but the majority of these titles have been given over to the unquestioning promotion of the metropolitan gay lifestyle, and the commodities and practices that help to shape it.

This is not to suggest that earlier titles such as *Him*, *Gay News* or *Capital Gay* were solely political in content, nor were they only concerned with reporting gay-related news and current affairs. From the outset, the gay press had sought to inform its readers of issues affecting their personal and political life *and* provide 'lighter' lifestyle articles that appealed to what can best be termed a gay sensibility[14]. *Attitude*'s arrival, however, redrew this map.

Published by mainstream publishing house Northern and Shell, *Attitude* was characterised by high production values, glossy heavyweight stock, full-colour printing and lavish fashion photo shoots. It identified itself as a gay man's publication and in this sense it was comfortable with its sexuality; it placed itself somewhere between the heterosexual men's titles such as *For Him Magazine* (now known as *FHM*), *Arena* and *GQ*, and the urbanite staples of this period, namely *The Face*, *I.D.*, and *Dazed and Confused*. The magazine's instant (and continuing) success is a testament to its accuracy in articulating the aspirations and desires (though not necessarily the needs) of the consumer-driven metropolitan gay male subculture. Its success has brought with it a number of pretenders to the crown,

---

14 I use 'gay sensibility' with reference to Bronski's discussion of it (see Bronski, 1984: 159).

including *AXM*, *Fluid* and *DNA* all echoing *Attitude*'s ethos of glossy fash-mag images and good-looking male models dressed by couturiers such as Gaultier and D&G.

The birth of this new type of gay magazine must inevitably be understood within the wider context of the growth of a male magazine market in Britain over the last fifteen years. Crewe (2003: 92) identifies Britain in the early nineties as a period in which 'style titles' such as *GQ*, *Esquire* and *Arena* spoke to (and by extension created) the figure of the new man – 'a sexually progressive, affluent and style-conscious consumer' and a precursor to the metrosexual of the 2000s. He identifies a tension between discourses of hetero-patriarchal dominance and the socio-cultural wars waged by second-wave feminists in the previous decade. *Attitude* is also a product of these contested sites of discourse and power. Its refusal to reproduce the news magazine format of the 1980s and failure to engage with any form of sustained political debate, places it not outside of, but rather integral to, British gay male history. *Attitude* is a product of the Section 28 marches, of the demonstrations that demanded equal rights and protection from discrimination for lesbians and gay men. While the GLF's *Come Together* magazine and *Attitude* appear to be poles apart, it should be recognised that the former paved the way for the latter. We must once more acknowledge the irony of the GLF. The commercial aspect of the gay scene – including magazines such as *Attitude* and *AXM* – owes a debt to the earlier radical Left-wing movement for creating the necessary ideological space in which such a market could be forged.

Attitude and its competitors articulate a post-political gay consumer voice that has been established in the space created by the GLF. Battles for equality may rattle on but by and large the middle-class, Western-educated male homosexual has won *his* battle (or had it won for him). He can be an out gay man *and* a lawyer/doctor/architect/policeman. He can earn just as much as his heterosexual counterpart and *Attitude* provides the mouthpiece for those who want to help him spend that salary on 'gay-friendly' goods.[15] *Attitude* is, in effect, a monthly manifesto for metropolitan gay male subculture. Along with like-minded publications such as *Boyz*, it both produces and is produced by the metropolitan model. As Burston (1995: 100) has written of the latter:

> You only have to digest a few pages to understand that, these days, it is not only possible to pursue a life of 'Gay' pleasure without sparing a thought for gay politics – it's what's expected.

As I shall discuss in Chapter 4, the metropolitan subculture found between the covers of such magazines has also become a significant trope within gay men's

15 And I use the term 'gay friendly' here whilst not wishing to acknowledge any kind of socio-political alliance or concern (as in the case of eco- or environmentally-friendly) but to identify a plethora of products that conform to and are emblematic of the metropolitan gay lifestyle.

digital culture, and one might apply Burston's statement to the popular dating and sex websites that gay men use today. Faced with the lack of political discussion, digital forms of communication have also provided a space for those voices that are not found within the gay press today. I shall pick up on this in my discussion of the online barebacking subculture in Chapter 6 and will explore this in more detail. Arguably the history of the gay press, and its most recent incarnation, has meant that sexual subcultures 'outside' of the metropolitan model have had to forge new communicative sites from which to speak. However, there is one final trope that I feel requires consideration here if we are to fully understand the contexts in which gay men in Britain first began integrating digital practices into their everyday lives.

Killer in the Village: AIDS and the British gay community[16]

HIV/AIDS must be central to any study of recent British gay male history. The virus has shaped and influenced the identities, practices, politics and desires of gay male subculture via the associated discourses of disease, blame and risk (see for example, the work of Weeks, 1990 and 1991; Edwards, 1994; Burston, 1995; Rayside, 1998 and Sinfield, 1998). Yet while HIV/AIDS remains central to any such discussion, the relationship between the virus and this subculture has altered over the last twenty years. Proving this is not difficult and we need only look to the work of Rofes (1998), Scarce (1999), Reaney (2000), Signorile (2002) and Dean (2009) for further evidence of such change. In Chapter 6 I will draw on much of this work to illustrate how one of the most dramatic shifts in attitudes towards the virus has been manifested online. The majority of the scholars I mention here are based in the United States and HIV/AIDS is a truly global pandemic. Learning from scholars, researchers and activists from across the world has been the key to understanding not only the virus but also reactions and responses to it. But while there are of course similarities in terms of routes of transmission, most affected social groups and prescribed methods of protection, from the outset HIV/AIDS has formed culturally specific relationships with those it has affected, and this has resulted in the British narrative of HIV/AIDS differing from the narratives established in other countries.

In the introduction to this chapter I mentioned the global aspect of metropolitan gay culture and Altman (1994: 13) identifies the importance of recognising such mobility when he states that the 'international travel' and 'interaction' of American gay men was one of the primary reasons behind 'relatively high infection rates ... in places as dispersed as San Juan, Sydney and Zurich'. The 'tracking' of HIV/AIDS has been a Western (and especially US) pre-occupation since the beginning of the pandemic. This is perhaps unsurprising given the fact that, with the first

16 The quotation in the title refers to the first detailed British television account of HIV/AIDS, a BBC *Horizon* programme aired in 1983 entitled *The Killer in the Village*.

reports of the disease emanating from the United States, HIV/AIDS was originally regarded as a North American phenomenon which, having established itself within the gay enclaves of New York, San Francisco, Miami, Los Angeles and Chicago, migrated to the UK as a result of global travel. Identifying the 'alien' responsible for bringing HIV into the USA carried with it concerns for national security, quarantine and border control and there was a recognisable need to locate HIV/AIDS as something 'un-American' and wholly Other. Shilts's (1987) best-selling novel *And The Band Played On* articulated this need and dramatised the searching and ultimate identification of 'patient zero', the man who supposedly introduced HIV into the American population. The fact that the book was turned into a film by HBO in 1993, despite the patient zero hypothesis being discredited, confirms not only the USA's need to apportion blame but also the political (as opposed to scientific, for example) motivations behind such searching[17]. The reporting of the first British AIDS death in *Capital Gay* (1981), which ran the headline 'gay man dies of US disease', demonstrates how HIV/AIDS was originally positioned as not only a gay disease[18], but an American one too[19]. In an interview with Garfield (1994: 242), Holly Johnson (lead singer of eighties pop group *Frankie Goes To Hollywood*) recalls first hearing about the new disease at a London nightclub:

> We went to Heaven one night, and there was a sign up saying, 'Tonight, all the music we play will be dedicated to the memory of Patrick Cowley, who died of A.I.D.S.' People were saying, 'What's this disease? What's this AIDS? What does it mean?' One of the guys had a vague idea, because as an air steward with British Airways he'd heard about it in America.

Johnson's recollection is notable for two reasons. Firstly, it emphasises the link perceived between HIV/AIDS and the USA as well as the relationship between international travel (and international work) and the spread of the disease. Secondly, it indicates that in the earliest years of the epidemic, knowledge (and rumour) about the virus emanated from within gay subculture rather than from official sources.

There are similarities between the British and American narratives of HIV/AIDS. The groups initially most affected were the same (gay men, IV drug users, haemophiliacs and other blood transfusion receivers) and reactions to the virus (anger, fear, denial, hysteria) were also similar. But this meta-narrative belies

---

17 'Patient Zero', flight attendant Gaëtan Dugas, was identified as a promiscuous *Canadian* gay man. His nationality was of utmost importance, the idea being that AIDS *had* to have come from a foreign invader.

18 AIDS was originally known in the USA by the acronym, GRID, which stood for Gay Related Immune Disease.

19 Engel (2001: 90) has identified the initial belief in British gay communities that AIDS as an American phenomena and later (largely as a by-product of the Government's national campaign) how gay men were 'marginalized … from AIDS and HIV work'.

the formation of local identities, relationships and discourses that developed out of specific cultural milieus and which were structured, in part, by the different timescales that operated in the two different countries. Additionally, while the British gay community's response to AIDS borrowed heavily from American strategies, important statistical, temporal and epistemological differences between the two countries resulted in altered experiences of HIV/AIDS.

Named after one of the first people to die of AIDS-related illnesses in the UK, the Terrence Higgins Trust (THT) was set up in 1982 and became Britain's first national HIV/AIDS awareness group[20]. Although gay-friendly, THT did not identify itself as solely gay in focus. That said, it has always devoted a large percentage of its work to raising awareness of HIV/AIDS in the gay community, and the majority of its initial membership were LGB identified. From the outset, however, THT aimed at educating, protecting and caring for *everyone* at risk. While there is no confirmation that the Trust drew directly from the earlier gay civil rights movement, similarities between the organisation and other gay groups are apparent. For instance, THT marries lobbying and campaigning tactics similar to those used by CHE, with the grass-roots consciousness-raising style of the GLF. This multi-faceted approach has allowed THT to remain the leading HIV/AIDS charity in Britain and has also allowed it to respond to HIV/AIDS on a variety of levels, something that is arguably the key to its success.[21] THT, together with the London Lesbian and Gay Switchboard, was responsible for the first awareness campaigns in the gay press. In 1983 *HIM Monthly* ran THT adverts that featured a helpline number for those concerned about HIV infection, and Switchboard began offering information on HIV as early as August 1983. In the same month, the Gay Medical Association (GMA) produced a leaflet designed to raise awareness amongst the gay community. By today's standards, the advice given by the GMA appears somewhat vague and inaccurate[22], though it must of course be remembered that the routes of transmission were at that time still unconfirmed. Inaccuracies aside, such work was integral to alerting gay men to the burgeoning crisis and offering information at a time when there was still no response from the British government. With no information being produced by the Health Education Authority and with doctors still having little to no idea what they were dealing with, these early interventions from within gay subculture were the lone voices responding to gay men's fears and anxieties about the coming plague and the gay press provided the means for these voices to be heard.

20 Later becoming a formal organisation, THT received charitable status in January 1983 (see Terrence Higgins Trust – history of organisation, online).

21 Altman (1994) discusses the importance of a pre-existing LGB identified community to the successful formation of HIV/AIDS organisations in the early 1980s.

22 For instance, in the same publication, the GMA (UK) suggest that avoiding partners who seem in 'ill health' is a sound safe sex strategy, giving rise to the spurious notion that HIV infection can be 'read' through physical symptoms.

While Watney (1994) criticises the gay press for its patchy coverage of HIV/AIDS during the early years, it is clear that during this period attempts were made to inform and to offer organisations a means of reaching their target audiences. King (1993: 29) cites a 1986 study in which 56% of respondents stated that they had found useful information on HIV/AIDS in the gay press. Similarly, Altman (1994: 21) identifies the gay press as being 'particularly important' during the formative years of the epidemic, 'acting as a vital tool in mobilizing the community'. It was through the press, NGOs and benefit nights such as the one mentioned by Johnson above, that HIV/AIDS was pushed to the forefront of the British gay consciousness from 1983 onwards. Today THT continue to conduct outreach work in clubs and bars, cruising grounds and public sex environments (PSEs). Many of my gay male students find themselves mixed up in sexual health and AIDS education work during their time at university and World AIDS day continues to be marked on the gay scene with large donations being raised each year for local and national charities supporting and caring for gay men affected by the virus.

With all this in mind it is perhaps surprising to find Sinfield (1998: 89–91) commenting that:

> What is troubling about AIDS in Britain is that we may seem to have passed *beyond* it, but actually we have not properly passed *through* it ... *as a community*, North-west European gay men have not lived with AIDS in the way US people have lived with it – and represented it.

Considering the initial response to HIV/AIDS, the fact that gay men are still identified as the group most at risk of contracting HIV in Britain, and that the majority of AIDS-related deaths in the UK have been within this social group, Sinfield's statement seems on first reading, to be at best odd, at worst, ignorant. Of course it is in fact neither. The key to understanding such an assertion lies not in the representation of HIV/AIDS, but in living with the *material reality* of the disease. It was initially expected that the British epidemic would follow the same trajectory as that witnessed in the USA. Focusing on quantitative rather than qualitative data, it was presumed that gay men would start developing and then dying from AIDS-related illnesses in similar numbers to those seen in New York, San Francisco and Miami. But these forecasts turned out to be inaccurate and there are a number of reasons for this, though as Watney (1994: 224) identifies, it has little to do with State intervention.

Firstly, there is the issue of time difference. By the time gay men in Britain were exposed to the virus, initial research into HIV had already begun and safe sex strategies, in their most rudimentary form, were being drawn up and implemented.[23] This time lag meant that condom use was promoted in Britain much earlier in the

23 Treichler (1997: 39) asserts that the 1983 pamphlet, *How To Have Sex in an Epidemic* was the first 'official' publication that espoused the condom code and the need for gay men to use the contraceptive when having penetrative sex. Watney (1994: 19) states

epidemiological narrative than it was in the USA. British gay male subculture has often been somewhat 'behind the times' in comparison to its US counterpart, whether it be fashion, music, politics or even drug use. In the arena of HIV/AIDS, this transatlantic delay proved to be crucial in implementing safe sex strategies much earlier on in the UK narrative than was possible in the USA. King (1993: 30) compares data drawn from survey cohorts in the early years of the British epidemic to data taken from San Francisco and New York-based studies. He concludes that by the time the immune deficiency disease was identified in 1980, the HIV virus had infiltrated extensive networks of gay men in both of the US cities. By comparison, the British prevalence rate was one quarter of that found in the USA, and changes in sexual behaviour, due to increased awareness in Britain, were crucial to this disparity.

The second reason behind this transatlantic difference in HIV/AIDS trajectories lies in the varied response rates from central governments. One could never applaud the British government of the time for being quick to respond to the growing crisis, but while it was slow in developing a strategy for dealing with HIV/AIDS, it was still faster out of the blocks than the American Administration. Four years after AIDS took its first British victims, the government were only just formulating a strategy for dealing with the crisis, a crisis that had already affected thousands and which, just two years later, had claimed 1,460 British lives (Avert – AIDS statistics UK, online). Yet the governmental response in the USA was even slower. According to AEGIS (AEGIS, online) it was not until 1988 that a government-sponsored AIDS awareness campaign was rolled out in the United States. Given that the first American AIDS victims were (retrospectively) identified in 1978, it was ten years – an entire decade – before the American government funded a national awareness campaign to combat the disease. This ten-year gap is undoubtedly a major factor within the epidemiological narrative of AIDS in America, leading Vito Russo to assert in 1988 that 'If I'm dying from anything, I'm dying from the President of the United States' (Act-up, online).

In addition to time lag and governmental (in)action, there were also subcultural differences that need to be taken into account. The commercial sex culture of bathhouses, saunas and back rooms that was a part of the American gay scene during the late 1970s and early 1980s meant that the virus was able to spread with an alarming rapidity. King (1993: 62) states that:

> There can be little doubt that one of the factors that facilitated of HIV among gay men in the gay centres of the United States … was the existence of bathhouses and back rooms as designated sex facilities.

Rotello (1997: 58–60) similarly identifies commercial PSEs as central to the initial spread of the virus. New York in the mid-late 1970s (for example) had a thriving

---

that in the same year, the *British Medical News* advised gay men to use condoms during sex.

commercial scene and back issues of magazines such as *Michael's Thing*[24] contain advertising for the East Side Sauna, Ansona 73 bath and health club, Broadway Arms Baths, The Club Baths and the Wall Street Sauna. By contrast, British gay male subculture in the late 1970s had relatively little to offer by way of commercial PSEs. There were a few saunas and public baths in major towns and cities, (the Burlington All-Male Health Club on Old Bond Street in London being one such example) but they were comparatively few and far between.

Thus while a gay man living in New York in 1980 could have sex with multiple partners in the space of one evening at a bathhouse, in London gay men were often restricted to either going to a bar or club and meeting someone, or hanging around a dark and often dangerous cruising ground in the hope that someone might pick them up before the police did. Britain has a rich history of gay public sex, but before HIV/AIDS it was never as commercially organised as it was in the USA. Today, the picture is markedly different and advertising for saunas, gay gyms and other sex-on-premises venues fills the pages of bar rags, and even the glossier monthlies mentioned above.[25] But the epidemiological framework for understanding the spread of HIV, suggested by Rotello in 1997, does not fit neatly with the history of British gay male subculture.

These differences in chronology, intervention and subculture mean that although HIV transmission did occur in Britain, it happened at a rate far slower than that found in the USA. While the latter reported 107,840 cumulative AIDS cases by 1988, the former reported 2,471 (Avert, online). At the time of publication, over 18,000 people have died of AIDS in Britain (THT, online). In the USA, this figure stands at over one million (Avert, online). These figures should be understood as relative to the size of the populations in each country[26], but it remains clear that in the language of its military officials the 'collateral damage' of HIV/AIDS has been far greater in the United States than in Britain. This is not to belittle the 18,000 plus British deaths, many of which could have been prevented through earlier government intervention (in the form of both research funding and awareness-raising) on both sides of the Atlantic, but it does allow us to identify key differences between the British and USA situation.

---

24 A weekly listings magazine for the New York gay scene.

25 Also of note is the fact that this new commercial sexual culture appears to be far more accepted within contemporary British gay male subculture than it has been before. In Chapter 5 I will discuss the history of public sexual culture in gay Britain. In contrast to the clandestine meetings in toilets and other public spaces, these commercial venues are increasingly becoming an accepted – and acceptable – part of urban gay life. I have witnessed a marked increase in the use of such venues by friends and acquaintances and it seems that today, along with participation in a back room of a club, or visiting a sex-club such as Hard-on or Hoist, going to a sauna (perhaps at the end of a night out) is becoming more and more normal for a larger and larger number of gay men.

26 Proof of the UK's difference to other Western HIV epidemics is evidenced in Watney's (2000: 2) assertion that the British have suffered 'a disproportionately small epidemic … by comparison with demographically similar countries such as France'.

So when he writes that gay men in Britain 'haven't passed through AIDS' in the same way that American gay men have, Sinfield is not denying the reality of British people living with HIV, he is identifying the different realities that exist worldwide in relation to the virus. Writing over a decade ago, at the height of the epidemic, Watney (1994: 244) also identifies these differences:

> It is still statistically unlikely that even in inner London the average gay man will knowingly have met someone living with AIDS, let alone been affected by death on a large scale.

Both subcultures have been immersed in HIV/AIDS discourse for nearly thirty years, but while gay subculture in the USA witnessed death and grieving on a massive scale, its British counterpart has by and large been grieving for *what might come*. This mourning for a deferred 'gay holocaust'[27] remains an important theme within British gay culture. The most powerfully felt dimension of the disease in Britain has been the abstract fear it has instilled in a population that has rarely witnessed widespread death as a result of HIV infection. And it has been this abstract fear – articulated through discourses of awareness, prevention and regulation – that has had the most powerful effect on gay men's lives:

> In a classic catch-22, gay men were stymied by HIV. We read the reports from San Francisco and New York about the 'gay plague'. The only victims that we knew were public figures: Rock Hudson, Halston, Liberace and Nureyev. But the London gay scene was under siege. (Sherwood, 2001: 3)

It was originally fear that prompted many gay men to change their sexual behaviour in the 1980s and many saw promiscuity as high-risk behaviour. But as an understanding of both the virus and safe sex grew within gay subculture, promiscuity could no longer be considered as a 'reason' for getting HIV. This was confirmed in a Project Sigma report (Hickson *et al.*, 1993: 94–95) that found there to be 'relatively less risk [of transmission] generated by casual sex than in relationships'. This conclusion may sound surprising but the research found that condom use in casual sexual interactions was much higher than in stable long-term relationships. In many respects this research laid the foundation for later advertising campaigns that targeted gay men in relationships. Such research, however, did little to silence those who saw HIV/AIDS as both a moral issue and an excuse to cast moral judgement. Right-wing politicians were joined by outspoken figures such as James Anderton, the (then) Chief Constable of Greater Manchester, in claiming that HIV/AIDS was God's response to homosexuality and that gay men were 'swirling around in a cesspool of their own making' (Sharratt,

27 In using the term holocaust here I acknowledge Larry Kramer's, (1990) *Reports From the Holocaust*, which is emblematic of both the level of devastation AIDS caused in America, and the type of activism that it prompted.

1987, np). Such attacks illustrate the ideological blurring of sexual behaviour and lifestyle that has occurred as a result of the virus. It is this blurring that allowed Sir Rhodes Boyson, then MP for Brent North, to comment that:

> AIDS is, to me, a part of the fruits of the permissive society. The regular one-man, one-woman marriage would not put us at risk with this in any way. (quoted in De Jongh, 1988, np)

The moral right justified HIV/AIDS as the 'natural' consequence of sexuality gone awry; it was the grisly but justified result of the gay man's (apparently innate) promiscuity. Watney (1994: 78) acknowledges this line of argument when he writes:

> [There is an] implication of collective guilt on the part of those indulging in sexual activity outside of marriage, a guilt which focuses most sharply on those who in any case are not legally entitled to marry one another, gay men, whose morality is judged against familial standards and, of course, is found wanting.

Guilt and punishment repeatedly appear as central themes in the pre-liberation history of Western homosexuality and they were deployed once more by reactionary elements in the government and the press to demonise non-heterosexual relations for 'causing' HIV/AIDS. It is hardly surprising that during a period in which the British government was advocating a moral crusade against non-heteronormative familial relations (Section 28), the virus should be used as reason against 'promoting' homosexuality. Considering the media's employment of such rhetoric, it is also unsurprising that the myth of homosexual promiscuity as the cause of HIV pervaded the very community such rhetoric sought to demonise.

Gay culture continued to be criticised throughout the 1990s by writers such as Kramer (1990) Rotello (1997) Signorile (1997) and Sullivan (1998), who saw it as promoting promiscuity and therefore HIV transmission. These writers' own homosexuality meant that (unlike the church, the state or the press) when each commentator spoke, he did so from *within* gay culture, conferring on his speech a degree of experiential authenticity which, in some eyes, legitimated his judgemental critique of how other gay men lived their lives.

For example, in his 1998 memoir/manifesto *Love Undetectable* Sullivan discussed his HIV positive status together with his views on the Catholic Church before claiming that all our political energies should be put into fighting for the right to gay marriage[28]. Sullivan's promotion of marriage operates on two levels. At first sight he appears to be campaigning for gay rights, for the legal and equal recognition of gay partnerships and the rights that this would entail. However,

28 Goldstein has quoted Sullivan as arguing against 'anti-bias laws' stating that harassment, discrimination and hate-crime are no longer necessary issues for the gay political agenda (Goldstein, 2000: 18).

a closer reading reveals that Sullivan's promotion of gay marriage employs a configuration of homosexuality based on monogamy at the expense of other queer identities and relationships. Importantly, HIV/AIDS is cited as a reason for gay monogamy and the repression of other configurations of homosexuality. Once more promiscuity becomes something to be treated, something wrong and deviant:

> My heterosexual friends, of course, instinctively saw my sexual life as a concession to carnality, an unthinkable lapse into irresponsibility – and I do not wish to deny that at some obvious level, it was … but understanding promiscuity is a necessary first step to transforming it, and transforming it into something more meaningful and dignified and loving is, perhaps, the most difficult bequest of the last two decades. (41–42)

Sullivan's promotion of monogamy merits comparison with the discourses surrounding the British Civil Partnership Act. Both Sullivan and the legislation seek to increase the rights of some gay people while affirming the belief in a 'correct' and valid version of homosexuality: one that conforms to societal norms and echoes the regulatory institution of marriage. This is confirmed when Sullivan states that *true* gay liberation comes with marriage, and that the older achievements were akin to nothing more than 'temporary occasions of desire snatched in the shadows' (Sullivan, 1998: 68).

While awareness campaigns have sought to promote safer sexual activity *regardless* of sexual lifestyle, cultural commentators such as Sullivan have used the virus as a platform upon which to promote monogamy as a *culturally* acceptable method of safer sex behaviour. Watney (1996: 18) sees HIV/AIDS as providing the means for a 'wholesale desexualisation of gay culture and experience' and this stands in opposition to the 'multiple encounters, shifts of sexual identification, actings out, cultural reinforcements' integral to the formation of a gay identity that 'desublimat[ed] the inherited sexual guilt of a grotesquely homophobic society'. Bronski (1997: 121) goes further and criticises the HIV/AIDS awareness campaigns themselves for devaluing and distancing its target audience, claiming that the use of advertising that relies on a consumer mentality serves to alienate gay men who do not conform to a particular body type or lifestyle:

> Promoting safer sex as a more 'fun' alternative to unsafe sex plays on the same underlying erosion of self-worth present in all advertising … The cult of the beautiful body and consumerism shape other gay male community responses to the epidemic.

The British government's first advertising campaign aimed at gay men fell foul of this consumer culture. The series of adverts featuring black and white images taken by Herb Ritts[29] and Jean Batiste Mondino used predominantly white, semi-naked models of catwalk calibre. In doing so the adverts served to perpetuate the 'body beautiful' aesthetic and stood in contrast to the reality of most men's lives, not to mention the ravaged body of the AIDS patient. The advertising copy may have promoted safer sexual practices but the images promoted body fascism, Euro-centrism and alienation. In a subculture that already has an increased investment in visual signifiers, the adverts served to re-iterate the gold standard that many gay men found themselves unable to match.

Conclusion

Section 28, HIV/AIDS, the gay press, the rise and fall of political activism, monogamy, condoms, the commercial scene, queer theory and identity politics: gay male subculture since 1984 has seen upheavals, tensions, triumphs and defeats that pervade its consciousness and will continue to do so for many years to come. Such pervasiveness extends to the digital environments, and structures the spaces and practices of gay men's digital interactions. I would go so far as to say that it is not only possible to recognise how the discourses of politics, commerce, lifestyle and health have permeated gay men's digital culture, it is imperative that we acknowledge these forces if we are to fully understand how and why gay men's digital culture looks, feels and operates the way it does. The integration of new media technologies and practices into gay male subculture can be seen as both the consequence of these histories and a response to them.

I shall return to these themes throughout the following chapters, reframing and refocusing my attention upon them according to the differing contexts in which they are encountered in digital forms and practices. The notion of a metropolitan gay male subculture, for instance, resonates throughout my discussion of gay dating/sex websites, and the process of identification and consumption that circulate through user profiles are structured by the rhetoric of a decidedly metropolitan construction of gay identity. Elsewhere, in Chapter 5, the metropolitan is evacuated, temporarily, as I explore how and why some gay men are using digital and physical spaces to 'queer' dominant understandings of gay sex and gay culture, momentarily stepping outside of this framework for multiple reasons.

In Chapter 6, the discourses of HIV/AIDS prevention work provide a springboard for my analysis of barebacking subculture as it operates within online environments. My case studies illustrate the variety of nuanced and complex responses gay men have formed to HIV/AIDS in the 'post-retroviral' era of the virus, where new drug regimes have radically extended the lives of HIV positive people. These responses are articulated in very different ways but their conclusions are often similar: the relationship between HIV/AIDS and gay

---

29 Ritts having made his name photographing the gay icon, Madonna (see Garfield, 1994).

male subculture is shifting radically and such a shift requires articulation and consideration. Understanding the connections between the history of HIV/AIDS and these new sexual subcultures is crucial if sexual health awareness campaigns are to remain effective. Finally, in Chapter 7, my discussion of digital cruising, whereby men are deploying mobile-locative technologies in order to interact with one another in everyday space, can be seen as a reflection on the continued political and social status of gay men in contemporary Britain. Digital cruising is not, in itself a consciously political act but, like the cybercottage of Chapter 5, the political history of gay male subculture is woven into the very fabric of these communicative acts. My discussion identifies the tense relationship that gay men (indeed all LGBT people) continue to have with public space and recognises both what has been achieved since the days of the GLF or of the Clause 28 rallies, and what remains still to be done.

However, before I begin exploring specific instances of gay men's digital culture I want to (re)connect with some of the broader themes that have underscored and framed my discussion in this chapter. In an effort to suture material and digital realities together and provide a discursive 'bridge' between this chapter and the in-depth analyses found elsewhere in this book, in the next chapter I offer a new critical framework for analysing and interrogating gay men's digital culture. This framework acknowledges the histories discussed in this chapter, while having in its sights the contemporary digital landscape of gay male subculture. It forms the theoretical architecture for the ensuing case studies and informs the methods by which these studies are produced. Yet, in building on my discussions here, it remains rooted in the recent history of gay male politics, culture and activism and as such, resolutely refuses to be located in solely the physical or the digital spheres of gay men's lives.

Chapter 3
Cybercarnality: Identifying a Critical Pathway through Gay Men's Digital Culture

As expressed in the introductory chapter, this book sets out to explore the relationship between contemporary gay male subculture and new media technologies, particularly the Internet. As any researcher of digital culture knows only too well, studying something as large and amorphous as the Internet can sometimes feel like a Sisyphean task; never-ending in its scope and, (as websites, practices, programmes and cultures evolve and move so rapidly), at times repetitive, the terrain often shifts and is forever changing. I addressed this issue in the introduction, commenting on the inevitable need to locate any such study within a specific time, place and context, while recognising how the learning contained therein might also speak to wider practices and spaces, and across time. To this I now add the point that digital culture can never be studied as a whole, but must be distilled, concentrated down and examined in ways that are, at best, fragmentary. Even breaking one iteration of digital culture – the Internet – up into the spaces created by and for, a particular subculture, for example, proves to be overwhelming in its scope. How can we, for instance, study 'gay cyberspace', when the sheer volume of websites, chat rooms, forums and other forms made by and/or for gay men, is immeasurable? Heavy-handed taxonomies offer us very little reward.

Yet, at the other extreme, the focusing on a single digital space can at first sight appear to be a rather blinkered view of gay men's digital culture, suggesting an ignorance of the vast constellation of data available in order to focus on a sole website or chat room or forum. Such charges can indeed ring true if due care isn't taken in considering *what* should be studied, *which* fragments warrant investigation, *how* we can learn about other similar spaces from the examination of a chosen few, and (perhaps most importantly) *why* these snapshots of digital life can be considered emblematic of wider internet cultures and subcultures. In short, such fragments should be considered important not only because of (or perhaps in spite of) their own specificity, but also because of what they serve to *illustrate*.

The digital spaces and practices explored in the ensuing chapters are examples of such fragments. We might consider the accompanying analyses products of a 'mining down' into the fabric of digital life in order to sample the fabric from which it is woven. Through such mining, I am aware of both the specificity of that space, but also the way in which that space can be read as symptomatic of wider issues, arguments and practices occurring in gay male subculture today. Thus, the case studies function as symbols of experiences and practices that in turn operate at a higher level, once removed from that of any single website or forum.

But can the multifarious iterations of gay men's digital culture be drawn together? Do the experiences of users of Gaydar, members of a barebacking website or men who Bluejack weave together in ways that produce a more cohesive understanding? Beyond the single website or chat room, is there a larger story to be told? A meta-narrative that – if not wholly explaining gay men's digital lives in their entirety – at least goes some way to pulling together otherwise disparate and unrelated spaces under the broader banner of gay male digital culture?

In this chapter I shall attempt to address this issue in order to consider the possibility of forming such a meta-narrative. Let me be clear, the aim of this chapter is not to propose a universal consensus regarding the nature of such environments. Nor do I wish to suggest that all gay men use digital media in the same way, or that there is an overarching truth about cyberspace waiting to be discovered 'out there'. Rather, what I will outline here is a *way of talking* about an array of cyberspaces constructed and populated by gay men. Specifically what I propose is a critical model that identifies commonalities that operate across a range of gay men's digital practices and digital spaces, and which provides a framework for discussing those commonalities within the context of metropolitan gay male culture.

The principal aim of this chapter then is to create a discursive framework through which the spaces, practices and subjects of gay male digital culture can be understood and through which specific themes that pervade, underpin and inform that culture can be articulated and foregrounded. I use the term 'discursive' here in the Foucauldian sense and identify the productive dimension of discourse, and the nature of its production – power:

> We must cease once and for all to describe the effects of power in negative terms … in fact, power produces, it produces reality; it produces domains of objects and rituals of truth. The individual and the knowledge that may be gained of him belong to this production. (Foucault, 1977a: 194)

The framework I propose here relies on an acknowledgement of the shifting and transitory nature of language, knowledge and power. Foucault (1976: 99) writes that 'relations of power-knowledge are not static forms of distribution, they are "matrices of transformations"' and the model I outline here articulates the 'polyvalence of discourse' (100), appearing, at times, to operate in contradictory and paradoxical ways. Likewise, in acknowledging that it is through discourse that 'power and knowledge are joined together' (ibid), the framework I seek to propose in this chapter does not suggest a static hierarchy of power but the *production* and *mobilising* of power. Foucault writes that '[d]iscourse transmits and produces power; it reinforces it but also undermines and exposes it, renders it fragile and makes it possible to thwart it' (1976: 101) illustrating this through the example of the 'sin against nature': sodomy. In historical, religious and scientific discourse, the resulting power produced served to both articulate the punishment/treatment of the sodomite/homosexual *and* mobilise a method for subverting and countering that same power (whether through a silencing or through a reversal of discourse).

The power identified here should be understood as operating in a similar fashion. Thus, for example, the discourse of monitoring and observation I identify below (a discourse of panoptic self-surveillance) is on the one hand being deployed as a means of exerting power over gay male culture (Gaydar) and simultaneously being used to subvert such power (as in the case of the cyber-cottage in Chapter 5). Additionally, the interstices created by race, gender, class, nationality and religion mean that while we often talk of gay culture as (positively) unified or (negatively) homogenous, the reality is far more fragmented and contested. This fracturing of the whole and the tensions that this inevitably exposes similarly demonstrates the mobilising of discourse for contrary means. As Kendall's (2002) work demonstrates, the Internet does not precipitate a levelling of the playing field; relationships of power that were previously established offline often get invoked in online environments, their effects remaining just as tangible. Grounded as it is in both contemporary and historical contexts: 'discourse must not be referred to the distant presence of the origin but treated as and when it occurs' (Foucault, 1997b: 25).

Butler (1990: 92) draws on Foucault's rejection of the 'sexed' body, writing that 'the body gains meaning in discourse only in the specific context of power relations' and that 'sexuality is an historically specific organization of power, discourse, bodies and affectivity'. Such an acknowledgement allows Butler to formulate a theory of performativity that identifies the political dimension of gender parody:

> which does not assume that there is an original which such parodic identities imitate … Indeed the parody is *of* the very notion of an original. (ibid: 138)

Butler's work has shaped queer and feminist interpretations of digital media (Macrae, 1997; Plant, 1997; Wakeford, 1997; Stone, 1998; Harraway, 2001) and has provided a framework for interrogating gender 'play' and gender 'confusion' online. While the spaces explored in this book are arguably resistant to the *conscious* acts of gender play often referred to in the work cited above, they all remain invested in specific performances of gender, and as such can be explored from this perspective:

> In the place of an original identification which serves as a determining cause, gender identity might be reconceived as a personal/cultural history of received meanings subject to a set of imitative practices which refer latterly to other imitations and which, jointly, construct the illusion of a primary and interior gendered self or parody the mechanism of that construction. (Butler, ibid: 139)

Finally, in setting out a loose critical framework for analysing and understanding gay male digital culture, this chapter seeks to provide a bridge between the material-historical discussion of British gay male culture outlined in the preceding chapter, and the more focused critical analyses of contemporary gay male web spaces that inform the following chapters. If Chapter 2 can be thought of as providing the context in which gay male culture began to immerse itself within the digital, this chapter should be understood as drawing on elements of that context in order to shape an awareness of these recently formed environments and practices.

Cybercarnality

Chiefly, I want to suggest a new term – *cybercarnality* – that can be deployed in multiple ways in discussions of gay male digital culture, as a means of signposting the identification of, and critical engagement with, tropes that have become prevalent across a constellation of digital spaces and practices created by and for gay men. As such cybercarnality can be read as a mechanism that operates from within the singular text – working at the granular level – but which also fastens that text to an ever-increasing number of sites in which similar practices, subjects and ideas proliferate.

Before we can begin to use the term of course we must firstly identify and define it, and the rest of this chapter will henceforth deal with this task of definition. Cybercarnality refers to the formation of a particular discourse that has come to structure and permeate gay male digital culture. This discourse operates at the level of content (via digital images, official and unofficial language, user-generated content and user-created content) and at the level of form – what we might otherwise call the 'architecture' of such spaces. It is by no means the only discourse in operation in any one site and it does not necessarily operate in the same way across the spectrum of spaces it pervades. As I shall demonstrate later, cybercarnality inhabits spaces that are supportive of a metropolitan gay identity as well as spaces that are counter-metropolitan or subaltern. However, while its outcomes and uses may vary greatly, the underlying 'code' of cybercarnality – and the socio-cultural context of its production – remains the same. Cybercarnality can perhaps best be understood as providing a means of acknowledging and identifying two specific tropes prevalent in gay cyberspace. These tropes coalesce in the production of online subjectivities and fashion interactions between those subjectivities. Inevitably they also influence gay male subculture as it exists across a myriad of digital, physical and 'hybrid'[1] spaces. These two tropes are identified as: a) the pornographic remediation of the gay male body and b) technologies of self-surveillance and corporeal regulation.

My analysis of the first of these tropes, that of pornographic remediation, owes a great debt to theories of sexual representation, particularly the work of

1 My reference to 'hybrid' space builds on the work of De Souza e Silva (2006).

Kappeler (1986). Gay male subculture's multiple investments in the rhetoric and representational strategies of pornography has been identified previously by many scholars (see, for example Stoltenberg, 1991; Dyer, 1992; Champagne, 1997; Mercer, 2000; Radel, 2001). But Kappeler's work on the *structures* of objectification that lie behind sexual representation provides, I believe, a productive foundation upon which to build a framework for understanding the remediation of an eroticised gay male body through digital technologies. Like Kappeler's objects of study, this remediation is invested in visual culture, however it departs from her feminist study through the incorporation of the attendant themes of HIV/AIDS and masculinity, which continue to circulate in and around gay male pornography, and which structure the content and form of gay male sexual representation in the West.

Meanwhile the ontology of the second trope lies within systems of discipline and surveillance. Whether through the medical discourses of psychiatry and psychoanalysis, sexology, phrenology and genetics or the judicial powers of governments, law courts and the police, such mechanisms have simultaneously constructed and codified male homosexuality within Western cultures since the nineteenth century.[2] As Foucault (1976: 43) famously writes of the 19th century, where once 'the sodomite had been a temporary aberration; the homosexual was now a species' and the production of this new 'species' lay in the development of technologies of surveillance that both produced and were produced by discourses. In *Discipline & Punish* Foucault (1977: 192) identifies these technologies as transforming men into 'docile bodies' and the homosexual, discursively produced in the 19th century, immediately became subject to mechanisms of *examination*:

> The examination is at the centre of the procedures that constitute the individual's effect and object of power, as effect and object of knowledge. It is the examination which, by combining hierarchical surveillance and normalizing judgement, assures the great disciplinary function of distribution and classification, maximum extraction of forces and time, continuous genetic accumulation, optimum combination of aptitudes and, thereby, the fabrication of cellular, organic, genetic and combinatory individuality.

While gay men (at least in the West) are no longer categorised as either criminal or mentally ill, regimes of power that centre on examination, and its attendant processes of identification, classification, recording and (re)coding, remain influential within contemporary Western gay male sub-culture. In Britain, the Civil Partnership Act of 2004 demonstrates the continuing relationship between legislation and homosexuality, while HIV/AIDS, and an attendant discourse of prevention, continues to resonate within gay male culture, medicalising sex acts in order that they may be open to scrutiny, inspection and evaluation. This second

---

2 For a discussion of the legal and social history of gay men in Britain see Jeffery-Poulter (1991) and Weeks (1990).

trope therefore draws upon a dual heritage while demonstrating how these regimes of power have been taken up by gay men themselves in numerous ways, and deployed through technologies of self-surveillance and self-regulation in an effort to be healthier, fitter, sexier, more desirable and – ultimately – 'better'.

These two tropes, which will be explored in detail shortly, form the axis upon which cybercarnality can be charted and fuel its operation as a mechanism through which the gay male body is constructed, consumed and regulated in digital environments. Cybercarnality thus denotes the (re)production of the gay male body in virtual spaces, through which the individual, group and gay culture as a whole, communicates, negotiates and experiences that space. In contrast to the historical (and overwhelmingly heterosexual) perception of virtual realities being non-corporeal, gay men's digital culture has long been preoccupied with the re-emergence, re-imagining and re-evaluating of gay male corporeality. And cybercarnality, I shall argue, offers a method for understanding and interrogating this pre-occupation.

Of course, an interest in the 'carnal' gay male body pre-dates the Internet. As mentioned briefly in Chapter 2, the gay press has long been involved in revealing and eroticising the male body. Magazines such as *Timm*, *Him* and *Spartacus* were as invested in an erotic coding of masculinity and the male form as contemporary web spaces are. More recent publications such as *AXM* and *DNA* regularly offer images of men that sit somewhere between fashion-spread and porn-shoot. It did not take digital technologies for men to become objects of a homoerotic gaze; we've been looking at each other 'in that way' for decades[3]. And the shift in gay newspaper coverage, from political discussion towards the promotion of specific sexualised lifestyles, inevitably converges with a discussion of the commodification of the gay male body. Cybercarnality builds on this, making the processes of visibility and commodification more explicit and extending them into new spaces. The primary difference between existing media forms that incorporate the eroticised body of the gay man, and newer, digital environments then, is that while the former have evolved and adapted according to changing consumption practices and socio-political contexts, the latter are founded upon such processes; they are built out of, and cannot be imagined outside of, this erotic economy of gay male corporeality. It is to the erotic dimension of cybercarnality then that I now turn my attention.

Trope 1: Pornography and representation

Any discussion of gay male pornography would be epistemologically flawed if it did not acknowledge the tremendous influence that feminism has had on the formation of critical debates surrounding the explicit representation of gay male sexuality. Second-wave feminist thought was responsible for providing both

3 See O'Toole (1997) for a discussion of the history of (gay) pornography.

the critical tools with which to engage in discussions about pornography, and for mapping the terrain of that discussion. As sexually explicit material rose to the top of the feminist agenda in the 1970s, debates surrounding the causes and effects of pornography served to imbricate feminist women and men into critical discussions surrounding sexual subordination and objectification, as well as the (male) glorification of that subordination. In the introduction to *Men Confront Pornography*, Michael S. Kimmel (1991: xi) quotes B. Ruby Rich's challenge to feminist men:

> Finally, here's a proper subject for the legions of feminist men: let them undertake the analysis that can tell us why men like porn (not, piously, why this or that exceptional man does not), why stroke books work, how oedipal formations feed the drive, and how any of it can be changed.

At the time of its original publication (1982), one faction of the North American feminist movement had been rallying for over five years against what it saw as pornography's celebration of female subordination and objectification. Pornography had become the most urgent issue for many radical feminists by the late 1970s, with the formation of Women Against Violence in Pornography in San Francisco, 1976 (Macnair, 1996: 13) and Women Against Pornography in New York, 1979 (Strossen, 1995: 73). While these organisations started off as anti-censorship (seeking instead to promote protest against pornography, thus avoiding conflict with the First Amendment), by 1983 they had radically shifted their opinions.[4] In Britain, Women Against Violence Against Women was set up in 1979 and, along with its American counterparts, helped to ensure that 'by the 1980s radical feminism and its anti-pornography agenda had become dominant within the feminist movement as a whole' (Macnair, ibid).

By no means all feminists advocated positioning pornography as a fundamental concern of the feminist struggle. Clark (1991) criticised the intense focus on pornography, which he saw as being at the cost of other feminist issues and Wilson (1992: 19) similarly demanded an expansion of the debate arguing that the narrow focus on pornography had led to other material forms of oppression and subordination being taken off the feminist agenda. Nevertheless pornography arguably remained a central point of focus for many second-wave feminists. Of course this is not to suggest that feminist discourse on pornography has been

---

4 The climax of this shift being the drafting and (momentary) success of an anti-pornography law drawn up by Andrea Dworkin and Catharine MacKinnon. Whilst the law – twice adopted by the Minneapolis City Council and once by the Indianapolis City Council, in 1984 – was challenged and ultimately quashed on the basis that it violated the First Amendment, it demonstrated the venom with which one branch of the feminist movement (a branch that was intellectually evolved – both authors of the law being lecturers at the University of Minnesota) were willing to attack graphic depictions of sexuality and sexual activity.

wholly against such material. Arguably one of the contributing factors behind the academic interest in porn has been the way in which discussions about sexually explicit material polarised feminists, regularly positioning them in opposition to – and attacking – one another. While the rallying cry that pornography was the theory, rape the practice (Morgan, 1980: 139) was loud, from the start there were voices of dissent from feminists who actively resisted subscription to the pro-censorship anti-pornography dictum. Some of these 'pro-porn' feminists struggled to justify what they saw as the censoring of free speech, while others saw such lobbying for censorship as curbing (female) sexuality[5] and criticised the surprising bed-sharing occurring between anti-porn feminists and the new Right[6]. Williams sought to recuperate elements of the pornographic stating that it was 'fundamentally a discourse, a way of speaking about sex' (quoted in Macnair, 1996: 91). Elsewhere she asserted that while there is 'no escape from the power and dominance of the masculine heterosexual norm', it is in pornography that 'opposition to the dominant representations of pleasure can emerge' (Williams, 1992: 262). She cited bisexual pornography, lesbian pornography made by and for lesbians, S/M porn and gay male porn as spaces in which the 'perverse' might operate as an 'important resistance' to the 'dominance of the heterosexual masculine pornographic imagination' (ibid). While the primary focus of both pro- and anti-porn feminist discourse continues to rest on the relationship between female subordination and pornography, gay male porn has never been wholly exterior to the debate. Indeed gay men became just as much a target as their straight counterparts during the firebrand anti-porn rallies of the 1970s. A speech, made during a 'Take Back The Night' protest in San Francisco, 1978, by Andrea Dworkin, offers one such example of this blistering critique:

> Force and/or convention designate some males as females or feminized. The plethora of leather and chains among male homosexuals, and the newly fashionable defenses of organized rings of boy prostitution by supposedly radical gay men, are testimony to the fixedness of the male compulsion to dominate and destroy that is the source of pleasure for men. (Dworkin, 2000: 42)

---

5 In the introduction to her reading of the Marquis de Sade's work, *The Sadeian Woman*, Angela Carter (1978: 3) wrote that 'pornographers are the enemies of women only because our contemporary ideology of pornography does not encompass the possibility of change, as if we were the slaves of history and not its makers, as if sexual relations were not necessarily an expression of social relations, as if sex itself were an external fact, one as immutable as the weather, creating human practice but never a part of it'.

6 Wilson notes that whilst political support for censorship came primarily from the pro-family, heteronormative Republican party, British political support came from the Labour opposition. This support, she argues, was offered in an attempt to rid the Labour party of its libertarian image in the face of a changing moral climate, where permissiveness was recast as deviance (see Wilson, 1992: 15–27).

MacKinnon (2000: 132) later referred to a court case in which it was reported that 'a gay man inflict[ed] the abusive sex learned through using pornography on his male lover, who tolerate[ed] it because he learned from pornography that a man's violence is the price of his love'. This link between gay male pornography and misogyny was later re-enforced by Stoltenberg (1991) when he criticised gay male sexual cultures for celebrating homophobia and misogyny. For him, gay male porn was 'eroticized power disparity … eroticized subordination' (254). Whilst the act of anal sex was not itself misogynistic, for Stoltenberg, the imposition of a gender hierarchy on gay sex turned it into an act of control and domination:

> [I]f you and your sex partners are not genitally different but you are emotionally and erotically attached to gender hierarchy, then you come to the point where you have to impose hierarchy on every sex act you attempt – otherwise it doesn't feel like sex. (235)

Homophobia is rooted within the gender hierarchy of patriarchal society, of that there is little doubt. We need only consider homophobic verbal abuse to see the link between homophobic attitudes and female oppression within contemporary culture[7]. It is also clear that gender hierarchies continue to operate in gay male pornography (tops vs. bottoms, active vs. passive, jocks vs. boy bitches). However in criticising gay men's pornography of misogyny, Stoltenberg, like his radical feminist predecessors, has been accused of obscuring the particularity of gay male pornography, and of submitting it to the same gender hierarchy imposed by feminist critique on heterosexual men's porn. In short, viewing gay pornography through the same lens as heterosexual porn – and condemning it on the same grounds – suggests a reliance on, and investment in, the very same hegemonic understandings of gender difference that such critiques set out to dismantle. McNair (1996: 130) for instance, identifies the need to evaluate gay porn for what it is first and foremost – non-heterosexual. He states that:

> In so far as it celebrates and articulates 'deviance', [gay pornography] subverts and challenges the still-dominant homophobic culture, becoming to that extent a political text.

He concludes that:

7 The homophobia of playground terms such as 'cissy', 'pansy', 'queen' and 'wuss' reveal not only culture's displeasure with the (presumed) homosexual but also the despised status of the feminine. 'Tomboy' (one of the few gendered terms applied to 'masculine' girls) by comparison does not carry the same displeasure, largely because the masculine occupies a celebrated status. In attacking a girl or being too butch, culture is mocking her failed 'attempt' to be as a good as a man. In attacking a boy for being femme, culture is criticising him for attempting to associate his biological sex – and therefore all men – with the second-class gender identity of femaleness or femininity.

> Gay male pornography is, from this point of view, an important part of the struggle for social recognition and legitimation of a marginalized sexual community. (ibid)

Responding to anti-porn critiques, the political potential of gay male pornography is often cited in defences against censorship. Strossen (1995: 167) echoes McNair's argument writing that:

> In light of the long-standing and ongoing legal and societal discrimination faced by lesbians and gay men, materials depicting and exploring their sexuality are especially important, serving to educate, liberate and empower.

Others have argued that 'pornography, like other expressions of sexuality, must be put into context, viewed through cultural, social, political and economic filters' (Clark, 1991: 28) appropriate to that sexual sub-culture, rather than solely through the frameworks applied to 'normative' hetero-porn. Discussing the appropriation of mainstream narrative themes such as the Wild West, Watney (1996: 73) underscores the political dimension of much gay male pornography, writing that, '[g]ay culture invariably works in this way on pre-given forms of a heterosexual culture with its objects 're-placed' … and homosexualised'. Watney also reminds us that 'it is important to remember that sexual identification on the part of gay men, is always mobile, able to assume different roles and positions, which are always also power relations' (ibid). All of which suggests that gay pornography should not be so easily equated with 'straight' pornography and warrants further investigation. This is not to suggest that Stoltenberg's or MacKinnon's arguments are wholly incorrect. Dyer (1992) criticises the archetypal gay porn narrative noting the implicit gender subordination that can be read in gay porn's focus on anal penetration, the performance of hegemonic masculinity and its institutional racism. However, responding to earlier 'wholesale' criticisms of gay porn, he goes on to challenge the anti-porn argument, suggesting that gay pornography can be celebrated as both an art form and a political resource. Central to his argument is the recognition that within gay porn we witness, to varying degrees, the affirmation of male-male desire from *within* the culture that both produces *and* consumes it. Echoing Ehrenstien's assertion that 'the pornographic is the obvious, absolute, unmistakable' (Dyer, 1992: 124) he writes:

> Gay porn asserts homosexual desire, it turns the definition of homosexual desire on its head, says bad is good, sick is healthy and so on. It thus defends the universal human practice of same sex physical contact (which our society constructs as homosexual); it has made life bearable for countless millions of gay men. (ibid: 123)

A similar defence has been launched by Burger (1995: 4) who argues for the inclusion of pornography within any historical account of gay male culture in the US and the UK:

> As a dimension of political practice, it abets the reshaping reformulation, and rethinking of gay male culture and its role in society. In short, pornography makes gay men visible.

Still others have problematised the association of the (gay) active-passive dichotomy with the subordination of women (Edwards, 1994: 88), the lack of understanding regarding the fluidity of roles in gay porn narratives (Pendleton cited in Williams, 1992: 245), and the failure to recognise the hegemonic disruption evident in *all* pornography (Tucker, 1992: 270).

Discussions of the role of gay pornography, and its political position within the culture it caters to, were reinvigorated in the 1990s as pornography began to be read through the lens of public health discourse. Since the mid-1980s, HIV/AIDS prevention programmes targeting the gay community have co-opted the aesthetics and discourses of pornography in an effort to educate men about the virus and normalise condom use. McNair (1996: 103) notes that there are now in circulation 'increasing numbers of 'educational' materials which offer instruction in safer sex, using images that, in other contexts, would be defined as pornographic'.[8] Patton (1991: 45) identifies the creation of a 'pornographic vernacular' in safe sex promotions:

> Sexual vernaculars are learned contextually: members of various language communities experience cultural recognition not through visual identification, but when performances – *what is said* – are meaningfully decoded by another person.

These vernaculars are increasingly employed in an effort to construct awareness strategies laden with specific sub-cultural significance. While reluctant to assert that safe sex in gay porn results in safe sex amongst its audience, Patton (1996: 3) does identify an important relationship between pornographic discourse and safe sex education. Her work underscores the growing consensus amongst researchers that gay male culture *invests* in its pornography – and for a variety of reasons – in a way that straight male culture just doesn't.

Much of the 'pro-gay-porn' discussion suggests that gay culture has a complex and multidimensional relationship with sexually explicit material. Patton (1995), Clarke (1991), MacNair (1996), and Williams (1992) all agree that gay male

8 Conversations with health promotion workers confirm this assertion, and they speak of managers of STI clinics and other testing facilities refusing to allow certain advertising campaigns to be displayed in their spaces owing to the graphic nature of the images and the overtly sexual connotations of posters and other materials.

pornography serves a variety of functions (entertainment, education, validation, identification) that are either not present within its straight counterpart or, if they are, operate alongside other more culturally acceptable texts and forms that offer similar pleasures and instructions. For Dyer (1992: 124) such an investment also points to the fact that gay porn is *productive*:

> A reading of *Meat*, or a look at gay porn, indicates really rather obviously that the sexuality described/represented is socially meaningful … In principle then gay porn is a form of representation that can be the site and occasion for the production of bodily knowledge of the body.

Gay porn can thus be considered a 'field of documentation' (Foucault, 1977: 189) and in doing so, the productive power of its documentary must be acknowledged. Indeed, homosexual pornography pre-dates the establishment of a gay identity in the West and thus must surely be considered a constitutive documentary process, serving to help produce the 'homosexual'. O'Toole (1999: 64) records early porn loops featuring homoerotic and homosexual content being available by the early fifties in the UK and the USA, while McNair (1996: 16) notes that the sudden rise in gay porn texts in the 1970s was part and parcel of the emerging gay identity. This is arguably one reason why gay men situated in or having access to metropolitan gay male subculture are more comfortable discussing, purchasing and critiquing their pornography than heterosexual men[9]: there is a level of cultural validity attached to gay pornography that is not currently found in its straight counterpart[10]. Metropolitan gay male subculture, and its attendant identities, draws heavily on pornographic representations such as those offered in gay porn films, gay magazines, gay chat lines, and now gay digital spaces. We cannot talk about gay male culture in Britain without acknowledging just how central pornography has been to the construction and maintenance of that culture. However, whilst the content of gay male pornography has been the subject of many of these discussions, the structure of pornography, the specific mode of representation, has often been overlooked.

This oversight was, in part, addressed by Kappeler (1986) in *The Pornography of Representation*. Beginning with a discussion of torture photos from South Africa, Kappeler moves on to interrogate a diverse range of images and cultural practices in order to form a critique of pornography in terms of its structural components.[11]

---

9 Testing such an assertion simply requires going into a straight sex shop and then into a gay sex shop. The level of chatter, the aesthetics of the store, even the visibility of the shop front are noticeably different.

10 And indeed gay pornography may in fact be the primary link between their own isolated existence and an otherwise remote and inaccessible metropolitan gay culture. Burger supports this idea when he identifies Oklahoma, a traditionally Conservative state, as being the largest consumer of mail-order gay male pornography (see Burger, 1995: 37).

11 Contemporary meaning circa 1986, the time of its first publication.

Central to this critique is a re-writing of Berger's (1980) essay *Why Look at Animals*[12] in which Berger approaches the subject of representation by examining why the animal kingdom has, since the dawn of representation, been a focus of our attention. Kappeler rewrites Berger's essay, translating it into a feminist context where 'woman' replaces 'animal' in order to demonstrate how the evolution of gendered representation is tied to the development of a gender hierarchy suited to a patriarchal capitalist endeavour. In doing so, Kappeler demonstrates how the position of 'woman' in society shifts from one of 'mutual recognition' (man and woman as active subjects), to one of 'observed', achieved through subordination and tokenism, which she likens to Berger's animal-pets.

Key to Kappeler's argument is the loss of the real or 'wild' woman. This figure has been domesticated, tied to the home of the man who possesses her in the same way that an animal is 'owned' by a zoo or collector; 'in the case of the female-pet, she is the creature of the life-style her owner imposes on her and her lap-dog' (75) However, despite such ownership, the desire for the 'real' woman, the 'pre-domesticated' form, lives on.

> Alongside the domestication of women household pets, the institutionalization of the sterilized, desexualized self-sacrificial angel in the house, there arises a day-dream of the wild animal-woman, the sexual beast, an image which is becoming ever more pressing toady after a long suppression of desire. (ibid)

It is at this point that the representation of woman-animal appears in culture and Kappeler likens this to Berger's zoo. In the same way that the zoo tempts the tourist with the promise of investigation, knowledge and comprehension, so the peep show, the porn magazine and the skin flick promise the opportunity of seeing women, or rather of seeing 'woman' the figure that has disappeared within, or rather because of, culture:

> Peep shows signal a period where women are disappearing from daily life, where the category of woman 'has lost its central importance' and man-made mind concepts of women have been co-opted into other categories; where the act that women can observe 'us' has lost all significance. (Kappeler, ibid: 76)

Kappeler does not suggest that women are shackled to domestic life or that they are denied access to the public sphere: 'it matters little that there exist as many women as ever' (ibid). She is acutely aware of what she calls 'the absorption of individual women into public life' but she is also aware that this absorption serves to remove such women from the category of woman; '[t]he ever-growing achievements of individual women have been singularly ineffective in the rehabilitation of the

---

12 Taken from his collection of essays *About Looking* (1980), which also included the *The Uses of Photography* and was the follow-up to his influential book and BBC television series *Ways of Looking*.

category of women' (ibid). One need only think of the language used in employment legislation to see an erasure of woman[13]. As Kappeler states when discussing the anticensorship argument:

> In the arena of debate, 'public' debate is pitted against feminist debate, without any apparent contradiction. ... Whilst recognizing the opposition as gender-specific – feminist argument, the rights of women – the 'public' voice and the 'human' rights lobby do not identify themselves as gendered. (18)

From 'woman-zoos' Kappeler moves on to explore other cultural interpretations of women, identifying the fact that at the point where society rendered women invisible, female dolls became more and more life-like and, in turn, and began to inform us of what women should be. These doll-stereotypes are no longer contained solely within the domain of women, and it is at this point that Kappeler's work begins to open itself up to interpreting other forms of gendered representation. She notes that Action Man, GI Joe and other action figures illustrate the formation of 'mind-people' of the male gender:

> Thus the large-scale manufacture of people toys corresponds with an increased ideological diffusion of gender stereotypes – 'mind people' – the process of the recategorization of woman leading the way, but now being followed by a recategorization of man. (78)

And further:

> Experiments are being made of male strip-shows for a female audience: the establishment of women-zoos prefigures a possible introduction of men-zoos. (78)

Echoes of Kappeler's argument here can be found in Campbell's (2004: 163) assertion that 'American society has become permeated by an idealised image of the male body' and that this body is 'just as impossible for most men to achieve as that idealised image of the female body imposed on women'. In identifying the relationship between 'people toys' and other idealised images of gendered bodies, and the categorisation process at work within culture, both Kappeler and Campbell appear to call for a recognition of what might best be termed a political-economy of representation, demonstrating how such images are embedded in structures that work towards the 'distillation of power' (78); human over animal,

13 Where women were previously denied access to the sphere professional work, they are now legally entitled to, on the basis of human rights; their gender is bracketed off as unimportant or undesirable. Men, by contrast face no such bracketing off. Hossfeld (1995) engages in a similar discussion regarding gendered difference – and their bracketing off as irrelevant when it suits employers and managers – in her analysis of Silicon Valley workplace politics.

man over woman, capitalism over subject. Of this final stage, Kappeler remains vague, stating only that there has been 'a formation of a capitalist elite of economic and ideological subjects' (ibid). Her precision, momentarily faltering, is ultimately restored in her final analysis of representation, one that highlights the inevitably failure of representation:

> The visit to the woman-zoo cannot but disappoint. And of course, nowhere in the zoo can a man find the look of a woman, the sign of an encounter (not that he is actually looking for it). (79)

The woman-zoo, the representation of woman, offers no satisfaction for the man because what he is looking for, consciously or otherwise, is not there:

> The look between man and woman – both looking as active subject – has been extinguished. The woman zoo extends beyond the metal slots and shutters of the peep show. The cultural space of women, captured and framed in imaged is one big SHOW WORLD. There remains but one kind of look: looking *at*. Man gazing at woman *one* way. (79–80)

Kappeler's work offers a radical intervention into the pornography debates. Her focus on the structures of representation – the form rather than the content of pornography – opens up a new avenue of investigation and allows us to move beyond the 'good vs. bad' debate – one which appears to be burning itself up with little progress. The ramifications of her analysis operate in contexts beyond feminism (though ultimately they cannot be separated from a feminist critique of patriarchy) and beyond the purely pornographic. For example, broadening out the 'mind-people' concept, it is not difficult to see how Kappeler's argument can be mapped on to a reading of gay male culture. Horne and Lewis (1997) have previously noted the importance of the visual within gay culture. Being *seen* in gay spaces, for example, continues to play an important role within the formation of a gay identity where:

> gay subcultures are noted for their higher-than-average investment in the visual, much of which these days is consumed in the gay-coded, relatively safe space of the urban gay village. (104–5)

However, while this intense focus on visual representations can be politically useful, it may also lead to more politically ambiguous consequences, serving the 'capitalist elite' identified by Kappeler above.

In Chapter 2, I discussed a shift in focus made by the gay press, away from news and politics to lifestyle, fashion and consumption. This transition has arguably been supported by what D'Emilio (1992) calls the transformation of the material reality of late capitalism. His argument, grounded within a political-economic reading of queer culture, is that 'capitalism has created the material conditions for homosexual desire to express itself as a central component of some individual's lives' (269). Late capitalism has indeed recognised gay men and (less so) women as valuable members of an increasingly mobile workforce in which single, independent men with no dependants fit the worker-mould required for a 'flex-worker' (Castells, 1996: 265) means of production. While the ideological effects of capitalism are slower to 'welcome' the (middle-class, white, able-bodied) gay man[14], an attendant culture of conspicuous consumption has developed both within and outside of gay subculture in order to harness the surplus capital being generated by this 'affluent' workgroup. This, the ideological dimension of capitalism, interpellates the gay male subject, both producing him, and instructing him in the modes of consumption appropriate to his newly recognised and validated lifestyle. And it is at this point, the point of consumption, that the 'recategorization of man', and 'ideological diffusion of gender stereotypes' identified by Kappeler can be found. What does a gay man look like? Look among the pages of *Attitude* and *Gay Times*, *The Advocate* or *DNA*. Or take a peek at the cast of Bel Ami's most recent DVD titles. There you will find what a gay man is 'supposed' to look like. Of course, looking at *GQ* or *Men's Health*, the same could be said for heterosexual male culture – up to a point. Images of idealised body types are not confined to gay culture. However, while straight male culture has a vast array of resources upon which to draw when constructing and maintaining identities,[15] the gay man, growing up and developing a sense of self within a world that positions him as 'other' and never 'just' a man, is far more reliant on such representations. The ease with which gay men can talk about the 'types' of men that they desire, or the types of gay subjectivity with which they identify, is unsurprising given the taxonomic processes that appear to structure this highly visual culture. As we shall see in the next chapter, this process of representation, categorisation and *legibility* is structuring gay men's digital spaces, and the methods by which gay men construct their online identities, and interact with one another.

It is Kappeler's understanding of the politics of representation, together with a critically informed discussion of the cultural significance of gay male pornography that forms the basis of cybercarnality. I shall return to this shortly but before I do, it is necessary to move beyond the pornographic and briefly explore a secondary theme that currently pervades gay male culture (and to a certain extent gay male pornography), and which also informs our understanding of cybercarnality.

---

14 D'Emilo points out that while shifts in the material effects of capitalism undermine the heterosexual nuclear family (opening up a space for other sexual identities and lifestyles) the ideological effects continue to privilege the family – and exile queer lifestyles for their corrosive effects on the 'building block' of society (1992: 263–271).

15 And after all, as his gender and sexuality assure that not only is he a member of the power-holding class, the straight man is also, consequently, always first and foremost 'just' a man.

Trope 2: The gay male body under surveillance

Foster (2000: 449) asserts that the opportunities afforded by the Internet make an involvement with new technology 'attractive to people who have been historically "stigmatized as ... trapped" by the bodies that mark them as marginal'. Interestingly he includes the gay male body within this assembly of marginal bodies suggesting that in the virtual world, queer bodies are always visibly queer: cyberspace offering a 'spectacularised gayness' (ibid). Such visibility stands in stark contrast to historical understandings of gay/queer male cultures, which have often been marked by their *in*visibility (Weeks, 1990). As discussed in Chapter 2, specific emphasis was placed on coming out – on gay visibility – within early GLF politics, and this focus can be understood as a response to the situation of gay men. Unlike members of other minority groups, gay men have not been 'trapped by the body': their bodies have been indistinguishable from their oppressors.[16] This has been a cause of tension and mistrust for both the dominant power-holding group and those whose difference *is* inscribed upon their body. As Bersani (1995: 66) writes:

> Gay men are an oppressed group not only sexually drawn to the power-holding sex but also belonging to it themselves ... We are in fact pariahs among minorities and oppressed groups ... as white middle-class gay men, we are too much like our oppressors, which means we can never be sufficiently oppressed.

The opportunity to pass successfully within the power-holding group, indeed (for many gay white men in Britain) the fact that one is born into this group, sharing early on in life the privileges assumed by heterosexual men, has been detrimental to the formation of inter-minority group affiliation. We need only think of the split that occurred within gay rights campaigning during the 1980s to see how gender politics served to undermine the relationship between gay activism and feminist groups. [17]

Such an ability to 'pass' has also instilled a sense of paranoia amongst the power-holding group. While women, ethnic minorities, the disabled and (to a lesser

---

16 Of course homosexual men have been making themselves known for centuries. From the Molly Houses of the 18th century, to the carnation-wearing dandies of the 19th, to the pink triangle pins, leather caps, tight white vest tops, moustaches, muscles, manicures, sun-tans and mincing flappery of the 20th century, homosexual men have coded their bodies to signify their queerness to others. That said, the body of homosexuality is neither static nor a priori recognisable.

17 Such privileging of masculinity was a constant criticism made by women during the GLF years, causing them to split off and form radical feminist groups (Power, 1995). Similarly, the racism identified within British gay male culture by gay men of colour (Cole and Allen, 1994) was also seen as being the result of a culture that was, in every other respect made up of privileged white men.

extent perhaps) religious minorities have been easy to identify (and thus exclude) from positions of power, the male homosexual has been the imperceptible traitor infiltrating the boardroom, bathroom, changing room and bedroom. This anxiety over the invisibility of the homosexual man stems from the belief that the hidden homosexual is hell-bent on 'recruiting' innocent heterosexual boys and 'stealing' patriarchy's prized progeny. Albeit inadvertently, gay male pornography has served to fuel this anxiety, regularly employing a range of narratives that focus on young, heterosexual men being 'turned' for the (viewing) pleasure of the homosexual audience[18]. In a peculiar validation of queer masculinity, the predatory homosexual has been projected onto the cultural landscape as a figure whose strength is such that he can turn any straight boy gay. Such fictions might in fact reveal a truth: gay men not only look like straight men, they may in fact want to sleep with them too (Bersani, 1995: 673–4).

The homosexual moves through heteropatriarchy's most intimate spaces and witnesses his most vulnerable activities. To add insult to injury, while he himself may not identifiable, the homosexual not only sees hegemonic masculinity stripped down to his boxer shorts, he may well also be *eyeing him up*. The resulting paranoia this generates amongst the dominant group operates at an individual and cultural level. It is the source of countless medical studies that seek to 'identify' homosexuality and it is inscribed in law in the form of anti-gay legislation. Section 28 may have ostensibly been about promoting family values, but the legislation was motivated by fear. A homosexual panic gripped the British government during the 1980s as Margaret Thatcher warned of a queering of Britain, unless the promotion of such a 'lifestyle' was stopped in its tracks (Weeks, 1990).

Throughout the West the paranoid fear of the 'hidden' and 'secretive' homosexual has pervaded and informed State policies. In the USA homophobia, in the real sense of the word – a *fear* of homosexuality – has become a legally recognised rationalisation for violent acts, including murder, against homosexually identified individuals. Suffredini (2001) uses the infamous 'Jenny Jones murder' to highlight how the 'homosexual panic defence' has been used in Court to successfully sway Jury verdicts. Central to this defence, is the notion of humiliation and objectification that the defendant feels they have faced at the hands of the victim – because of their sexuality; in such cases homosexuality *itself* serves to mitigate such violence.

On a larger scale, both Hitler's final solution and McCarthyism both incorporated such paranoia, and oral history records and archive material reveal that in post-WWII Britain the identification of homosexuals became a matter of

18 These range from the 'gay-for-pay' scenario where a 'straight' performer is offered financial reward in return for homosexual sex, or the 'duped' scenario where the 'regular' guy is tricked into having a gay 'encounter' to narratives that employ less explicit invocations of heterosexual masculinity. These narratives often fetishise particular careers (armed forces, emergency services, blue-collar/construction) or particular leisure activities (motorbiking, contact sports, camping) in order to appropriate the implied heterosexual masculinity before queering it through gay sex acts.

increased judicial and media concern.[19] Such examples illustrate Best's (2010: 8) assertion that 'surveillance practices have long been tied to various forms of social control' and demonstrate how practices of tracking, monitoring and identification are inextricably linked with issues of power, namely power over the subject.

If legislation and politics produced technologies and discourses to identify and 'draw out' the 'hidden' homosexual, medicine provided the framework for a panoptic self-surveillance and self-monitoring of the gay male body. During the 1980s, HIV/AIDS served to underscore the historical fear of the queer, as Britain and the rest of Western world struggled to understand this strange and devastating new virus. New methods of queer surveillance were developed and validated through medical discourses as the 'gay plague' looked set to take hold. Strategies and technologies that addressed harm-reduction, containment and public safety were developed throughout the 1980s and 1990s and many of these interventions have not only targeted gay men, but have, in the process, identified them, rendering them visible to the State.

In Chapter 2, I discussed the impact that the virus had on British gay male subculture and HIV was seized upon by governments as an opportunity to collect data on this invisible minority under the auspices of health promotion and infection reduction. Although mandatory testing and identification never materialised in Britain, Bersani (1995: 19) was correct when he stated that 'nothing has made gay men more visible than AIDS' and that '[t]he heightened visibility conferred on gay men by AIDS is the visibility of imminent death, of a promised invisibility' (21). Prior to HIV/AIDS, the world of gay male sexuality was almost as invisible as the gay male body. While sex had become a dominant discourse within Western society by the 1950s, with Kinsey claiming that 37% of American men had engaged in a homosexual activity at some point in their lives[20] (causing moral outrage (*Gay History Today*, online)), little was known about homosexual sex other than 'standard' acts such as anal-genital penetration and oral-genital stimulation (mirroring heterosexual 'norms'). Kinsey may well have identified various homosexual activities, but he didn't provide a comprehensive discussion of homosexuality.

In spite of Gay Liberation, gay male subculture throughout the 1970s remained, to the mainstream at least, a murky world of experimentalism, promiscuity and 'strange' sex acts – or at least that is how it was perceived by mainstream culture[21]. The 1980s shone the harsh light of the medical examination on gay sex

---

19 See Hall-Carpenter, 1989; Weeks, 1990; and Jeffrey-Poulter, 1991.

20 Kinsey's first sex study *Sexual Behaviour in the Human Male* sold out upon publication in 1948.

21 Films such as *Cruising* (Friedkin, 1980) often presented gay male subculture as dark and 'underground' as dimly-lit bars and smoke-filled discos became signifiers for gay space. This practice of queer signification pre-dated Gay Liberation (see Russo, 1987:142) and continued to be deployed throughout the 1980s and 1990s in films such as *Philadelphia* (Demme, 1993) and *Priest* (Bird, 1994). While gay sex was rarely depicted in any detail the

as the burgeoning health crisis provided a legitimate motivation for detailing and documenting gay male sexual cultures.

However, unlike the legislative/dictatorial attempts to quantify, qualify and control specific populations, these processes of investigation and surveillance were not meted out by the State through force or coercion. As Foucault (1977: 203) reminds us:

> By this very fact, the external power may throw off its physical weight; it tends to the non-corporal; and, the more it approaches this limit, the more constant, profound and permanent are its effects.

Just as the investigation was not seen as forceful, so the consequences and end results were understood as anything but repressive (at least not to begin with). Indeed it could be argued that the very success of such investigations in Britain lay precisely in them *not* being seen as enforced by officers of the State. Instead, these new practices were heavily invested in a panoptic understanding of society; an understanding that relied on the formation of a self-governing subject of surveillance during a time of perceived crisis:

> The plague as a form, at once real and imaginary, of disorder has as its medical and political correlative discipline. Behind the disciplinary mechanism can be read the haunting memory of 'contagions', of the plague, of rebellions, crimes, vagabondage, desertions, people who appear and disappear, live and die in disorder. (Foucault, 1977: 198)

Trading on the (very real) possibility that death was coming their way in the form of a 'gay plague', gay men accepted the opportunity to begin talking to doctors, counsellors and researchers about what they did between the sheets, and out on the streets. Sexual diaries were kept, recording encounters in minute detail (Coxon, 1996), and health promotion agencies drew up lists of sex-acts, providing both the scientific and colloquial names for each practice.[22] Gay men were invited to get tested, and when they did, they divulged sexual histories, which were documented for future research: research that led to guidelines being put into place advising gay men to take charge of their sexual habits:

> the examination leaves behind it a whole meticulous archive constituted in terms of bodies and days. The examination that places individuals in a field of surveillance also situates them in a network or writing; it engages them in a whole mass of documents that capture and fix them. (Foucault, 1977: 189)

---

clothing and 'underground' aesthetic invoked in such scenes suggested that such sex was strange, deviant and possibly dangerous.

22 See, for example, the *National AIDS Manual* (online).

Without any doubt (and, as has been discussed in Chapter 2) these measures not only ensured that gay men in Britain were educated about HIV, it served to halt the decimation of the British gay community and saved hundreds of thousands of lives. All this notwithstanding, it remains a fact that during the first fifteen years of the AIDS crisis, gay male culture was subjected to intense scrutiny and documentation which, whatever its motivation, led to the formulation of a hierarchy of sexual practices within the gay community. As we shall see in Chapter 6, the response of many commentators to bareback sex draws attention to the continuation of this hierarchy and the cultural investment made in it by gay male culture.

Such a hierarchy was not constructed in an ideological vacuum. The dominant discourse of heteronormative sexuality also permeated gay male sexual cultures at this juncture. Watney (1996: 76) notes how criticisms of promiscuity (or rather the pornographic representation of such promiscuity) served to 'equate the possibility of HIV infection with quantitative rather than qualitative aspects of sex' during the AIDS crisis. Thus we see cottaging[23] – which has relatively little to do with unsafe sex acts, being focused predominantly around oral and masturbatory practices (Humphries, 1970), nevertheless being targeted by sections of the British police in the late 1980s due to an increasing 'awareness of AIDS' according to some.[24] Similarly, sexual practices that found no ostensible comparison within the dominant heterosexual culture were often subjected to questionable evaluation and condemnation, including from within the gay community itself.[25] Group sexual cultures, promiscuity and polyamorous relationships, all of which had been more commonly associated with gay male subculture than with mainstream society in Britain, were all called into question. Meanwhile, the reality, that you are only as safe as the sexual acts you engage in, became increasingly overshadowed by the promotion of monogamous life-long partnerships. While one could argue that the latter dictum, for the most part, implied and supported the former, it is important to identify the intrinsic difference between the two; the former statement is predicated on medical research, the latter belief is built upon hegemonic understandings of monogamy, sex, and sexual relations.

Indeed, hegemony was at the centre of much HIV/AIDS work. As identified in Chapter 2, the ideological position of homosexuality in the West has radically changed over the last fifty years and this shift in acceptance (as well the limits to such tolerance) informed governmental and extra-governmental approaches to HIV prevention. The problem was not homosexuality per se, as perhaps it might have been in the 1950s: in the 1980s it was a matter of national importance – indeed national security – that if homosexuality was to exist, that the 'correct' form of

23 Cottaging, the practice of having anonymous sex in public spaces, is discussed in detail in Chapter 5.

24 Namely the Gay London Police Group (GALOP) as quoted in Bowcott (1989, np).

25 See Chapter 1 for a discussion of the moralising of AIDS from within the gay community.

homosexuality, and the right type of homosexual, be recognised and validated. This brings us back to the argument made in the previous chapter regarding the validation of metropolitan gay male subculture which, far from being the antithesis of all things heterosexual, is in many respects, running parallel to it, providing a stable platform for the continuation of the homo-hetero binary.

I mentioned above the fact that HIV/AIDS-surveillance has not been solely the province of official regulations alone and the acts of scrutiny, examination and control, were taken up by numerous agents – including gay men themselves – during the AIDS epidemic. We might think of this multiplicity of surveillance in terms of Haggerty, and Ericson's (2007: 108) surveillant assemblages:

> A great deal of surveillance is directed toward the human body. The observed body is of a distinctly hybrid composition. First it is broken down by being abstracted from its territorial setting. It is then reassembled in different settings through a series of data flows. The result is a decorporealized body, a 'data double' of pure virtuality.

While not holding to the belief in 'pure virtuality' identified here (as will be demonstrated throughout this book, gay male subculture is the antithesis of such decorporealization), the mechanisms of surveillance that Haggerty and Ericson identify, (and the conceptual tools of Deleuze and Guattari that they employ), do fit with the proliferation of surveillance that gay male culture has met with since the 1980s. Extending Foucault's disciplinary machine, Deleuze's control society (1992), offers a critical framework through which HIV/AIDS surveillance can be read. The Terrence Higgins Trust, for instance, run STI testing facilities in gay saunas in London, and have been providing outreach education work in bars and clubs since 1994[26]. Gay men do not 'escape' such practices of surveillance in their social spaces; the nightclub becomes the classroom; the sauna becomes a testing clinic. Deleuze (1992:179) notes that 'in disciplinary societies you were always starting all over again', identifying the transition from school to barracks to factory and the different discrete systems one became plugged into (and unplugged from) when entering or exiting such institutions. By contrast, in the control society, 'you never finish anything – business, training, and military service being coexisting metastable states of a single modulation, a sort of universal transmutation' (ibid). Deleuze refers to medicine as one such system of control and, it would seem, gay male subculture has come under this new form of discipline. If disparate *spaces* become enmeshed into on-going and unbounded systems of surveillance, so does *time*, as gay men are 'disciplined' into forms of perpetual monitoring and control – 'what was now needed was an intense, continuous scrutiny' (Foucault, 1977: 174). We should remember, for instance that, 'HIV testing is not always a one-off occurrence. For many people, decisions to test will be made many times in their sexual careers' (Flowers and Church, 2002: 50).

26 Source: Terrence Higgins Trust (via email correspondence).

A discourse of personal responsibility became prominent in the mindset of many gay men during the HIV/AIDS crisis. Writing in 1995, Signorile identified this as a reaction to 'fear and sadness':

> I realise that I owe it not only to myself but to my sexual partners to know my HIV status. If I find I am negative, I have a responsibility to keep myself that way, to overcome urges to act in ways that put me at risk – no matter what fuels them and no matter how difficult they may be to fight off. (121)

Signorile has since become a vocal opponent of barebacking and of the bareback scene and it is not difficult to agree with his sentiment here: 'taking the test' seems the right thing to do. However, putting personal beliefs aside, (not to mention the fact that testing is a key defence in the fight against HIV infection) Signorile's argument identifies the production of Foucault's (1977: 137) 'docile body' within gay male culture. 'Urges' are to be 'overcome' and behaviour held in check as the gay man subjects himself to the disciplinary mechanism of HIV testing ('techniques of classification and tabulation' (156)) that brings within an 'infinitesimal power over the active body' (Foucault, 1977:137).

Since the late 1980s gay men have been invited to get tested regularly for the virus – and a host of other STIs. In part, this is merely the gay-specific variant of a broader cultural shift, in which the British population has been increasingly encouraged to regulate diet, appearance, mental and physical well-being. However, gay male subculture surpasses the general population in its methods and means of self-surveillance, control and discipline. It is something of a paradox that a culture so often criticised for being hedonistic and carefree is simultaneously enmeshed in strategies of self-surveillance, self-discipline and self-control. These strategies include gym-training and specific forms of body-sculpting, ranging from the increasing of pectoral and bicep muscle through to botox, liposuction, tanning and implants. The use of anabolic steroids and 'natural' workout enhancement drugs appear to be increasing within gay gym culture. Within metropolitan gay male culture today working out seems to have relatively little to do with *maintenance* and more to do with *modification*: 'a body is docile that may be subjected, used, transformed and improved' (Foucault, 1977: 136). Consider, for example, Amico's (2001: 361) description of the Auroroa nightclub patrons:

> Muscles are, in fact, abundant at Auroroa, perpetually and conspicuously on display ... Many sport tattoos, especially the angular, abstract sort which have become known as 'tribals' ... Bodies are uniformly hair free – the results of waxing, depilatories, shaving or electrolysis ... Of course, *not all have reached this 'pinnacle' of physical development*; there are many whose shirts stay on ... and whose clothes are less revealing. (author's emphasis)

Self-improvement and the notion of achieving an ideal body, the 'right' body, appears to be a central tenet of metropolitan gay male subculture. Indeed Amico goes so far as to state that '[f]etishisation of the 'ideal' or 'perfect' male body is widespread in certain gay communities … and is manifest in advertising and visual materials' (ibid).

From the physical, self-scrutiny moves to the psychological with the identification and eradication of effeminate personality traits. In search of the ideal 'gay' masculinity, self-tests and questionnaires such as Channel 4's 'Gay-O-Meter' and websites such as straightacting.com[27] have become popular within gay subculture. Whilst such tests are generally regarded as 'harmless fun' they articulate two important points. Firstly, that the identification of homosexuality continues to be a preoccupation for both the mainstream and the margin, and secondly that being seen to be gay continues to be problematic for many gay people. We may brush such quizzes off as nonsense but can we continue to do so when gay men proudly announce their (straight) rating score in their online dating profiles, provide links to such tests, and use such strategies to highlight their 'conformity' to 'regular' masculinity?

Campbell (2004: 189) concludes that 'modern matrices of power have utterly permeated the human body' and that 'it is this body entrenched in power relations that is reproduced in cyberspace'. In many ways, matrices of power mirror those that are deployed by a patriarchal society on women but with one important difference. Women remain identifiable and therefore open to control and regulation *prior* to such techniques of surveillance: their gender, or more precisely the patriarchal construction of gender difference, *identifies* them as subjects to be surveyed, investigated and controlled. Gay men, by comparison are not only regulated by such systems, they are also rendered *visible* via such processes. It is within this context that we must consider the recent legislation surrounding gay partnership rights as discussed in Chapter 2.

The 2004 Civil Partnership Bill has been applauded by Stonewall as a positive move towards bringing lesbian and gay relationships on to an equal footing with heterosexual marriage and this is no doubt true. However, the formation of a partnership register must also be understood as a strategy of identification and surveillance. While heterosexual marriages are similarly documented, the implications of such documentation are most powerfully imagined and felt by a minority group that historically has had good reason to fear identification, chiefly because of the legal and extra-legal violence that such identification has so often brought with it. Furthermore, and has been discussed in the last chapter, the British government's decision to recognise one type of non-heteronormative relationship serves to further undermine other forms of queer intimacy and partnership, while also (re)validating the hierarchy of sexuality and sexual behaviour that emerged during the HIV/AIDS crisis.

27 Straightacting.com has previously branded itself as 'your masculine gay guy hangout'.

Cybercarnality – in practice

What I am suggesting here then, is that the two tropes I have outlined above, and which reverberate across metropolitan gay male subculture, can be used to inform an analysis of the digital spaces and practices employed by gay men in contemporary Britain, and by extension, the West. To repeat myself, I am not positing cybercarnality as an attempt to form a universal 'rule' for investigating these spaces. However, I am suggesting that through the invocation of a meta-narrative, one that is fluid and dynamic enough to encompass and articulate the contradictions found between divergent spaces, we can begin to identify and interrogate the processes of (self)representation and (self)surveillance that pervade and constitute a myriad of digital spaces inhabited by gay men today. Furthermore, I propose that it is through such a meta-narrative that we can begin to comprehend why metropolitan gay male subculture has become so heavily involved in such environments, and so immersed in digital technologies of mediation.

But what can it tell us? What does it prove? Such questions cannot be fully answered in this chapter alone. Instead, in the four chapters that follow, the concept of cybercarnality is deployed in order to develop an analysis of the space in question: one that both highlights the specificity of that space and identifies commonalities between it and other seemingly different gay cyberspaces. Cybercarnality is thus used as a tool of critical reflection, appearing towards the end of each chapter in order to reinterpret the findings and articulate them through the framework set up in this chapter. However, while the deployment of this framework must take place within the context of the case studies, two assertions can be made here, in this chapter, in order to provide a clear understanding of how this meta-narrative operates and what it sets out to identify and illustrate.

Assertion 1: *There is a distinct and specific relationship between the digital body and the physical body in gay male cyberspace*

Firstly, cybercarnality acknowledges the practices of embodiment central to gay men's investment in digital communications. As we shall see in the following chapters, a preoccupation with bodies, chiefly eroticised bodies, is apparent within gay men's digital culture. As Dowsett *et al.* (2008: 128) comment in their discussion of barebacking websites, 'bodies that matter are those that are successfully sexualized'. In foregrounding what we might call the 'remediation' of the gay male body, cybercarnality identifies the relationship between digital and non-digital aspects of gay culture, and also acknowledges the central role gay men's bodies play in bridging the supposed divide between the two.

Even when text was sovereign within virtual environments, gay male online culture appears to have foregone the opportunities made available by the technology to create new and fantastical digital bodies. Unlike the spaces examined by Macrae (1997) or Stone (1998), sites designed for, and populated by, gay men do not engender a sense of corporeal 'play'. As I shall demonstrate in the next chapter, Gaydar profiles have always been heavily invested in notions of the real and of the authentic. In part this is achieved through visual cues as Gaydar has, almost from the outset, allowed users to upload images of themselves. Campbell's (2004) study demonstrates that a preoccupation with 'translating' the offline body into online contexts – rather than creating 'new' bodies using the resources available to the user – governed gay cyberculture long before the advent of profile pics and Internet movies:

> The body remains present in cyberspace because what we refer to as 'the body' is at once a physical form and a discursive configuration apprehending the physical. (6)

Campbell here makes an important intervention in the theorising of (dis)embodiment in digital contexts. At the same time he implicitly identifies the next question in this line of investigation, namely what is the political implication of this embodiment and what methods – what discursive frameworks, what representational strategies – are deployed in the fashioning of the gay male body online? This chapter – and indeed, this book as a whole – seeks to address these questions by investigation how digital remediation serves as a point of reconnection with both the individual body and the cultural body of gay male culture. In doing so, it also identifies how this remediation draws heavily upon pornographic structures invoked elsewhere in gay subculture. Jackson (1995: 130) identifies this, writing that historically gay pornography 'meets an "urgent need" in preserving secret sexual realities of oppressed minorities, and in foregrounding the vacillating dynamics of power and resistance'. He calls for the integration of pornography into studies of gay male representation, stating that:

> gay pornography represents a long tradition of visual texts and visual environments produced by and for gay men – which means it provides prototypes and paradigms for specifically gay male spectatorship, specularity, and visibility. (ibid)

The increased investment in the visual by gay culture identified by Horne and Lewis (1997) similarly pervades digital environments and informs the methods by which the gay male body is mediated online.

It is the role of cybercarnality then to identify both the 'translation' of the gay male body into digital environments, *and* the specific techniques of representation that are deployed by gay men themselves in this translation. The pornographic gaze – that structure of looking that promises knowledge of the 'real' (Kappeler, 1986: 76) becomes embedded within the architecture of gay male cyberspace at this point. It is present in the design of gay male dating sites and it is present in the poses struck by men in their profiles. It is evident in the textual interactions that take place in the cybercottage and it governs the way in which men understand and 'read' each other's bodies in the online bareback community. It also serves as a point of contact between men as they interact across mobile platforms, in everyday public life.

Cybercarnality thus highlights the processes of commodification apparent within gay male digital culture as the pornographic lens through which bodies are represented online engenders questions of objectification, knowledge production, and consumption. At one end of the scale, this commodification results in an expansion of Kappeler's argument; the entire cultural apparatus of gay male subculture becomes so immersed in practices of representation that the individual cannot be understood outside of the 'mind-images' that circulate within that culture and which are produced by the 'capitalist elite of ideological and economic subjects' (Kappeler, ibid: 79). At the other end of the scale and as will be seen in Chapter 6, such commodification exploits the gay male body, risking it for commercial gain in order to satisfy a desire that it itself has created. This then, is the first assertion that I make in the name of cybercarnality: *that there is a distinct and specific relationship between the digital body and the real body in gay male cyberspace and that this relationship is intimately tied up with the structures of looking and of consumption that are to be found in gay pornography.*

Assertion 2: *A history of surveillance permeates and manifests itself within the digital spaces of gay male culture*

If gay male digital culture remediates the body and does so through a pornographic lens, then it also provides the means for watching that body, in multiple ways and with multiple consequences. Campbell (2004: 147) warns against seeing the bodies that inhabit digital worlds as 'inherently liberating' and suggests that the 'hyperawareness and monitoring of the body' found within contemporary culture is not limited to the physical worlds we inhabit. Cybercarnality reveals how questions of surveillance are written into the architecture of gay cyberspaces. Whether cruising for sex or maintaining and updating his profile, the gay man is continually involved in a process of surveying, regulating and controlling both his own identity, and those other identities that he comes across in that environment. Practices of looking, and of being looked at, are intrinsic to gay male culture. They are embodied in the technologies and discourses of medical surveillance highlighted above, and at the other end by the sexualised practice of looking – cruising – that occurs in both gay spaces (sites that are demarcated as gay or gay friendly) and non-gay space (out on the street for instance, or in a public toilet).

Given the attendant history of surveillance that runs throughout the history of gay male culture in the West, it is unsurprising that such a theme should become so pervasive in the digital spaces of gay male subculture. To even consider cruising/dating sites such as Gaydar without an awareness of the levels of surveillance involved in such spaces, or to conceive of activities such as cyber-cottaging without a discourse of surveillance being invoked, is impossible. Spaces and practices are being constructed and deployed as methods of intense scrutiny and surveillance although this is not to say that gay male subculture is using online spaces purely as a policing tool. Indeed the production of surveillance techniques is simultaneously countered by responses to such issues of surveillance. Here we see the formation of a '"reverse" discourse' (Foucault, 1976: 101), as surveillance is no longer a top-down system of control but becomes mobile. As I will demonstrate, the bareback community uses online space in order to negotiate sexual encounters outside of – but in response to – the framework of surveillance imposed upon gay male sexual practice. Meanwhile, much of the erotic potential of the cybercottage lies in its relationship with surveillance. Risking surveillance by the authorities is a major factor – and incredibly important to the erotic charge – of the cybercottage. In this space, men avoid State surveillance while all the time maintaining a surveillance of each other. Meanwhile, the new mobile practices that are gaining popularity in gay male subculture are predicated on surveying the spaces in which one moves through in order to identify other gay men. As such, the second assertion I make in the name of cybercarnality positions *gay male subculture's involvement with digital communication technologies as mobilising new techniques of (self)surveillance for multiple reasons and with diverse effects.*

Cybercarnality offers a bridge between 'offline' gay male subculture and 'online' gay spaces (a binary that is, in fact, largely illusory), between cultural theory and new media practice, and between surveillance and embodiment. It is through a discourse of cybercarnality that we can draw together common themes and arguments that run through otherwise disparate and conflicting spaces. And it is through a discourse of cybercarnality that we are able to forge a more coherent understanding of the key motivations behind gay male subculture's involvement with new media technologies. In the following chapters I shall demonstrate how this discourse can be applied to each individual case study, in order to illustrate the practices of embodiment and surveillance that are structuring gay men's digital culture. The ultimate aim of cybercarnality is not to criticise or to promote or to evaluate that which it is applied to. Rather, it's purpose is to *understand* it, from a particular perspective; one that is aware of gay men's history, and the wider themes permeating gay male subculture, but which also identifies shifts and modulations within that subculture (and, perhaps within that history) via new forms of communication and through the invocation of new spaces, practices and voices. It is to this 'new' digital world that I now turn my focus.

Chapter 4

'From the Web Comes a Man'[1]: Profiles, Identity and Embodiment in Gay Dating/Sex Websites.

Every day in Britain thousands of men use digital platforms to search hundreds of databases in order to retrieve information about other men. This information is delivered in both textual and visual formats via search mechanisms that filter results according to the parameters defined by the operator. These search facilities are often highly developed, allowing operators to outline a detailed array of criteria and 'rules' to ensure that the information retrieved matches the operator's requirements as closely as possible.

In the information economy, where data is a commodity (Castells, 1996), the amount of access an operator has to such information often depends on the level of subscription purchased in advance. Some databases charge more for access to larger files (such as MP4 or QuickTime files) and operators who cannot afford the higher subscriptions may find their access is restricted, search results limited and the amount of information that can be viewed, reduced. Irrespective of subscription, however, and like most databases, the requesting of, searching for, and retrieval of information occurs silently. That is to say, while there are exceptions to the rule, most systems allow operators to disable data-tracking, allowing information stored on the database to be accessed and viewed without detection or data footprint. This 'silence' allows the operator to search through vast amounts of data and discard results that don't sufficiently meet the brief set, without fear or concern that those who have supplied the data will be aware of this rejection. This is the world of gay online dating.

Of course, most of the 'operators' using these databases today, right now, probably as you read this, would not recognise themselves or their activities in the description I have just given. The men who are currently logged on to sites such as Manhunt, Gay.com, LadsLads, Recon, DaddyHunt, DudesNude, LushLads, Mothership, Gaydar, Mand8, or Fitlads (to name just a few) do not see themselves as 'operators', nor do they regard their activities as being a form of 'data mining' or 'information retrieval'. I have never heard of anyone going to one of these sites in order to 'perform an advanced search based on multiple criteria'. And while I've heard people talk about 'online communities', 'social networks' and

1 This catchphrase was used during an advertising campaign in December 2002, for the Gaydar dating website.

'cruising sites' nobody has ever referred to these websites as databases. We don't 'access data' – we look at pictures of guys and read about what 'danishot' or 'fuckt2006' or 'Bunsboi'[2] is into, and when they might be free to meet up with us. We don't use these databases to analyse data and refine search methods. We use them to meet other men, to chat to friends and strangers, to keep in touch with acquaintances and to arrange sexual encounters that might range from a romantic date on a Wednesday night through to a weekend-long P'n'P[3] gang-bang involving two or three 'power bottoms' and a bunch of 'aggressive tops'.

The dry, dusty and deeply unsexy world of database building, organisation and searching is what drives many of these websites, and without the database they could not exist. But it is the front-end of such databases that gay men are plugged into, in their tens of thousands, and these front-ends are given a smart, shiny 'chrome' (Stallabrass, 1996: 86), which serves to attract users, promising an ever-more engaging, more enjoyable and more exciting experience. This chrome also provides site owners with an opportunity to advertise the supposed uniqueness of their database – their own individual take on online dating/cruising, whether that be catering to a particular fetish, or type of body, or age, or location. Whether such claims to uniqueness and originality are accurate or not is questionable. Underneath the sheen and the publicity, many of these websites may in fact be peddling the same types of experiences, the same types of bodies and the same ideological messages as each other.

Over the last ten years much has been written in the gay and mainstream press about these gay dating/sex websites (for example Flynn, 2003; Simpson, 2003; Meiring, 2006; Smith, 2008 and Strudwick, 2009) and this fashion for looking up and 'hooking up' with men online has long surpassed the transient status afforded a trend or fad. In the introduction, I mentioned the reference that the TV series *Queer As Folk* (1999) made to gay men's use of dating/sex websites and in the intervening ten years these sites have become an integral part of gay male subculture in Britain. While there is undoubtedly a level of fatigue generated around using such websites, and while they are by no means used by all gay men, dating/sex websites continue to pervade the everyday lives of many gay men today, both in Britain and further afield. In doing so, they provide the starting point for my close analysis of gay men's digital culture.

In this chapter I focus on that most ubiquitous of online forms, the user profile, and expose it to a variety of analyses in order to consider the relationship between this form of self-representation and contemporary gay male subculture. I explore the user profile as it is deployed, circulated and consumed on Britain's most

2 At the time of writing this, these usernames have not been registered with Gaydar, and are intended to be understood as indicative of the types of names taken up by users when creating profiles on this site.

3 'P'n'P' refers to 'Party and Play' and is an American acronym that has migrated to the British gay male scene. It refers to sex (often with multiple partners and sometimes incorporating BDSM or other 'hardcore' practices) while using recreational drugs.

popular gay male dating/sex website, Gaydar. Positing the profile as a complex object that operates on multiple levels, I begin my investigation with a summary analysis of the main components of the profile, before deploying a psychoanalytic reading that draws critical strength from feminist film theory. Encapsulated within the profile are the dyadic issues of identification and objectification and the first theoretical frame I utilise not only offers the opportunity to explore both of these concerns, but does so through the rhetoric of the visual, a rhetoric that has a deep and lasting resonance within gay male subculture, not least within the purview of identification – of both Self and Other.

The user profile and narrative cinema are, of course, different forms, and I am keenly aware of the need to provide a multidimensional approach to this digital object. This I achieve through a secondary analysis, the intellectual hinterland of which is marked out by the work of visual theorists such as Barthes (1980), Horne and Lewis (1997) and Jones (2002). Chiefly, I consider how relationships between browser (the spectator) and user (the spectacle) might be complicated through Barthes's notion of the '*punctum*' (1980: 28), which might be best described as affecting a piercing or 'pricking' (116) – a jolt of recognition in the browser, when he encounters a particular image or profile. Having established the multiple points of connection that operate between user, browser and profile, I move towards a final 'meta-analysis' of Gaydar and its profiles in order to consider how a discourse of cybercarnality (as outlined in the previous chapter) structures both the identities that inhabit this space and the practices of legibility and validation that operate on Gaydar – and by extension – other dating/sex websites.

Gaydar.co.uk: 'What you want, when you want it'[4]

For anyone who has even the loosest association with contemporary British gay male subculture, my choice of case study is hardly surprising. For over ten years, Gaydar has been the most popular gay website in the UK. Set up in 1999 by Gary Frisch and Henry Badenhorst, the website was ranked No.1 within the category 'Lifestyle – Gay and Lesbian' by the site-ranking company Hitwise in 2002 (QSoft Consulting, online). Six years later the same company ranked Gaydar the most popular dating website (irrespective of sexuality) in Britain (ibid). In 1999 Gaydar reported a worldwide membership of 3.8 million (ibid) and despite an ever-increasing number of competitor sites, Gaydar remains the number one gay dating/sex website in the UK today (ibid). It is arguably the most well known gay Internet company in Britain, and is a recognisable global brand with a raft of digital and non-digital enterprises. In Britain, Gaydar has had a visible presence at Manchester Mardi Gras, London Pride and Brighton Pride for several years. This presence often includes a gang of muscle-bound men wearing white briefs and

4 This slogan has adorned the homepage of the Gaydar website and continues to do so at the time of writing.

sporting the Gaydar logo on their bare chests, who give out lanyards and whistles during the parades. In 2009, Gaydar also staged a one-day event – Soho Live – in London's gay village and both Profile and Lo-Profile (a bar and club in Soho) are owned and operated by Gaydar.

The 2002 Hitwise classification of Gaydar within the lifestyle category is an accurate description of both the brand and the website, which has historically striven to offer more than just online contact advertisements. While profiles remain at the heart of the Gaydar experience, additional services have been scaffolded on to the site over the years, changing and evolving over time, depending on technological developments and popularity. These services have included; chat rooms based on location, fetish and other interests; a digital radio station (Gaydar Radio) featuring contemporary dance music and gay-oriented news and chat; a newsletter (in conjunction with RainbowNetwork); a virtual email service; an online shopping mall (Gaydar mall); venue listings; e-cards; Netmeeting facilities; escort listings; Instant Messaging; and Flesh – a selection of pornographic galleries and stories organised according to theme (run by thenumber.com). While many of these services are no longer available to users, others have gone from strength to strength (Gaydar Radio being an multi-award-winning example) and remain integral to the stable of online services owned and managed by the parent company, QSoft Consulting Ltd.[5]

Access to many of these services has been subject to membership status and while basic membership to Gaydar has always been free, those who opt for the 'upgraded' membership are provided with enhanced services and tools. Looking at the variety of services it has offered, together with its relationship to wider gay male subculture, it is clear that since its inception, Gaydar has sought to position itself as more than simply a database of potential sex partners. It has striven to be recognised as a space where men (and arguably to a lesser extent women[6]) can meet, hang out and chat. As one advertisement for the site proclaimed in 2002, 'It's not just a website, it's a world' (*QX International*, March 2002: 2). This echoes Mort's (1996: 175) assertion that since the 1970s homosexuality in Britain has become organised around more than 'just' a set of sexual practices, increasingly offering gay men and women a 'proliferation of ways of living'. This fits in with Sinfield's (1998: 6) 'metropolitan' gay male subculture, as outlined in Chapter 2. Reflecting on the emergence of a gay village in Soho, Mort writes that 'the search for sex was run together with music, dancing and all the paraphernalia of style which had been forged in the culture of the marketplace' (179). A similar sentiment can be found in the work of Weeks (1983), D'Emilio (1992) and Valocchi (1999).

---

5 Gaydar Radio has won a host of awards including 'Best Digital Terrestrial Station, 2007' at the Sony Radio Academy Awards, 'Best Radio Station' at the 2006 BT Digital Music Awards and 'Commercial Radio Station of the year' (2007 and 2008) at the Arquiva Awards. (QSoft Consulting – Awards, online).

6 QSoft Consulting also own Gaydar Girls, a similar site to Gaydar, aimed at lesbian and bisexual women.

Positioned as a lifestyle website, Gaydar provides the necessary environment for metropolitan gay male subculture to flourish online and, as a result, can be understood as maintaining and reaffirming the shifts that occurred a decade earlier in the gay press (as discussed in Chapter 2). Furthermore, as evidenced by the subscription fees, the (now defunct) shopping mall and the pornographic e-zine, Gaydar promotes and endorses the twin practices of consumption and commodification central to the success of metropolitan gay culture, imbuing Britain's most popular gay web space with 'the culture of the marketplace' identified above.

This culture is echoed in the promotional strategies of the parent company, QSoft Consulting, who describe themselves as a 'network of complimentary new media' and who confidently state that 'QSoft IS the gay market' (QSoft Consulting, online). Campbell's (2005: 665–666) reading of gay lifestyle website PlanetOut identifies the 'Janus-faced' attitude such websites have towards their consumers and the same can be said for Gaydar, which 'present[s] two distinct identities depending upon the position of the viewer' and which 'employ[s] techniques of panoptic surveillance, combining automated modes of data-gathering with the enticement of patrons to participate in their own surveillance'. In providing a raft of services, Gaydar provides an opportunity for gay men to connect with one another to an extent that has been previously unimaginable. We need only consider the vast difference between the gay men who choose to meet other 'like-minded' individuals via Gaydar today and those who, forty years earlier, found solace, sympathy and similarity on the end of the Icebreaker's phone-line mentioned in Chapter 2. While it is a misnomer that the Internet has eradicated the loneliness many gay men face when coming to terms with their sexuality, it is the case that websites such as Gaydar have provided important resources to combat the isolation and marginalisation that growing up gay in a straight world often engenders.

In providing this resource, such websites also provide an efficient and powerful method of reaching an attractive 'new' audience of consumers. Echoing the metropolitan ideal of what it is to be a gay man, the marketing rhetoric of QSoft promises potential advertisers a captive audience of '18–35 year old single people with high disposable incomes' who are 'well educated, well travelled, early adopters' and who are 'media savvy, demanding [and] vocal' (QSoft Consulting, online). If this were not enough to tempt the most conservative of advertisers, the company go on to explain why the gay market is a good market:

> Why Target the Gay Market? Spending power. The gay market has the disposable income to purchase your product or service. With no school fees, child support, or wedding for which to save, the average 30-year-old gay man has the disposable income of a 50 year old middle manager, and the spending habits of a 20 year old. … Because you want the Mainstream Market. The gay consumers friends, colleagues and family are all part of the wider community. Who better to target as an ambassador or your product than the person in the group with the money to purchase, and the inclination to innovate? (ibid)

The emergence of a gay economy (Hewitt, 1995), manifest in the discourse of the pink pound, has not been missed by mainstream advertisers looking to exploit the success of gay civil rights and cash in on this new lifestyle-oriented subculture and commercial gay websites have provided a means of tapping into this market:

> Although the community faces of these portals suggest that self-disclosure is a prerequisite to inclusion and romance, the corporate face of *PlanetOut* Partners suggests that such personal information aids in rendering gays and lesbians ready consumers. While these community faces gesture to the varied tastes in entertainment, news and leisure of LGBT communities, the corporate face speaks only to the economic interests of target marketers. (Campbell, 2005: 677)

The ideological tenets of capitalism may have been relatively slow to adapt, (D'Emilio, 1992) but the material reality of capitalist society has provided a space in which consumption can turn the sexual deviant into a 'good' productive citizen.

It is important that the commercial dimension of Gaydar be identified if we are to gain a full understanding of the website, but while the economic underpinnings are an important factor in comprehending this space, for the most part, the material underbelly of Gaydar, while unsavoury to some, remains an integral and seemingly unavoidable facet of Gaydar life. Although financial concerns structure the website and inevitably influence decisions made regarding its design and focus, paradoxically they rarely interrupt the daily ebb and flow of user's routines online. And, while Gaydar continues to strive towards being recognised as a lifestyle website, offering its consumers the chance to spend their money in a variety of ways, it is the user profiles – and the identities contained within the – remain the major draw for users.

Constructing 'me' on the Internet

Creating a user profile on Gaydar is reassuringly simple. By inputting relevant information into each field, or selecting items from lists of values (LOV), anyone with a computer, an Internet connection and five minutes can create a simple profile. For convenience, a template is used for creating each profile, allowing information to be split up into a number of categories and while the template has been amended and edited over the years, the general layout has remained remarkably stable. The categories roughly translate as:

> *'About Me'* – a personal statement written by the user. This is often six or seven lines long, and briefly describes the individual. There are no restrictions as to content. This section can be left blank but many users include a short description of themselves and their purpose for being on the site. Some members include poems or song lyrics, while others feature

sexually explicit descriptions. A range of different discursive styles and modes of address are employed and the choice of what to include (or not) is entirely up to the user.

'What I am looking for' – a personalised message to readers. Again, the content of this is at the discretion of the user. People often use this section to describe the kind of person or kinds of practices (sexual, social etc) that they are looking for.

'General' – This is a list of generic sentences, chosen by the user from a master list (e.g. 'I am a single Gay Man', 'I am looking for no strings sex', 'I am looking for couples/groups'). Gaydar supplies the LOV, and the user can only choose options from the list.

'Personal and other information' – split into two sub-sections, the first provides information on body type, shape, size, age, practice of safer sex, whether the user smokes, drinks, uses drugs and star sign. The second relates to hobbies and interests, including favourite food, author, film, music, bar, club, country and city.

'Keywords' – This LOV is split up into seven sections: Fetishes; Types I Like; Sexual Activities; Languages; Sports and Fitness; Religious Interests; Leisure Activities. Users can select one, none or more from the LOV, which then feature under the appropriate heading in the final profile. Profiles are searchable according to the 'Keywords' section. Thus a browser interested in a particular body type can use the Keyword search engine to generate a list of users with the corresponding body type.[7]

'Communicate' – in this section (aimed at the imagined browser) anyone who has looked up the profile can email the user, send a message via the instant messenger service, email the profile to a friend, save the profile in a virtual favourites file and make notes on the profile.

'Profile rating' – at the bottom of each profile, a rating/notes facility is displayed allowing browsers to rate the profile using emoticons. These comments do not appear on the profile, but form a private record for individual browsers.

Apart from the rating system, the above information is presented in text form, the web page being formatted automatically by the software and headed with the title

7 The 'keywords' section of the profile template was added to the user profile in 2004 and since this time has expanded in size and scope. Keywords currently relate to sexual acts, sexual preferences, fetishes and non-sexual activities.

'profile for [username]' along with geographical location (the location set by the user as their 'home' location), the number of hits the profile has received and the age of the user.

Although it is not mandatory, users often include at least one digital image in their profile and photos can be marked 'private', allowing access to fee-paying members only. In less than fifteen minutes any individual can create a profile, provide a digital image and place himself in circulation on the Gaydar database. As users can access this database across the world, building a profile on Gaydar is akin to becoming a part of a global gay village that spans Europe, the Americas, Africa, and Australasia. Services such as Gaydar Travel[8] and Gaydar Positioning Service (GPS)[9] illustrate both the global nature of the database and the pervasiveness of the service (not to mention the increasing dissemination of a metropolitan gay male subculture). In a very short time you can create a profile, upload an image and join the global party that is Gaydar. The ease and speed with which you can create a profile on Gaydar, however, belies a complex discussion surrounding the construction of an online identity through the Gaydar profile. For while it is feasible to create and post a profile with minimum effort, the choice of username, the images selected, the selection of information to be included (and excluded) all raise questions regarding the representation of subjectivity online.

Considering the context in which the profiles I am discussing are found, it would seem that the profile is created by the user in order to *attract* activity: the main purpose of the profile is to 'sell' the subject to the community of browsers. However, this selling of the subject is also closely intertwined with notions of purchase. Coupland (1996) utilises Giddens' (1991) work on the commodification of the individual within late modernity to construct an analysis of the discourses of commodification at work within heterosexual lonely-hearts columns. The main assertion held by Coupland is that the process of commodification held within 'mediated dating' is not uni-directional, but bi-directional; 'as a discourse practice, such advertising is involved not only with the promoting or 'selling' of selves but with the attracting or 'buying' of others.' (191)

While the looks-personality dichotomy Coupland identifies in dating advertisements does not comfortably fit the structure of the user profile[10] and whilst there is a marked difference between the fixedness of the advert and the fluidity of the profile, elements of the model do translate into the online equivalent. Gaydar profiles simultaneously display the user as an object to be 'browsed' ('About Me')

8 Gaydar Travel allows user to upload holiday and travel dates to the service, allowing browsers to see when 'non-local' users will be visiting their region.

9 'GPS' allows users to identify their geographical location (via postcode) and then triangulate the distance of other users. Once set up, the user can use the 'who's online' service to identify users who are in close proximity.

10 Coupland identified the fact that visual markers were reserved by users for describing themselves, whereas personality markers featured more heavily in descriptions of the ideal mate, their 'purchase' (Coupland, 1996: 190–193).

and construct him as the discerning consumer, whose ideal image we as browsers must fit in order to succeed ('What I am looking for'). This consumer/consumed dichotomy is integral to the structure of the profile and can be articulated through the multiple acts of spectatorship involved within the user profile.

Narcissistic identification, gay spaces and the user profile

Mulvey's seminal essay (1975) on the visual coding of narrative cinema offers a powerful socio-political analysis of film, which has since been widely utilised in critical readings of film, television, digital media and performance (see for instance, Neale, 1983; Holland, 1996; Sandell, 1996; Derné and Jadwin, 2000 and Drummond, 2003). Bassett (1994) has suggested that the psycho-dynamic trope of Lacan's mirror stage (the origin of Mulvey's analysis) might be a useful tool with which to analyse the performance of gender and identity within cyberspace, in the same way that feminist film theory has done so. Meanwhile Knight (2000: 22) observes that the digital practice of webcam communication ('camming') allows 'women to understand, participate in, and profit from the specular economy' that Mulvey originally identified. All of these analyses revolve around the twin concepts of looking and being looked at – of identification and objectification – central to Mulvey's original argument and within digital environments we can indeed consider the computer screen as 'setting up a mirror along Lacanian lines', (Bassett, 1994: 40) although, as I shall discuss below, an analysis of Gaydar on this axis produces somewhat different reflections to those found by others.

> [Having missed much of the queer celebrations 'in honour' of the Queen's Golden Jubilee] I fully intend to make up for it this weekend though – fly to Scotland for Carl's birthday … the Scot's won't know what's hit them – I'm moving my 'Gaydar profile' to the 'Glasgow room' as we speak darling (well, as 'Uhurah' in Star Trek would have said – I need all my 'Hailing frequencies open'!!) Varda [sic]! Chris – by email.[11]

The quotation above is taken from an email sent to me by a friend with whom I used to communicate with via email and different forms of instant messaging. In this message (sent from his desktop PC at work) he explains the process by which he plans to organise his weekend away in Scotland. The motivations behind moving his Gaydar profile from one location to another are numerous. Aside from finding out from 'locals' what bars and clubs are worth visiting, Chris's digital presence allows him to contact other gay men in Glasgow, namely for sex. From

11 Not real name. For ethical reasons all names and usernames have been changed in this chapter. Where appropriate, approximations that convey similar meanings, intents and identities have been used. All quotations have been quoted verbatim, including spelling, typographical and grammatical errors.

his message it is clear that Chris *identifies* with his profile, an image of his own subjectivity within this digital environment. That this identification is with an image *external to* him suggests that a process of alienation lies at the heart of identificatory processes as they are (re)articulated through the profile:

> It is an image that constitutes the matrix of the imaginary, or recognition/misrecognition and identification, and hence of the first articulation of the 'I' of subjectivity. (Bassett, 1994: 40)

This articulation is not new, but rather echoes the original alienation central to the formation of the ego:

> Recognition is thus overlaid with mis-recognition: the image recognised is conceived as the reflected body of the self, but its misrecognition as superior projects this body outside itself as an ideal ego, the alienated subject, which, re-introjected as an ego ideal, gives rise to the future generation of recognition with others. (Mulvey, 1975: 9–10)

Chris's motivations for moving his profile echo the commodified subject at the heart of Coupland's work and Chris is indeed advertising himself, positioning his profile so as to be ready to 'receive' messages from potential partner-buyers. But to see the profile as purely an advertisement would be to ignore the level of narcissistic investment involved in the creation of the profile. The process of creating a profile, of making choices regarding disclosure and non-disclosure of information, suggests that Chris (and by extension, any user) recognises and identifies with the 'I' of his online subjectivity: he is both the producer and the consumer of this text.

What lies at the heart of every profile is the question 'how do I want to be seen?' If we approach this question from the other side of the screen as it were, we must realise that reading profiles is never an unmediated act. While the screen, the space and the software provide the first point of mediation, the second point of mediation is undoubtedly the user who has created the profile. We, as browsers, are presented with a portrait (be it textual or otherwise) of the user through his own eyes: the profile is an externalising of the interior. To look at a profile is to see the subject *from his own position* – imagined or otherwise. Arguably one of the pleasures of browsing profiles lies in this process of mediation. How people translate their offline subjectivity into their online identity through their profile reveals more about that person than a profile could possibly contain. That is to say, the profile is as much a mechanism for self-identification as it is one of self-promotion:

> Here curiosity and the wish to look intermingle with a fascination with likeness and recognition: the human face, the human body, the relationship between the

> human form and its surroundings, the visible presence of the person in the world. (Mulvey, 1975: 9–10)

The user profile also represents a consciously constructed subjectivity that inhabits a space where *the natural assumption is that you are gay* – on Gaydar you do not need to act gay or speak gay, you can simply *be* gay. As identified by Horne and Lewis, (1997: 105) being seen in gay spaces continues to play an important role within the formation of a gay identity, and '[f]or many urban gays (or those who visit the city) the activity of seeing and being seen in a clearly gay-coded space (be it a bar, a Pride march, a café or a sex shop) is part of affirming and asserting an identity'. The introduction to the now defunct Coming Out Stories website, positioned the site as a 'safe and encouraging *place* for gays and lesbians' (comingoutstories.com, online, author's emphasis) and being seen to be gay remains an important aspect of establishing and maintaining a gay identity.

As I discussed briefly in Chapters 2 and 3, visibility, as a theme, dominates the history of gay subculture (see Weeks, 1990; Mercer, 1993; Hennessy 1995; Medhurst, 1998; Radel, 2001) and this is unsurprising given the fact that identifying as gay involves a conscious and (dis)continuous sequence of acts and performances. 'Coming out' is about making one's self, visible; throwing one's queerness into relief against a heteronormative background that would otherwise render it *invisible*. Throughout history queer people have undertaken projects of sexual signification, often in covert ways (see Holt and Griffin, 2003) and whether it be through the handkerchief code, the rainbow flag, the (appropriated) pink triangle or any one of a number of other symbols, gay men have been signalling their sexuality to anyone 'in the know' for centuries (see also Urbach, 1996).

These acts of visibility became politicised in the 1970s (see Power, 1995) and this prioritising of the visible continues to frame gay culture in the West today, where 'a sense of a recognisable identity may be variously signified by the wearing of certain clothes and the consumption of certain magazines, films, posters and the visual packaging of music (Horne and Lewis, 1997: 99–100). In opposition to 'mainstream' space, being seen in a gay venue confers a queer status upon the subject without further verbal or non-verbal queues. The space itself acts as a form of 'outing'. Thus being seen in a queer-coded space serves to render homosexuality visible, making the subject 'part of the scene' as it were – a member of the club (Dishman, 1995: 3).[12]

Non-physical space can also be seen to operate in similar ways and while websites are often coded as heterosexual by default (see Kendall, 2002 for further discussion), being 'seen' on Gaydar can offer a sense of 'place' while also operating as a marker of queerness. If, on Gaydar, everyone is assumed to be gay, then identifying as gay within online interactions is to identify as *normal*. The political dimension of this should not be underestimated, especially when we recognise

12 For a further discussion of gay/queer space, see LeVay and Nonas, 1995; Skeggs *et al.*, 2004; and Sibalis, 2004.

ch online spaces act as 'the reverse of the presumption of heterosexuality [found] in most offline spaces' (Campbell, 2004: 74). Consequently, the mediated subjectivities created within cyberspace often have the capacity to be *more* authentic than the offline identity of the user. While the content of Gaydar does not suggest that the website is explicitly designed to facilitate coming out, the structure and space in which it operates lends itself to this emancipating activity and suggests that the profile may operate, at least in part, as some form of idealised self. Within the context of contemporary metropolitan gay subculture the user profile can therefore be regarded as the latest tactic employed by an 'invisible' minority group through which the subject can be rendered *visibly* gay.

In Chapter 3 I discussed Foster's (2000: 449) notion that cyberspace provided the means for what he terms a 'spectacularised gayness' in order to highlight the visibility afforded gay men in digital environments. This claim, I contend, must be extended in order that it may acknowledge the presence of what Stone (2000: 524) refers to as a 'legible body'. Her argument, grounded within Butlerian lesbian-feminist thought, asserts that the body must always be understood as a 'culturally intelligible body' that is articulated, regulated and therefore subverted through the 'textual productions' that 'each society uses to produce physical bodies that it recognizes [sic] as members' (ibid). In this respect the Gaydar profile not only represents gay male subjectivity in cyberspace, it also operates as a medium through which that subjectivity is produced and maintained and creates a culture of legibility. The Gaydar profile, I am arguing, invites gay men to construct subjectivities that are (1) egotistical representations of the self and which (2) occupy spaces where homosexuality – not heterosexuality – is the default, where people assume you are gay unless you say otherwise. This posits Gaydar as a space in which gay men can undertake a project of (re)identification with the self, and in this sense it is surely a positive manoeuvre.

However, before we migrate to this gay utopia, we must acknowledge that Gaydar simultaneously satisfies the narcissistic gaze of the subject *and* the voyeuristic gaze of the Other. The ludic self-styling suggested by the likes of McRae (1997), Stone (2000), and Bassett (1994) is always accompanied, on Gaydar, by an unnerving sense of being watched. The reduction of the virtual gay male body to that of an object of desire suggests that gay men are involved in a process of commodification of the self at the very point at which they are rendering themselves visible and forming digital self-representations. The user profile encapsulates this dual relation of looking/being looked at and I will demonstrate that these two positions co-exist within gay dating profiles, suggesting that while users can and do identify themselves with a self-created image, they do so knowing that the profile will become an object in the narrative of desire of the Other.

Gaydar: What you want when you want it?

Type www.Gaydar.co.uk into your web browser and you arrive at the gateway to the Gaydar 'community'. The page provides access to the rest of the site and is headed with the Gaydar logo and the trademark catchphrase filled with hope and promise: 'what you want, when you want it'. For the first six years of Gaydar's life, and in case you were unsure of what exactly it was you wanted, a toned male body (Figure 4.1) appeared in the bottom left hand corner of the page to remind you of what you came for. This static image appeared on the Gaydar homepage for approximately the first six years of the site's existence and acted as a promise of what was on offer inside.[13] Arguably it also suggested an ideal of gay masculinity, *producing* the ideal at the point at which it *represented* it.

Figure 4.1 Desiring (the) object: The homepage image that greeted visitors to the Gaydar website for the first six years

© Chris Reynolds.[14]

13 This image has since been replaced by a scrolling set of images depicting men, in various states of (un)dress and either on their own, or with one or two other men. The diversity of body types represented echo the types of bodies identified elsewhere in the site, and this will be discussed later in this chapter.

14 I am indebted to QSoft Consulting for granting permission to reproduce this image here, and for assisting in elements of this research by answering emailed enquiries regarding usage statistics.

The cropping of the shot, just below the waistline, together with the slight darkness at the bottom of the image, suggesting pubic hair, whet the appetite and promised users more of the same if we ventured 'inside'. If the cropping of the image suggested nudity, the content suggested sexual activity. As seen in the image reproduced here, the model appears to be balancing himself, his hands outstretched as though pressing against a wall. The position of his head, the posture and his apparent nakedness work together to suggest a scene of fellatio, his eyes cast downwards towards the 'action'. In this sense, we identify with the model, taking his position, that of 'receiving' oral sex from an unseen partner. I have (very obviously) borrowed from cinematic techniques commonly employed by both straight and gay pornography in order to develop my reading here. If we were to embed this image into a standard pornographic narrative, the next camera shot would doubtless be from the model's eye view, looking down towards his kneeling accomplice. In this scenario, the nakedness of the model does little to reduce our identification with him. His toned physique, washboard stomach and suggested suntan are synonymous with a specifically metropolitan gay masculinity that contemporary urban gay male culture idealises and against which many gay men measure themselves. The model's dominance here is a sexual one (standing over the unseen fellator) and a cultural one (he is literally stood at the doorway to British gay culture's most popular online space).

However we can extend and complicate this reading by positioning ourselves behind or perhaps external to the model, moving our gaze from one of *identification with* the subject, to one of *objectification of* the model. The head bowed and the hands stretched suggest sado-masochistic overtones of power and domination as the model becomes the sexual object of the reader's fantasy; the anonymous faceless body captured and exposed for the audience's pleasure.[15] Thus, while allowing for an identification with the model, we must also recognise the potential for scopophilic objectification: to modify Lacan (1999), and in the style of gay male pornography[16], we want to both *be* the model and *have* the model.

Despite the site's recent redesign, which has seen this image withdrawn, I want to pay particular attention to this image for two reasons. Firstly because it demonstrates the need to modify heteronormative readings (or rather feminist readings of heteronormative texts) in order that they may adequately articulate the complex and specific relationship between subject and object encountered in gay male online environments such as Gaydar. This point I shall return to shortly. My second reason for lingering over this image is because it illustrates the

15 Note also the religious overtones of this image. The nakedness, the arms outstretched, and the bowed head make references to the central trope within Christian iconography; the body of Christ at the point of ultimate sacrifice; the crucifixion. This act of self-immolation is a central tenet of Christianity, one that might also be considered to be laden with an intense (homo)eroticism.

16 I particular, I am thinking here of the useful work undertaken by Dyer (1992) on the subject of gay pornography and identity/objectification discussed in Chapter 3.

'consumerisation of male sexuality' (Kibby and Costello, 1999: 352); a process whereby the male body, having been fully clothed for centuries, has recently undressed in popular culture and, increasingly, offers the potential for queer erotic appropriation.

Mulvey's 'gaze' theory argues that female characters in narrative cinema are subjects of/subjected to a voyeuristic gaze, through which they become 'coded for strong visual and erotic impact' (Mulvey, 1975:11). Subsequent analyses have identified the deployment of this gaze towards male subjects, though cinematic convention and an institutional nervousness surrounding the male body means that this remains fraught with anxiety. Neale (1983: 14) argues that film can offer a 'spectacle of male bodies, but bodies unmarked as objects of erotic display', and impresses upon the reader the fact that such a spectacle is 'marked not by desire, but rather by fear, or hatred, or aggression'. Echoing this, Holland (1996: 165) identifies a similarly displaced voyeurism in the (cinematic) figure of the cyborg, where 'violence displaces male sexuality (in our homophobic culture) by undermining any notion of the male body as a passive spectacle through narrative intervention, which justifies the camera's objectifying gaze by making him the object or perpetrator of violent action'.

Both Neale and Holland acknowledge the queer 'danger' inherent in male objectification, the former commenting that 'homosexuality is constantly present as an undercurrent, as a potentially troubling aspect of many films and genres' (Neale, ibid: 15). This undercurrent exists due to hegemonic understandings of gender, which scaffold sexuality to essentialist notions of masculinity and femininity. Thus the objectification of the male body remains problematic because it implies that it is open to the same objectification meted out on the 'passive' female body. If passivity is a feminine trait (as both cinematic convention and hegemony dictates) then the objectification of the male body is simultaneously a feminisation of the male body. Historically, such male effeminacy has been a signifier of homosexuality within Western cultures.[17]

This undercurrent also thrives on a cultural anxiety regarding the exposure of the male body (Neale, ibid). Exposure suggests acts of looking, uncovering and revealing, all of which can carry strong sexual connotations and this process of looking at the male body-as-object commands audiences to radically reorganise their reading of the male body.[18] Such reorganisation is not without its insecurities and uncertainties:

---

17 Indeed, before homosexuality was allowed to be discussed openly by British film and theatre censors, it was signified through the deployment of effeminate male characters. See Russo (1997), Tyler (1993) and Bourne (1996) for further discussion.

18 Think, for example, of the tight camera framing of women's genitals and the intense cinematic scrutiny of breasts, vaginas, and anuses which are so common in much heterosexual pornography.

> The male nude reappeared in art and popular culture in the late 1970s but it has been a nervous uncovering. New codes of masculine display are not fully written, and certainly not comfortably accepted …. (Kibby and Costello, 1999: 353)

While remaining a site of discomfort for the hegemonic order, ambiguities that coalesce around the nude male become the location if intense erotic investment within gay male subculture. Edwards (1994: 88) argues that a reversal of power-relations operates within gay visual culture, commenting that, 'the gay consumer of pornography is led to identify with the pre-given gay partner in eroticising the transgressive straight to gay partner due to the camera's *construction of the passive partner as subject and the active partner as object* (author's emphasis). Meanwhile, Watney (1996: 28) identifies the rupture that queerness effects within normative understandings of gender and power:

> Homosexuality problematises the causal identification of primary power with the figure of the biological male as masterful penetrator. It equally problematises the parallel identification of powerlessness and passivity with the figure of the biological female as submissive and penetrated. For the gay man is truly polymorphous: he may fuck and be fucked, and is as much at home in the one fantasy-position as the other.

As illustrated in my discussion of the Gaydar homepage image, uncertainties over how to read the nude male allow a gay male audience to identify with (be) the model and share in his experience, while simultaneously objectifying (having) him, by placing ourselves outside of the fantasy, and becoming voyeurs of the nude body. Working this line of thought through, we must inevitably identify a point at which the subject behind the user profile ultimately becomes the *both* the spectator *and* the spectacle, the subject *and* the object, the active *and* the passive. This unstable, shifting and 'versatile'[19] set of positions is deeply characteristic of Gaydar, which operates as a space where gay men are simultaneously invited to be agents of their own subjectivities, and objects of desire in the sexual narratives of others.

In the first of his three essays on the theory of sexuality (the essay that focuses on sexual aberrations) Freud (1905: 69) discusses the libidinal content of the spectator's look, suggesting that 'visual impressions remain the most frequent pathway along which libidinal excitation is aroused'. While feminist psychoanalysis originally organised the active/passive dyad inherent in scopophilia according to gender difference, Freud's original thesis suggests that both the active and passive elements of scopophilia may be contained within a single individual.

---

19 The term 'versatile' is used within contemporary gay male subculture to identify the sexual role of the subject. 'Versatile' is generally understood as a willingness to be either the 'passive' or the 'active' subject within penetrative sex.

> Whenever we find in the unconscious an instinct of this sort, which is capable of being paired off with an opposite one, this second instinct will regularly be found in operation as well. Every active perversion is thus accompanied by its passive counterpart: anyone who is an exhibitionist in his unconscious is at the same time a voyeur. (ibid: 81)

Gaydar's catchphrase is 'what you want, when you want it', not *who* you want, nor when *they* want it, and while users embark on a project of narcissistic identification through their profiles, they also implicitly position themselves as objects for consumption by the gaze of the invisible browser. Such positioning is most obviously located in the choice of images that users upload to their profiles.

Virtually visible

Digital images saturate the Gaydar database and vary greatly in terms of quality, size, content, sexual explicitness and relationship to the user. All Gaydar members, regardless of membership status, have been offered the opportunity to upload images to their profiles since the earliest days of the site. This, twinned with the increase in domestic broadband connections in Britain during the period 1999–2004[20] and decrease in price of digital image capture hardware,[21] has meant that visual representations of the body have been a key part of the Gaydar experience. Indeed, profile images (known in Gaydar parlance as 'pics' or 'pix') are perhaps the most (in)famous aspect of the Gaydar profile, known well beyond just the website membership.

The furore in 2003 surrounding the revelation that Labour MP Chris Bryant had a Gaydar profile focussed not on the written content of his profile but on the accompanying profile image. Tabloid culture ensured that the photo of the underwear-clad Bryant was reproduced by several newspapers and it was the visual, as opposed to the textual aspects of the profile that upset the conservative news press the most. Bryant's sexuality was not the shock revelation (he was neither closeted, nor had he been forced out of the closet by the media, having been open about his sexuality for a number of years), neither was his membership of Gaydar. What *was* shocking – for the likes of the *Daily Mail* at least – was the fact that the MP had posted a picture of himself almost naked, on a website for all to see (Glover, 2003: 13). While the likes of the *Daily Mail* found such behaviour aberrant, Bryant's photograph did not look particularly different in terms of style, quality and content from a number of similar images that litter profiles on Gaydar today.

---

20 OfCom (2004) reported a rise in UK domestic broadband connections from 17% in 2002 to 37% in 2004.

21 The convergence of camera and mobile phone during this period is particularly poignant here (see Gye, 2007 for further discussion).

Profiles containing images are marked in search results by a coloured dot denoting the content of images in the profile. The categories are as follows:

Red = Explicit Sexual Content
Yellow = Some Nudity
Blue = No Sexual Content

This colour code was added to the Gaydar site in 2002 in order to allow browsers to discriminate between profiles when downloading information[22] and correspondence with Gaydar at the time of the code's launch revealed the following statistics:

Blue – Nil nudity within profile – 75%
Yellow – Some flesh with profile – 14%
Red – Full nudity within profile – 11%[23]

Bearing in mind the fact that the middle category can reasonably be considered to contain erotic content in the same way that pin-up magazines are considered erotic (or indeed Bryant's photograph might be), 25% of all profiles with photos can be considered sexually explicit or otherwise sexual in the broadest terms.[24] Even the briefest of searches reveals that close-up images of body parts are a common feature of user profiles and these fragmented images of the body often include headshots of the user together with images that focus on specific areas of the body such as the chest, backside and genitals (though other body parts such as feet or back together with body markings such as tattoos or piercings can also easily be found).

For example, the profile for 'intojocks' opens with an image of the user standing in a subordinate position (hands on head, head angled downwards) against a non-descript background. This full body shot shows the user dressed in army fatigues, his face having been blanked out. Three other pictures feature on the user profile,

22 Upon implementing this system, Gaydar were specific in their reasoning, stating that 'if a user is in a public Internet cafe or at work, then they will most probably not want to view a profile which has pictures of a sexual nature' (email response from Gaydar support, September 2002). This leads into an interesting debate regarding public/private spaces and the tension between online and offline areas of public access. The issue of space will be explored in more detail in Chapter 7.

23 Email response from Gaydar support, September 2002.

24 It is interesting to note that the reply from Gaydar used a different scale to that displayed on the website, indicating that the categorising of photos is somewhat subjective. For example, a photo of the user sunbathing contains some nudity but may well offer no sexual content. Similarly, pictures of genitals may be considered sexually explicit by one user and only nude by another. The main image of the profile 'szero', taken from an elevated angle, is of a man, lying face down on a bed, fully clothed in a bomber jacket and jeans. His hands are handcuffed behind his back. Should this image be labelled with a blue or a red dot?

all of which centre on the user's groin, with and without the eponymous jockstrap. Repeating my earlier assertion regarding identification, Gaydar renders the body of 'intojocks' as always already gay in ways that the real body offline can never fully be. Yet 'intojocks' digital body, the body of his alienated ego-ideal, is simultaneously rendered an object of sexual desire through the voyeuristic gaze of the potential browser. If the images flip between subject and object, the profile text furthers this stating that the user is looking for 'rough sex ... toys and bondage' and that he is interested in 'sex in jocks'. The 'introductory' image confirms the 'butch' element of this profile (military attire being a pornographic signifier for fantasies of rough sex and/or bondage and humiliation scenarios) while the other images detail the particular *fetish* of the user.

Morton (1995: 307) argues that fetishes, while appearing to be ludic and liberatory, are in fact obstacles that 'guard against the encroachment of knowledge'. The virtual body of 'intojocks' similarly denies us access to the user, and fixes him as a sexual object in the same way that conventional film fixes the female as an object of (over-invested) desire, inviting the audience to consume her through the camera lens and through the gaze of the male protagonist. Of course in psychoanalytic film theory, the female object represents a problem to be solved. Her presence perpetuates the fear of castration central to the entrance into the symbolic system and '[u]ltimately, the meaning of woman is sexual difference' (Mulvey, 1975: 33). The woman embodies lack, representing both difference and the painful reminder of difference. Though bound by narrative, the woman comes to signify the anxiety of those who would wish themselves masters. Mulvey details two methods, 'two avenues of escape' (ibid) by which this penile anxiety is repressed through the narrative. These are (1) punishment of the female (sadism) and (2) disavowal of the castration (fetishism) and it is the latter that can be seen at work within the user profile. The fetish, or rather the object of the fetish, operates as a barrier to knowledge and the displaced penis is found within an object that is continually re-affirmed to ensure that 'it becomes reassuring rather than dangerous' (Mulvey, ibid: 14).

It is in the process of re-affirmation that we learn to identify the fetish. Mulvey cites 'over-valuation', 'a direct erotic rapport with the spectator' and a coalescence of 'object and screen space' as processes of affirmation (ibid). While we must acknowledge that the penis is far from absent on Gaydar, we can recognise the underlying castration complex encapsulated in the user profile if we comprehend the fetish as operating at a broader level than just the fear of penile loss, within the domain of the objectified. The castration complex is therefore not simply the loss of the penis, but rather the fear of being objectified oneself – of having done to you what has been done to the user presented in the profile. This unconscious anxiety is recuperated on Gaydar according to the conventions of the fetish. Echoing the 'compartmentalisation' of the textual body found in gay IRC channels (Campbell, 2004: 11), in the user profile tightly framed shots, a direct address to the spectator (achieved through hyperlinks, where single images open up on a blank page external to the profile), and the repetition of the fetish object leads to an over-investment in the object that affirms rather than endangers the object and its relationship to the spectator. The profile for 'intojocks' organises the subject as a fetish for the spectator.

The choice of username echoes this reductionism, objectification and fetishising of the body and explains 'the way identity plays out here' (Bassett, 1995: 544). Usernames are unique and regularly reflect the sexual desires ('bladder4u', 'passiverimmer', 'thongboi') or body type ('8inchcut', '2hungones', 'askinpig') of the user. Bearing in mind that a general search based on geographical location can find in excess of 1,000 profiles at any one time, the choice of username is an important step in creating a virtual body, and for attracting potential partners for specific forms of sexual activity.

This is not to contradict my original assertion that the virtual subject of the user profile is a point of identification for the embodied user. Rather, it builds on this claim in order to provide a more accurate understanding of the way in which the user profile functions. Campbell (2004: 113–114) suggests that within gay digital spaces 'the body is at once monadic and composite, a unified self and a collection of parts, a desirable person and an object to be desired'. In creating digital representations of the self, members of Gaydar are involved in complex processes of identity construction. However, because the object of the vast majority of user profiles is to satisfy sexual desire, these representations dismantle the body of the user and create a fragmented and unbounded sexual 'body-in-bits'. This body is then advertised on Gaydar to attract new sex partners. The scopic shift occurs at the point at which the profile encounters the voyeuristic gaze of the anonymous browser. As I shall discuss later, the relationship between surveillance and pornography – identified through the framework of cybercarnality – is key to this reorienting process, moving subjects into objects through the deployment of pornographic aesthetics in profile representations.

Psychoanalytic theories of visual pleasure such as Mulvey's remain a useful starting point for feminist and queer media analysis, though of course they are not without their blindspots (see Branston, 2000, for a comprehensive discussion of these), and a discussion of gay subjectivity, (while sharing feminism's interest in sexual politics) does not always fit the structures of thought set out by feminist criticism. As illustrated by the brief analysis of the Gaydar homepage image, psychoanalysis is useful to a point, but the gaze of a gay male audience blurs boundaries between being and having, subject and object, identification and objectification. Eroticising the body has different political implications for a social group who have historically been denied such pleasure (see Horne and Lewis, 1997 for further discussion).

Another factor, which requires us to move beyond psychoanalysis, is the specificity of digital media. The psychoanalytic frame that I have employed in this chapter was originally designed to suit narrative cinema, and although elements can be usefully appropriated in an analysis of the visual culture of digital phenomena, it cannot tell the whole story. We need a new framework, or at least a different framework, in order to further extend our understanding of the profile, especially if we acknowledge that some images do not necessarily fragment the user, but in fact strengthen the connections between subject, profile and browser.

'No pic no dick' – the role of 'face-pics' in user profiles

'Face-pics', those images that clearly show the user's face, normally in close up, are increasingly prevalent on Gaydar. This is not to say that everyone includes a face-pic. Many users choose not to and there is a degree of tension surrounding the decision to include a face-pic and whether to interact with someone who has chosen not to show their face online. Putting a face-pic on your Gaydar profile is the equivalent of putting your money where your mouth is; it demonstrates an investment in space that resonates with the argument regarding visibility in gay space discussed earlier in this chapter. A face-pic demonstrates your investment in this space and your willingness to openly identify as gay or bisexual. The cultural history, social tensions and competing discourses that make up gay male subculture are not separate from Gaydar, they are what constitute it. Thus within the architecture of Gaydar we can hear echoes of the GLF's rallying cry (for instance) to 'come out' and be 'proud'. This political history may not be consciously invoked by either the users of Gaydar or by Gaydar itself, but the discourse of gay civil rights is woven into the fabric of gay male environments both online and offline.

For example, just as being a closet queen in the mid-late 1970s became increasingly unacceptable to the newly out gay community, so writing a profile on Gaydar is no longer considered adequate. The face-pic articulates issues of self-identification, honesty and integrity and many users value this form of self-representation most highly, not least because they see it as validating the profile; to many it is an act of investment and confirmation that can never be afforded a faceless profile:

> '[I] am to be proud of who I am, get appreciation, let other users see me.'
>
> '[I choose to include a face-pic] in the interests of my own integrity. A photo implies that I am open and honest about who I am.'
>
> 'I have nothing to hide and receive a better response with pictures on my profile.'
>
> '[A]llowing people to see how I look makes them more comfortable – I am not afraid to be seen; most add photos to attract people'. [25]

25 These responses were generated from a small survey, run during the course of research, together with conversations with users of the site, during the course of wider research into gay male subculture.

Since the time of the 'cross-dressing psychiatrist' (Stone, 1998: 65), fears of online deceptions and scams have circulated within scholarly and popular writing about the Internet. Gaydar culture is not immune to such anxieties and concerns over veracity, honesty and integrity often translate into a fear of being duped into meeting someone who bears little resemblance to the description on their profile. While such deceptions may not cost users financially (the fraud not being a material one), they can be seen as both a nuisance and a waste of time and energy. Coté and Pybus (2007) highlight the levels of immaterial labour invested in spaces such as MySpace, and one might see a similar level of labour invested by the men who use Gaydar. Acknowledging the investment that users make not only in their profiles but in contacting other users, means that such deceptions are not only a nuisance, but render the user's labour unproductive and lacking exchange value; the pay-off does not reflect the work put in.

For many users, face-pics are considered a form of insurance against such deception, acting as a promise of what they can expect in real life.[26] Such insurance measures are often intimately tied to processes of self-identification on Gaydar. As the quotations above suggest, being *seen* as an out gay man is an important facet of these respondents' identity. Being 'proud' of who they are, questions of 'integrity', of not wanting to 'hide' or be seen to be 'afraid' – users ascribe a great deal of value to face-pics on Gaydar. Rather than objectifying the subject, respondents indicated that a face-pic serves to validate the user: a visual declaration that authenticates both the profile and the user. In a sense, the face-pic becomes a form of membership card, providing proof of legitimacy at the same time as it marks the user as *visibly* queer. This membership echoes Campbell's (2004) findings regarding the regular use of 'nicks' – nicknames – by users in IRC, where a level of 'ethical accountability' was at stake when such nicks were used by others.

Membership of course has its boundaries and some of the men I spoke to on Gaydar identified a transactional facet within such images. The response of one user, for example, who had chosen *not* to include a face-pic but had instead included only body images, underlines this transactional dimension. He explained that he 'would rather only send that [face-pic] to people who are willing to show their face-pics'. We might even think of the face-pic as a form of currency on Gaydar for, as the response suggests, there is a system of trade that users enter into via their images. Slater (1998: 111) identifies 'a concern … with reciprocity' in online environments where images are swapped and 'traded' stating that:

> Despite the fact that the supply of sexually explicit pictures on IRC is entirely free and apparently inexhaustible – beyond either scarcity or value – being ripped off or 'leeched' is a matter of constant, obsessive anger and regulation.

26 Though of course there are always cases where the picture is either out of date, particularly flattering or indeed, false.

The responses above suggest that a similar system of trade operates on Gaydar and that similar concerns with reciprocity pervade the user profile and interactions between users. Decisions behind such choices demonstrate the central role this type of image plays within what we might identify as the Gaydar economy. Like Slater's moral economy, this economy is not financial but functions on the level of subjectivity, imbuing user images with a level of 'social capital' similar to that found in gay IRC channels (Campbell, 2004: 156). Many of the men I spoke to, who had chosen to include a face-pic, often spoke derisively of those who remained hidden. Responses such as 'I chose to include photos because many ppl [people] are false and closets', or 'I wouldn't reply to a message without photo's [sic] attached' and finally, 'I will not respond to any profile without a picture and don't expect others to – it makes it look as if you have something to hide' are typical of the attitude displayed towards users who do not include an image of their face. Such users may be asked for an image prior to further interaction, establishing a transactional relationship with the intended contact, or they may be shunned for their perceived unwillingness to 'trade' identities and be open in the first place.

If this economy deals in subjectivity – be it the trading of images and messages, or an acknowledged investment in the space (through profile updates, detailed profile contents or membership status and recent activity) – then what is also being traded simultaneously is *trust* (see also, Lawson and Leck, 2006). Thus, being seen to not invest in this space (through not including a face-pic, for example), serves to dislocate the individual from this circuit of trust and place him in a zone of ambivalence. The 'faceless' user is a sub-prime investment – unknown and unseen he is treated with, at best, distrust, at worst, disdain.

Despite this danger of rejection some of the men I spoke to on Gaydar still felt that it was important that they remained 'hidden' owing to issues surrounding levels of 'outness' in other spheres of their life. Yet even these men confirmed the cultural, moral and social value of the face-pic:

> 'chose not to have photos in my profile for the simple reason i prefer to choose who sees my pic.'
>
> 'I have not included a facepic, as I would rather only send that to people who are willing to show me there facepics, and not otherwise. If I did put my facepic up, I would not know who is looking at my profile (maybe a friend), whilst they may know who I am.'
>
> 'no pic dont feel like advertising myself throughout the world.'
>
> 'My face pics are deliberately unclear because of my occupation. Full shots are sent privately to people if we get on.'

In all these responses, the economic facet of the face-pic is identified. In the first, the user acknowledges the value-system that he places on his face-pic: he wants to 'choose' who sees he image, only those who are *worth* it will receive his picture. In the second, the user employs a system of transaction involving trust, authenticity and confidentiality. Similar to the adage of 'you show me yours, I'll show you mine' the user is unwilling to invest his digital self in the Gaydar community unless his browsers do likewise. The third respondent clearly demonstrates the promotional dimension of user profiles (echoing Coupland, 1996) while the final response reminds us of the slippage that can often occur between digital and physical spaces. Whether or not a face-pic is included in a user's profile, the decisions behind the choice suggest that face-pics carry immense value on Gaydar.

Writing about the work of radical artists such as Claude Cahun and Cindy Sherman, Jones (2002: 950) observes that 'the self-portrait photograph is an example … of this way in which technology not only *mediates* but *produces* subjectivities in the contemporary world' and recognises the connection between these self-consciously radical photographers and more mainstream self-representations:

> The point … is to engage with such images … in such a way as to open out the question of how subjectivity is established and how meaning is made in relation to *all* representations. (Jones, ibid: 949)

Similar to Butler's (1990) work on performativity, Jones argues that the exaggerated performance of these artists destabilises modernist assumptions regarding 'truth', both the truth of the photograph and of a pre-given identity. It is unsurprising that such an approach to photography proves attractive to marginalised and sexually dissident subjects (Jones, ibid: 948). The average Gaydar face-pic may not be as explicitly involved in staging such a radical assault on conventional notions of identity as the artistic self-portraits analysed by Jones, but her thesis remains relevant nonetheless:

> The subject performs herself or himself within the purview of an apparatus of perspectival looking that freezes the body as representation and so – as absence, as always already dead – in intimate relation to lack and loss … At the same time, in their exaggerated theatricality, these works [of Cahun *et al.*] foreground the fact that *the self-portrait photograph is eminently performative and so life giving*. (Jones ibid: 949) [author's emphasis]

Gaydar face-pics work to validate the subject of the image and allow a level of identification between user and browser. As one correspondent commented, 'I like to know who I'm talking too and vice versa'. Users did not consider themselves as objectified by this process but instead embodied through this visual representation, as they felt a face-pic 'let people c who they [were] chatting 2 [sic]'. Face pics, it seems, perform an act of digital embodiment and are part of the project of 'affirming and asserting an identity' on Gaydar (Horne and Lewis, 1997: 104). Furthermore, to be a part of the Gaydar community you need to be *seen* to be a part of it.

Life, death and fridge magnets: Barthes' *punctum* and connection on Gaydar

This quality of photographic embodiment (something of a paradox given that the medium that is often seen as 'capturing' or 'freezing' the subject) was also identified by Barthes (1980) in *Camera Lucida*. While Barthes begins by linking the photograph with death, asserting that the freezing of the subject in a photograph highlights the inevitable death of that subject, he later suggests that the medium can create a 'rupture', which gives life to the image, embodying the subject through what he famously terms the *punctum*. This detail, which pierces the *studium* of the photographic image, is affected by time and detail, both of which serve to connect the viewer to the subject of the photograph.

The beautiful elusiveness of Barthes' *punctum* makes it somewhat difficult to quantify, yet a framework that identifies (if only in the most personal and, paradoxically, most abstract fashion) the relationship that may develop between subject and object is a tantalising prospect for any analysis that seeks to explore the relationship that develops between user, browser and image in an environment such as Gaydar. The reasons for this are numerous. Firstly, the *punctum,* in its ability to capture the viewer, drawing in and 'touching' him at a level beyond superficial criticism or remark may help us to understand the relationship between face-pic and browser on Gaydar. In opposition to the *studium*, which always remains in 'the order of liking, not of loving' (Barthes, 1980: 27), the *punctum* disrupts the distant and critical gaze of the viewer and effects a kind of counter-criticism, a reflection of the viewer:

> The second element will break (or punctuate) the *studium*. This time it is not I who seek it out (as I invest the field of the *studium* with my sovereign consciousness), it is this element, which rises from the scene, shoots out of it like an arrow, and pierces me. (Barthes, ibid: 26)

User profiles are designed to advertise the user, to attract the critical eye of the browser and capture his attention, though this may rarely be achieved. As with most forms of advertising, the profile is rather obvious in its intentions – it seeks out the browser in ways that are consciously foregrounded. This is unsurprising given the fact that the profile is a means of promoting the self, of marking the self to browsers:

> To recognize the *studium* is inevitably to encounter the photographer's intentions, to enter into harmony with them, to approve or disapprove of them, but always to understand them, to argue them within myself, for culture (from which the *studium* derives) is a contract arrived at between creators and consumers. (Barthes, ibid: 27–28)

But if we follow Barthes' line of argument through, the few times that the profile effects a kind of capturing – piercing – it may well be less a result of the user's intentions or anything within his control (lighting, framing, choice of outfit, decision to smile or not) and more to do with those 'partial object[s]' (ibid: 43) that appear by accident within the frame: a detail that leaps out of the image and which catches the browser's eye, his attention and his imagination. This aspect of accident is enhanced in most Gaydar face-pics by two qualities, namely their relative amateurism and their location. Face-pics (indeed a large percentage of the images found on Gaydar) are regularly situated within the domestic space of the home and these images are often taken using domestic digital cameras or low-resolution web-cams. Here the trend is to focus on foregrounding the user, while little attention is paid to the background. Yet the background often provides a wealth of clues about the user and their (life)style. These background details – these accidents – can also provoke *punctum*, since Barthes' use of the term stresses that it resides less often in the overt, central subject of the photograph than in incidental details which prompt unexpected recognition or recollection in the mind of the viewer:

> In this habitually unary space, occasionally (but alas all too rarely) a 'detail' attracts me. I feel that its mere presence changes my reading, that I am looking at a new photograph, marked in my eyes with a higher value. This 'detail' is the *punctum*. (Barthes, ibid: 42)

Like Barthes' *punctum,* the act of browsing Gaydar is an intensely personal and solitary form of active looking, in much the same way as pornography is.[27] For example when looking at the profile picture of 'hotMA2guy', it is not his clenched fist held up to the camera, his military style bomber jacket or his shaved head that catches my eye or reveals the user to me. Of course I identify the *studium* of the photograph immediately. What is being 'sold' here is transparent. I see a man in his early forties looking straight into the camera. I see his unsmiling face and the angle of his body suggesting the stance of a boxer or bouncer. I see the intentions of the user in this image, his reason for choosing it. I understand and interpret the signifiers in order to comprehend his performance of 'tough-guy' masculinity, the desire to portray himself as straight-acting or butch (desires that are arguably structured and

27 I here contradict Barthes in claiming that the *punctum* is present within pornography. Relying on the maintenance of a boundary between 'erotic' and 'pornographic' photography, Barthes felt that while the work of Mapplethorpe (for instance) could be 'redeemed', the pornographic photo was unary – untouching. I can understand Barthes's exclusion of the pornographic if by this term he only means those studio-produced images of the order of pin-ups and magazines. However, if we expand the meaning of this term to include more amateur, less stylised images, then we must begin to acknowledge the presence of the *punctum*. For the *punctum* is an accident, a partial object or detail, and in being so, it can be as present within the pornographic image as it is in other less explicit photos.

promoted by the site, and which I will return to below). I understand the image and I am not touched by its performance. The *studium* of the image does not affect me.

It is the background details, the kitchen in which this picture has been taken, the cheap table lamp, the fridge and, most important (for me, at least, for this is personal) the fridge magnets on the door, that hold my attention. They serve to reveal another side to the user, one that contradicts – though in no way consciously – the machismo that the image foregrounds. The magnets arouse an identification within me: similarly tacky plaques adorn my own fridge. Furthermore, that one of the magnets resembles one of my own, (perhaps the most garish), given as a token of affection by a young relative of mine, highlights the 'ownership' of the *punctum*:

> Last thing about the *punctum*: whether or not it is triggered, it is an addition: *it is what I add to the photograph and what is nonetheless already there*. (Barthes, ibid: 55) [author's emphasis]

In opposition to the *studium*, which can be reduced to the language of semiotics (signifier, signified, referent) the *punctum* is both in the photograph and outside of it, beyond the frame. Barthes comments on the portrait of a black family stating that 'on account of her necklace, the black woman in her Sunday best has had, for me, a whole life external to her portrait' (ibid: 57). The face-pic for 'hotMA2guy' reveals, through its *punctum*, a life completely external to both this image, and the pose.[28]

Jones (2002: 961) quotes Metz (1985) when she states that:

> the *punctum* 'depends more on the reader than on the photograph itself' … The *punctum* is that detail in the image that opens it to the depths of our fully embodied subjectivity by pricking our memory.

I want to ask 'hotMA2guy' where he got his fridge magnets. Did he buy them? Were they a gift? Does he even like them? Or does he keep them because, like me, he feels guilty about throwing away a present that was given with sincerity and love? The deliberate pose of the user freezes him in a death stare. It is the 'accident' of the fridge magnets that reveals more to me about the user than his mask of masculine performance can ever reveal. It is this unravelling of a narrative, partly owned by the user, partly owned by the browser, that creates a connection between Self and Other.

There is an erotic quality to this connection; a desiring quality to know more:

> When we define a Photograph as a motionless image, this does not mean only that the figures it represents do not move; it means that they do not emerge, do

28 Indeed, the pose, together with the username and text, serve to provide a well-rounded performance of butch masculinity, which it seems is the aim of the user and a quality he seeks in partners.

> not leave: they are anesthetized and fastened down, like butterflies. Yet once there is a *punctum*, a blind field is created (is divined). (Barthes, 1980: 57)

The amateur image is split into a *posed* foreground (studied, 'fastened down') and the accidental *quality* of the background. It is this quality that makes me pause at 'hotMA2guy''s profile. Such accidental, 'partial objects' catch me, halt my browsing and stay with me after I've moved on. To the list of attributes we can associate with the Gaydar profile then (identification, objectification, validation, investment) we must now also add *connection*.

It would be naïve to assume that this connection either predicates a meeting face-to-face or indeed any form of communication. It is similarly inaccurate to suggest that all browsers experience the effects of the *punctum* prior to contacting a user. When I talk of a connection being maintained through the image, I am not suggesting a physical or communicative link between subjects but an interiorising of the image and, at the same time, an acknowledgement of the exteriority of the image. The image validates both the existence of the user – 'that has been' – and also his (previous) presence in this space (Barthes, ibid: 96). Barthes writes that 'the photograph does not necessarily say what is no longer, but only and for certain what has been' (85) and in this sense, the image is a producer and judge of truth in a way that text cannot be:

> no writing can give me this certainty. It is the misfortune (but also the voluptuous pleasure) of language not to be able to authenticate itself. (ibid)

This certainty, carried within the image, is intensified within digital environments, for while digital images allow for an unprecedented degree of manipulation, the proof-of-life quality that photography continues to hold within contemporary Western culture can be evidenced in the statements quoted above regarding the implications a face-pic has for trust and validation on Gaydar. The *punctum* thus serves to confirm the existence of the user while also drawing in and 'arresting' the browser who happens upon his image in this digital environment. Identifying the potential power of the detail, of the almost mistaken and half-submerged partial object of the profile image, allows us to better understand the various facets of the Gaydar user profile. In doing so, we are able to acknowledge how the cultural practices of creating, maintaining and browsing profiles are intimately involved in projects of identity-formation, cultural affirmation, connectivity, membership and validation.

Rate me/validate me: Gaydar and the discourse of cybercarnality

In December 2004 Gaydar launched Sex Factor, a ratings-based competition advertised as 'a new, fun feature, which allows you to nominate and vote for your favourite guys on the site – or to enter yourself' (Gaydar, Sex Factor, online). Every month the votes for each entrant are counted before 'the hottest guys' are crowned 'Sex Factor winners!' (ibid). There are no prizes for being a top scorer, other than having your profile advertised on the leader board, but this has not stopped Sex Factor becoming extremely successful. On 21st December 2004 the following statistics were posted on the Gaydar site:

> In the first 5 days we have had over 30 000 entrants and more than 6.5 million votes have already been cast. (ibid)

At the time of writing this, some five years on from its launch, Sex Factor continues to be a popular feature on Gaydar, though its categories have been reduced from sixteen to thirteen.[29] Originally the categories could be roughly divided into three genres; clothing/fetishwear ('leather', 'rubber', 'uniform', 'sports gear'), age ('young guys 18–21' '22+', 'older guys'), and body type ('bears', 'cubs', 'skins & punks', 'muscle'). In many ways these categories echo those often found in the contact adverts of gay magazines and advertisements for pornographic chat lines. Some categories ('alternative/hip' and 'guy next door' for example) straddle genres, although even these tacitly suggest a certain age, body shape and clothing preference. Importantly, the categories identified on Sex Factor (which have been chosen by QSoft Consulting) focus entirely on the visual and certain guys win because they fit the 'look' that the category promotes.[30]

Built as it is around its central database of searchable user profiles, Gaydar embodies a process of perpetual classification and Sex Factor celebrates this classification, creating taxonomies of gay identity. Age, attire and body shape form the holy trinity of metropolitan gay male subculture through which identities are produced and understood and the popularity of Sex Factor illustrates the importance placed on such classification as it champions the pursuit of the most perfect specimen in each category. I am reminded of Kappeler's (1986) argument, which I drew upon in Chapter 3, and her work on pornographic representation allows us to identify the structural similarities between Sex Factor and gay male pornography. Kappeler's reading of culture suggests that images are embedded in structures that work towards the 'distillation of power' (Kappeler, 1986: 78) and I would argue that Sex Factor illustrates such a distillation of power, namely late capitalism's power over male homosexual desire and identity. Where Kappeler regards toy dolls (such as Barbie and Action Man) supporting an 'increased ideological diffusion of gender stereotypes' (ibid: 78) I would argue that the taxonomic processes at work in 'games' such as Sex Factor engender a similar experience where 'the remorseless diffusion

29 Since this time, the number of categories has not only been reduced but the specific age categories have been removed. A new 'couples' category has also been added.

30 Interestingly, there is no category for the 'chubs' identified and studied by Campbell (2004) on IRC. There is also no category for trans men, suggesting that some bodies cannot be comfortably accommodated in these digital contexts. It should also be noted that in every category, the top ten entrants are regularly all Caucasian.

of gender stereotypes, of ready-made and imperative life-styles, of regulated and uniform relationships … through the remorseless diffusion of their material basis – consumer goods – renders human subjects increasingly marginal' (ibid: 79).

Meanwhile, and somewhat paradoxically, though Sex Factor appears to separate users into discrete classifications, there appears to be a level of slippage between them, suggesting an underlying homogeneity. For example, many in the 'hip' category look as though they could also be in the 'muscle 18–30' category. Similarly, some of the 'older men' could also be 'bears'. It should be pointed out here that there are no guidelines as to what these categories mean and users are supposed to know *a priori* what the conventions of each category are. Thus, while there is a level of classification that fragments gay culture into multiple 'mind images' (ibid: 79), underpinning all of these is a particular aesthetic – a particular masculinity – that continues to be cultivated within metropolitan gay culture and which permeates Gaydar and similar dating/sex websites. For example, many of the top profiles feature men with remarkably similar bodies: toned, developed muscles, evenly tanned and (save for the bears and cubs) hairless. Indeed, many of the top profiles look similar to the images that adorn the Gaydar homepage, suggesting the further promotion of an idealised gay body. Arguably (and responding to Kappeler's argument) the emphasis in gay men's digital culture is not so much on 'regulated and uniform relationships' as it is on regulated and uniform *bodies*.

Of course this focus on the gay male body, and on regulating that body is not new to gay subculture (as I have discussed in the previous two chapters), but the advent of digital media technologies marks a definite re-inscription of the sub-cultural rules of engagement. Campbell (2004: 154) notes the formation of multiple hierarchies of male beauty, which he dubs the 'male beauty myth' in gay IRC channels, but acknowledges that the idealisation of a 'muscular, athletic, youthful, strong and principally white male body' has been evident since the end of World War II (162). Sex Factor appears to further re-enforce such hierarchies and such idealisation as it celebrates these rules and, by extension, integrates gay men into a system of self-representation and self-surveillance. It serves to illustrate the relationship between the way in which gay men understand themselves and patriarchal pre-occupations with self-surveillance and self-regulation, a key element within cybercarnal discourse. If, remembering Stone's (2000: 524) argument, the body is always a 'legible body' then Sex Factor is more than simply a game of 'hot or not', it is the end point of a much larger system of embodied scripting, which serves to write the digital subject into being using a highly codified language. This code, the code that both produces and frames the gay body in digital space, is the code of gay male pornography and the categories validated by Sex Factor map onto pre-existing genres in gay male porn.

As the table below illustrates, almost[31] every category available on Sex Factor at the time of its launch could be found in contemporaneous gay porn genres and can be identified in pornographic film titles released around the same time.

31 It should be noted that the 'rubber' and 'alternative/hip' categories are not mirrored in gay porn genres but, as the recent release column of the table demonstrates, these 'types'

Table 4.1 Sex Factor categories and their relationship to gay male pornography[32]

Sex Factor Categories	Gay Porn Genres	Recent Gay Porn Releases
Leather	Leather	Open Trench
Rubber	N/A	Gay Latex Dreams
Uniform	Uniform/Uniform Twinks/ Military Men/Cops	Top Secret
Sports Gear	Sports/Sports Twinks/Gym Guys	Football Orgy 2
Muscle (all ages)	Studs/Muscle Men/Young Studs	Muscle Fuck
Bears/Cubs	Bears	Manimal
Young Guys/Guys Next Door	Twinks/First Timers	Beachboy
Guys Next Door (31+)	Studs	Straight Men Fuck
Older Guys	Daddies	In Gear
Hip/Alternative	N/A	SkaterBoy

I am not suggesting that QSoft intentionally sought to mirror Sex Factor categories onto gay porn genres, nor am I suggesting that this taxonomic process is unique to Gaydar – far from it. As expressed in the introduction to this chapter, database searching relies on setting filters, parameters and rules, and such search facilities are common across a whole range of dating/sex websites. More often than not, these rules share a close relationship with the codified world of gay male porn. In demonstrating the crossover between Sex Factor categories and pornographic genres, I want to acknowledge the methods by which representations of the gay subject are increasingly influenced via a pornographic discourse, and that 'identity work' on sites such as Gaydar does not happen in a vacuum, but draws upon gay pornography, which in turn shapes our understanding of subjectivity in these – and other – spaces. One might of course argue that gay men have been appropriating pornographic codes long before the advent of the Web. This is undoubtedly true. However, the deployment of pornographic codes within digital forms such as the user profile, (which, we should remember is the space in which gay men may encounter other gay men for the first time), extends such appropriation to the point

can be found within contemporary gay pornographic texts.

32 Gay porn categories taken from the Gay DVD Sex Video Store (online) and the recent release list is compiled from Videoshop.com (online).

where identity work no longer scaffolds such codes onto a sense of self but instead uses them as the vocabulary through which the digital self is written into being.

Writing the self (through words or images) is integral to both the Gaydar profile and a discourse of cybercarnality, the discourse through which the gay male body is rendered visible and available for consumption on sites such as Gaydar. The user profile can be regarded as the latest tactic employed by an invisible minority group (Foster, 2000) through which the subject can be rendered *visibly* gay and cybercarnality signals the *way* in which this subject is rendered visible and reveals the particular frames of reference at work within the formation and maintenance of gay subjectivity online.

As Sex Factor demonstrates, subjectivity on profile sites such as Gaydar is not only represented but (re)produced through a pornographic lens. Of course the 'newbie' may not necessarily conform to these categories, but if he is to 'fit in' – that is, if he is to function, be understood, be found within search engines, and be picked up – then he will have to submit to the conventions of this pornographic discourse. This is not to say that those who do not fit neatly into the categories offered by Sex Factor cannot 'exist' on Gaydar but rather, that such subjects inevitably exists *in relation* to these categories. That is, individual subjectivity is defined against a pre-existing taxonomy and is judged against such classifications. I may not fit into any of these categories but I am comprehensible – legible – only in relation to certain age brackets, certain body types, certain fetishes.

Cybercarnality is at the heart of the user profile and the text and images used by many users to construct their online selves borrows heavily from pornography. Within many user-generated images the pose, mis-en-scene, clothing, and self-conscious realism signified through the background detail are reminiscent of conventions found in gay male pornography. Pornographic structures govern the modes of self-representation in the user profile and exhibiting the body on Gaydar relies on a specific language of display.

Even when references to specific pornographic texts are not visibly invoked, bodies are always understood through a pornographic lens; the body – be it represented textually or visually – is always framed by the promise of erotic investigation and sexual pleasure: *carnal* satisfaction. Bodies may be clothed and their poses may not appear pornographic but the structures of representation present on Gaydar (the methods by which we look and *see*) maintain a level of identification with the cybercarnal. The browser navigates to a profile in order to *know* the user. He looks at the profile in order to *discover* the real person the other side of the screen. But, just as Kappeler's peep show customers can never find the real woman, so the browser can never find the user's real identity within the profile. This is because the profile is designed with one look in mind – 'looking *at*' – and in being thus designed, the profile cannot provide a space for mutual recognition. Profiles provide a means of knowing (a way of seeing) the Other, and it is this knowledge that is inflected with, framed by and invested in the cybercarnal. If the browser and the user talk, it is through their profiles. If they meet offline for coffee or for sex their meet is still framed by the profile – this is because they experience each other initially as objects to be looked at, investigated, chosen and consumed. While a single image may provide a sense of connection, a *punctum*, this connection is ultimately bound by the frameworks of representation in which the image is located, frameworks that construct and permeate the user profile. The browser may be arrested, pricked by an accidental detail in the profile image, but his mode of looking, his approach, cannot be separated out from the cybercarnal.

Conclusion

Sedgwick (1991) states that any critical analysis of society must take into account the hetero-homo binary within our society, and this binary is apparent in discussions that centre on representations of the male body in contemporary Western culture. It is precisely because Western culture has been produced, distributed and consumed by and for the dominant gaze of the heterosexual male that any discussion of the male body should include a point of reference that is primarily homosexual. This is in part due to material-historical circumstances but it is also a result of the conventions of visual media such as narrative cinema, which 'teach' the audience how to decode gendered bodies, whom to assign sexual agency to, and most importantly, who to sexually objectify.

Through the adoption of a psychoanalytic framework we can see how the user profile embodies the twin practices of identification and objectification and the user profile is both a tool for (re)producing identity in digital space and a site of objectification. The browser is positioned as the unseen subject that consumes the user according to his own personal desires. In understanding this objectification, we might queer Kappeler's (1986: 61) central argument thus:

> under his aesthetic gaze, any [man], known or unknown, turns into the 'stranger', that object of no interest except for its capacity to stimulate the subject's feeling of life.

The user is seen but he does not know by whom. He is the silent object of someone else's narrative but he cannot reciprocate unless given permission by the browser.

Psychoanalysis alone cannot accommodate the culturally specific dynamics contained within the practices of constructing and consuming profiles. Any treatment of the male body, clothed or unclothed that frames it as an object to be consumed opens that body up to a queering of masculinity and thus such consumption must be read across different registers and within a different political context. Through the development of a second critical frame we can identify the plurality of meanings inherent within the user profile, which functions not only as a marker of identity, but also as a membership card and a proof of authenticity. We can also see the user profile as a point of mediation, connecting individuals together, though, as has been demonstrated through a discussion of the *punctum*, these connective possibilities may not be consciously known to either user or browser. Thus the profile can be understood as a text that serves to construct, articulate and legitimate identity within gay sub-cultural spaces online. As such, it is both a method of communication and a means by which men are rendered culturally legible in gay/queer digital environments.

Finally, through the acknowledgement of a cybercarnal discourse, which pervades the gay user profile, we are forced to recognise the intense and complex relationship that ties this writing of the digital subject to the generic – and gendered – codes of gay male pornography. The freedom to create, play with and mould identity in gay cyberspace is tempered by this meta-discourse of explicit sexual representation, which structures our understanding of digital identities here and frames our interactions with others in such spaces. This connection between pornography and gay identity pre-dates the user profile, but it is through the profile that such a relationship reaches its zenith, as the bodies we produce online, (digital bodies through which we are rendered visible, intelligible and knowable) are formed from, filtered through and recognised by the codes of pornography, codes which permeate gay male subculture at every level.

Chapter 5
Cruising the Cybercottage

In the last chapter I explored the most popular gay male website in Britain, Gaydar, in order to discuss how gay men are using digital media to produce, maintain and negotiate sexual identities. Throughout my analysis I tacitly relied upon a specific paradigm of homosexuality, namely the metropolitan model identified by Sinfield (1998) and outlined in Chapter 2. This lifestyle-oriented identity remains the most visible and widely acknowledged articulation of homosexuality in Britain (indeed throughout the West) today and fosters a concept of an unchanging 'fixed' gay identity in the same way that heterosexuality is conceptualised as natural, stable and immovable. Such claims to fixity have arguably helped gay men and women to claim a degree of civil and human rights within late capitalist Western societies, while simultaneously providing a point for entry into the political-economic structure of late capitalism through the marketing of a gay 'lifestyle'. As D'Emilio (1992: 12) states, the self-identifying 'out' gay subject may have been created by gay rights movements but it has only become accepted within the public sphere because it serves the interests of a changing economic system:

> Capitalism has created the material conditions for homosexual desire to express itself as a central component of some individuals' lives … Human sexual desire need no longer be harnessed to reproductive imperatives, to procreation; its expression has increasingly entered the realm of choice. (ibid)

Within this wider context Gaydar can be seen to operate in the same way as a conventional gay bar or club, as a commercial space that defines the individual and, to quote Jones (2002: 950) 'not only *mediates* but *produces* subjectivities' within that space. At the same time Gaydar interpellates users into flows of informational, sub-cultural and economic capital thereby translating these practices of identity formation into forms that support and feed proliferating networks of consumption.

But beyond the metropolitan model, digital ICTs also offer opportunities for other articulations of homosexuality, which grow out of cultures and identities that follow radically different trajectories to that of 'mainstream' gay male subculture. Such trajectories highlight the racial, geographical, gendered and class-based boundaries of metropolitan gay culture and often develop from positions of multiple marginalisation and a sense that 'gay' culture does not speak to or on behalf of all queer people. Weeks (1990: 33) reminds us that 'homosexual behaviour cannot be crammed into any one predetermined mould, because it pervades many different aspects of social experience'. Sinfield (1998), Corber

(1999), and Valocchi (1999) all identify the fact that this metropolitan urban-centric and Western understanding of homosexuality is but one iteration of male same-sex desire and that some identities choose not to (or cannot) access this lifestyle-driven subculture. Examples of such ICT use include queer working-class youths in rural America, who use the Web to fashion their own identities and publics (Gray, 2009); Taiwanese men who perform 'queered effeminacies' online (Lin, 2006); and diasporic queer Indians, who make use of the blogosphere to articulate their subjectivities at the intersection of sexual and racial marginality (Mitra and Gajjala, 2008).

In Chapter 3 I considered how the Civil Partnership Act of 2004 served to further validate and promote one form of homosexuality – the monogamous gay relationship – above all others. Such validation inevitably risks undermining identities and practices that fall outside of this 'straight-friendly' (or homonormative[1]) metropolitan culture. In this chapter, and Chapter 6, I map out and analyse three digital environments that diverge from the metropolitan culture maintained on Gaydar, and which appear to offer opportunities to deviate from 'mainstream' configurations of homosexuality. In Chapter 6 I shall demonstrate how the Web has been integral to the establishment of a new sexual subculture and the formation of a new discourse of gay male sex. In this chapter I focus primarily on a virtual environment dedicated to sexual practices that remain outside of the framework of 'normative' gay male sexuality. By dismantling the 'activity = identity' equation central to metropolitan gay culture, this environment caters to practices and (non)identities that are perceived to be marginal to that culture. To rely on an analogy for a moment; if Gaydar is the equivalent of a bar in London's Soho, in this chapter I want to focus on digital spaces that are comparable to gym changing rooms, motorway lay-bys, or department store toilets.

Studying this kind of digital space is not easy. Returning to my analogy for a moment, although bars in urban centres do change periodically, they rarely change from one day to the next: their identities, like their foundations, are relatively static. By contrast, toilets, lay-bys, back alleys and park spaces are never stable sites of homosexual activity or identity. What may be a public sex environment (PSE) on Thursday evening may well be nothing more than a public convenience on Friday morning. Furthermore, considering histories of police surveillance and hate crime, these sites often oscillate between homosexual and homophobic, and may in fact be both simultaneously (see Humphries, 1970; Flowers *et al.*, 1999 and Tomsen, 2006 for further discussion). We might consider these spaces as sites of queer 'tactics', employing De Certeau's (1984: xix) definition of the term:

1 I use the term 'homonormative' with reference to Puar's 2006 article on terrorism, nationhood and queer identities, in which the author identifies the methods by which a particular type of homosexuality has been co-opted by US heteronormative culture for a host of reasons, one of which being to ensure the further policing of 'non-normative' and 'non-nationalist' sexualities while at the same time positioning US society as embracing (some forms of 'correct') sexual diversity (see Puar, 2006: 67–88).

> I call a 'tactic' … a calculus which cannot count on a 'proper' (a spatial or institutional) localization, nor thus on a borderline distinguishing the other as a visible totality. The place of a tactic belongs to the other. A tactic insinuates itself into the other's place, fragmentarily, without taking it over in its entirety, without being able to keep it at a distance.

The physical sites of the public toilet and the motorway lay-by are not 'proper' – they are not owned or controlled by the queer identities that pass through them. Rather, they offer opportunities for momentary queer appropriation: for brief stealings of time – and pleasure – within the place of the heterosexual other (Tomsen, 2006). Similarly to the public toilet, the type of digital space I am concerned with here is far less stable, far harder to find and, for the most part, more short lived than the comparatively static Gaydar. It too is tactical rather than strategic. That is to say, the spaces informing my discussion in this chapter do not form cohesive *strategies* of power in the same way that Gaydar – in being constructed for and populated by gay men – does:

> Strategies are … associated with space, and specifically with those spaces, which are owned and operated by powerful dominant forces. Strategies operate in space, consolidating power over others who impinge on that space. (Bukatman, 2000: 160)

Spanning both the physical and digital worlds, public sexual cultures are the subject of both online and offline systems of security and surveillance. Such systems embody the strategic power that governs public space, although online, the law enforcers more often than not take the form of corporate bodies that offer web hosting services, who themselves fear prosecution for 'supporting' such spaces and practices.

Given the 'tactical' nature of the online space that forms the primary focus of this chapter a particular set of ethical questions must be considered. Using its actual name would disclose too much information about its location (both physical and virtual), and while such web-groups are not illegal, as will be discussed below, the (physical) activities that some members may engage in, or rather *where* they engage in them, could cause concerns for law enforcement agents. The implications of this will be discussed in more detail shortly, but in the context of methodological approach and ethical awareness, it requires important decisions to be made regarding the presentation of the group. Unlike other sites discussed in this book, the web-group does not attempt to attract a wide audience. While some have argued that all web pages uploaded are in the public domain, others have identified the difficulty of maintaining such a line of argument in relation to membership-restricted spaces, Intranets and 'private' discussion forums, web-groups and communities[2].

In shaping an ethically appropriate methodology, I acknowledge the influence that Bruckman's (2001, online) work has had on my approach. She identifies the challenge that humanities research faces when studying the Internet; a dilemma that stems from the fact that for many scholars located in this area, Internet research is not conceptualised, executed or recorded in the same way as it is in other disciplines. The starting point for any methodological enquiry must therefore be the acknowledgement that 'many humanities disciplines have not historically viewed what they do as human subjects research' (ibid). Faced with the dilemma of either exposing research subjects without proper permission or 'hamper[ing] our ability to understand the medium' (ibid), Bruckman devises a tiered system of disguise founded on an assessment of the potential harm that exposure could cause the subject. Seeing the issue of anonymity as a 'continuum of possibilities' (ibid) she organises four ethical positions from which to conduct research on the Internet. These range from 'no disguise' to 'heavy disguise' and it is the latter that I have chosen to adopt in developing my methodological approach to the spaces under investigation here:

- Heavy disguise.
- The group is not named.
- Names, pseudonyms and other identifying details are changed.
- Verbatim quotes are not used if a search mechanism could link those quotes to the person in question.
- Some false details may be deliberately introduced.
- For example, if you are studying a support site for a chronic disease, you might change the disease in published accounts.
- No one would likely recognize the subject (except perhaps the subject him/herself).
- Someone deliberately seeking to find a subject's identity would likely be unable to do so.
- Details that would be harmful to the subject if disclosed *may* be revealed, because the subject has been carefully anonymised. (Bruckman, 2001: np)

A pseudonym that reflects the general physical location of, and type of action sought by, the group membership has been chosen for the web-group under investigation. All names have been disguised and while posts have been quoted verbatim, these cannot be traced through freely available search mechanisms. False details have not been introduced as it was not felt necessary to do so, the other components of the heavy disguise position being adequately effective in

2 See Berry (2004) for a comprehensive discussion of this debate. I am indebted to David M. Berry for his thoughts and input into the shaping of the ethical dimension of this chapter's research.

anonymising both the space and its participants. Lastly, while the posts have been copied verbatim, specific physical locations have been anonymised or deleted. Similarly, the university (Midchester) referred to in the central case study is a fictitious name, though the descriptions of the student demographic and the city are accurate. Such levels of anonymity mean that sensitive information can be disclosed and analysed without any risk to the subject or the institution.

Such anonymity and non-disclosure is imperative when we recognise that the object of study here is a clandestine world in which anonymity (or at least imagined anonymity) is vital to its appeal, success and survival. This investment in anonymity means that research techniques such as interviews, surveys or ethnographic interaction are not appropriate. During the course of my research I 'lurked' on group email lists, 'lurking' being not uncommon behaviour in these web-groups. Many members, though visible to the group through their online status appeared to lurk, never posting or actively engaging with the group membership. Therefore my presence and (in)activity was not unusual. Lurking allowed me to gather data (primarily in the form of postings to the group) without the risk of it being compromised by my own intrusions. The combination of uncontaminated data collection twinned with the application of Bruckman's 'heavy disguise' position has allowed me to bridge the difficult gap between ethics and methodology, between respecting those who use such sites and interrogating their activities.

Uni_cock

Uni_cock is a web-group designed to provide a channel of asynchronous communication between men looking for casual sexual encounters both on the university site and in the surrounding city. Hosted for free by a major international web service, access to this group is subject to membership. This is simple to obtain, requiring only a valid email address and the user's confirmation that they are over 18. While the web-group provides a variety of services similar to Gaydar the majority of activity and communication is via short text-based messages posted to the group, which are then circulated to the membership via email. Uni_cock is dedicated to the facilitation of immediate sexual gratification within semi-public spaces.

In describing Uni_cock, and other spaces like it, I use the term 'cybercottage' to identify both the type of activity, the virtual location, and the cultural specificity of the web-group. 'Cottaging' is the British term for the practice of having casual (homosexual) sex in toilets, a 'cottage' being the slang term in British gay subculture for a public toilet (the North American equivalent being a 'tearoom'). While some of the spaces described as possible PSEs in cybercottages are not strictly speaking cottages (shower rooms and changing rooms in gyms, along with park spaces are regularly suggested as locations) the lack of an alternative term means that cottaging remains the most appropriate idiom by which to describe the activity sought through the web-group. The cybercottage can thus be defined as a digital space created for the sole purpose of negotiating casual sexual encounters between men in specific (semi)public spaces in corresponding offline locations.[3]

Public (in)conveniences: Cottaging in context

Before embarking on a detailed analysis of Uni_cock, a brief consideration of the complex role cottaging plays in gay subcultural history may be instructive. As an articulation of homosexuality that pre-dates the evolution of a gay identity, cottaging is representative of the type of covert homosexual activity often necessary in the first half the twentieth century. Burton (1985: 38) goes so far as to suggest that 'it is possible that men of whatever predominant sexual persuasion have been cottaging for as long as men have had the need to relieve themselves'.

Historical accounts reiterate the prevalence of this kind of activity in pre-Wolfenden Britain and, with no organised commercial scene to speak of, cottaging was often the easiest way of meeting other men (see also Weeks, 1990; Goldsmith, 1998; and Humphries, 1970). As such it is a recurring motif in the narratives of men growing up prior to Gay Liberation and the formation of an 'out' gay identity (Babuscio, 1988; Hall-Carpenter, 1989). Chauncey (2002: 293) reminds us of the relative 'newness' of such an identity writing that:

> The most striking difference between the dominant sexual culture of the early twentieth century and that of our own era is the degree to which the earlier culture permitted men to engage in sexual relations with other men, often on a regular basis, without requiring them to regard themselves – or to be regarded by others – as gay.

The cottage provided a site for such sexual relations between men to occur and the anonymity afforded by fleeting trysts in public conveniences supported this non-identification. I shall return to the issue of non-identification below. During the 1970s, gay activism developed a tense relationship with the clandestine world of cottaging (see Weeks 1990; Power, 1995; Sinfield, 1997). Sometimes it was deplored it for its secrecy, its reputation and its political apathy, while at other times it was defended as a legitimate part of a multi-faceted homosexuality, repressed by a hetero-patriarchal ideology of the nuclear family. For the GLF, cottaging as an activity was not the problem, rather the problem resided in the 'false consciousness'

---

3 One could argue that the term cruising is more general and, being often used in relation to looking for sex in public and semi-public spaces, would be more suitable. However the implication of sexual activity is not as definite. Cruising is as likely to take place in the aisles of a local supermarket as on Hampstead Heath and more often than not it does not result in sex. We could say that in this instance, cruising is understood as the invitation: cottaging is what happens when you accept that invitation.

of those who sought a sexual outlet in this way.[4] The predominant GLF mindset saw such men as closeted, devoid of 'gay pride', lacking in liberation, and, most probably, living seemingly heterosexual lives. Reflecting on the old beliefs of the GLF, Sinfield (1997: 210) writes:

> Once, we supposed that the opportunity to be openly gay would attract many husbands away from their marriages and save younger men from making such a mistake; so married homosexuals would die out as a breed.

While cottaging was difficult to denounce because of the sex-positive stance of the GLF, Sinfield's comment reveals the ultimate goal of gay liberation: the extinction of the 'married homosexual'. The belief that cottaging was the domain of the closeted drew strength from Humphries' (1970) work in this field. His study, conducted in 1960's America has long been used as evidence that cottaging is an activity engaged in primarily by heterosexual-identified men, despite the fact that there was very little possibility of identifying as anything else during this period.[5]

While the GLF rhetoric can be understood as an exercise in consciousness-raising, (see Chapter 2) it must also be noted that such discourse was modelled upon (or perhaps has since been manipulated into) a dynamic that collapsed sexual identity and sexual difference. In other words, it assumed that the married man who 'indulged' and the cottage queen who lingered by the urinals were both closeted homosexuals. This understanding of sexual difference has been the mainstay of the gay civil rights movement but it is problematised by the cottage, which effects a blurring of the homo/hetero divide and, in doing so, poses as much of a threat to the stable, differentiated gay identity maintained by the likes of Stonewall as it does to heteronormativity. As Tatchell (1999: 46) has identified, '[a]nything that clouds the distinctions between straight and gay is deemed suspect and dangerous' and not only by heterosexuality.

In the 1980s cottaging, as a form of public sex, became caught up in the snowballing moral panic over HIV/AIDS. Gay was good but gay sex was not. Dean (2009: 20) eloquently describes the period as a time when 'you could feel better about being gay as long as you felt worse about being a slut', and Kramer's epic op-ed *1,112 and Counting* (1983: 22) illustrates how this message became crystallised within Anglo-American gay culture through some of its most vocal spokespeople:

> I am sick of guys who moan that giving up careless sex until this blows over is worse than death. How can they value life so little and cocks and asses so much?

---

4 Indeed the first public GLF demonstration in Britain took place at Highbury Fields (in London, November 27th 1971) and was in response to the arresting of a young man accused of 'indecency' i.e. accused of cruising the area for casual sex. See Walters (1980: 12) for an account of this demonstration.

5 See Griffith (1998) for further discussion of Humphries' work.

> Come with me guys while I visit a few of our friends in intensive care at NYU. Notice the looks in their eyes guys. They'd give up sex forever if you could promise them life.[6]

Because it has always been about casual sex, cottaging was seen as contributing to rising HIV transmission rates, and because it was anonymous and furtive, comprising of 'secret' codes and gestures and a degree of opportunism, cottaging was seen as playing into the hands of those who saw homosexuality as nothing more than a bunch of dirty old men preying on the innocent. The fact that neither of these assumptions was accurate did not matter. Cottaging had long been regarded as deviant by the mainstream and, in a bid to raise funds for HIV research and care, the gay community were quick to distance themselves from any bad old habits that might muddy the waters and jeopardise their progress.[7]

At the time of writing, cottaging remains illegal in Britain, the most recent review of its legal status being in 2003, by way of the Sexual Offences Bill. This legislation, which sought to replace the 1956 Act of the same name, abolished discriminatory laws that previously prevented gay men from engaging in sexual practices in private, while allowing the same practices to be carried out by heterosexuals. As with most forms of legislation that involve sexuality, a storm of controversy surrounded the Bill, not least because it seemed to make provision for both heterosexual and homosexual practices in spaces that were 'outdoors but in an isolated place where one would reasonably expect not to be observed' (Burrell, 2002: 6).

Yet while the Act did change laws regarding sex in semi-public spaces for both heterosexuals and homosexuals, a new offence covering *all* sexual behaviour in public was introduced. Confused? You should be. For while the Bill appears to decriminalise sex in public but unobservable spaces (for example in the cubicle of a public toilet), the then Home Secretary, David Blunkett, contradicted this by stating that the new law regarding all sexual behaviour deemed unacceptable is designed to *include* cottaging. When questioned on the topic of public sex the Home Office review team were quoted as saying that 'the discreet couple should not be penalised' (Clarke, 2002: 6–7). Yet in the same article Blunkett was said to be 'anxious that the law should be drafted so it will still outlaw 'cottaging', or men having sex in public toilets' (ibid). In light of my earlier discussion regarding the promotion of monogamy and the 'good gay couple' it is interesting to note that

---

6 Following on from the success of his award-winning novel, *Faggots*, and celebrated AIDS play, *The Normal Heart*, US writer Larry Kramer co-founded the Gay Men's Health Crisis in 1981. He has been a vocal member within HIV/AIDS campaigning. This quotation is taken from a six-page article published in *New York Native* (March 14–27 1983) in which he takes stock of the burgeoning AIDS crisis and demands action from all quarters. See also Kramer (1990) for a discussion of this article.

7 See Redick (1996) for an insightful discussion of the relationship between HIV/AIDS activism and public sexual cultures.

the 'discreet couple' is invoked by the review team here as that which should be protected – and afforded rights. Single gay or queer men, it seems, are not afforded such sexual freedoms under the new legislation[8].

The Bill has served to close legal loopholes regarding the sex offenders' register, and sex crimes carried out using the Internet have also been detailed in the legislation. By contrast the legal position of gay public sexuality appears to be even more vague than before. It is within this context that an analysis of the cybercottage must be understood.

Queering public (cyber)space: The case of Uni_cock

In one of the earliest discussions of a gay men's digital culture, Shaw (1997: 136–7) draws parallels between the search for a gay IRC channel and the search for a gay bar:

> Ask a gay man for simple directions to the local gay bar. Under the viaduct, over the railroad tracks, down a dirt road, across an alley, in the back door of a non-descript building, or shrouded from the street by smoked glass windows – it is quite difficult to find. Word of mouth will tell you it's there; a patron will show you the way. … Similarly, IRC exists as a word-of-mouth community. Logged on to a local server, there are no signs saying this way to IRC. Once arrived at, given that as many as 5,000 channels exist at a given time, finding the online gay community proves equally difficult.

Shaw's analogy of the 'camouflaged' gay bar does appear to be somewhat outdated, even by the standards of the 1990s, but it should be noted that while many local gay bars and clubs are increasingly visible today, *some* gay spaces continue to be difficult to find and remain intentionally off the beaten track.

For example Legends, a popular mainstay of the Brighton gay scene, is sited prominently on the seafront with a terrace out the front and Pride flags hanging in the windows. It is not difficult to identify Legends as a gay bar, and it is not difficult to find. What is (or rather *was*[9]) difficult to find was the Schwartz bar, a leather and rubber fetish club, also situated on Brighton seafront. Housed in the cellar of Legends, Schwartz was a popular hangout for Brighton's leather and gay BDSM community, but unless you knew exactly where it was and when it opened, you

8 See Johnson (2007: 526) for a detailed review of this legislation, its history and its gender/sexual bias. Johnson also identifies the point I make here, that wider law reform surrounding homosexuality continues to support a dichotomy between well-behaved 'good' gays and dangerous 'bad' queers.

9 Perhaps signalling the narrowing of Brighton's queer culture, the Schwartz bar has since closed and Legends has been extended into the basement space to provide a more 'mainstream' club/bar experience for its patrons.

would never stumble across it accidentally. Shaw's statement, while perhaps too general, is worth considering when bearing in mind both the similarities between digital and physical spaces and the disparities between different expressions of homosexuality in Western contexts. If the metropolitan identity is visible within both mainstream and gay male cultures, the figure of the leather clone, for example, remains in a cultural twilight, partly stereotype and partly mythical but largely unseen. The same can be said for spaces such as Uni_cock. In contrast to the sponsorship deals and full colour advertisements for Gaydar found within the national gay press, invisibility seems to be a key factor in the maintenance of Uni_cock.

Like the leather bar, there is little chance of the average browser (gay or straight) stumbling across Uni_cock's homepage. There is no banner advertising to drive traffic to the site and search engines fail to reveal the address for the web-group. My own discovery of, and journey to, the website is perhaps emblematic of the group's invisibility. Having initially been told about the cybercottage by a friend, it was not until the URL was written down and handed to me that I was able to find the group online. This is not to say that I was invited to join the group in any formal sense. Rather, as Shaw illustrates above, it demonstrates that while the space is always there, knowing how to get to it is quite a different matter: 'word of mouth will tell you it's there; a patron will show you the way'.

This invisibility is important to Uni_cock for a number of reasons. Firstly, the group caters to men based at or nearby a specific geographical location, Midchester University, and the immediacy of the offers of/requests for sex means that only men working at or near the university are able to meet up at the designated times, often within an hour of posting:

> 14:07: Hi, I am about now ready and waiting for cock ... will be around [name of building] toilets for the next hour or so ... let me know guys!
> 14:46: ne1 around now? message back
> 12:32: hi [name], i'm up for one right now and i'm in [campus building]. You about and what are you wearing.

Though occasionally members may post advance notices to the group in order to arrange 'meets' in advance, usually later in the day/evening:

> 11:30: any 1 about later today for a nice long suck off in [university] bogs??? message me if up 4 it....no time wasters please..
> 13:58: I'll be around tonight after 10.... is anyone ever around then???

This immediacy emphasises the temporal and spatial variations between Uni_cock and other, more visible, gay digital spaces. For example, Gaydar offers its members the opportunity to chat with people from all over the world and hopefully find that special someone. By contrast, Uni_cock will get you 'blown' within half an hour and offers its membership little else. The web-group has no interest in forming a national or international membership – it is strictly local and relies on being so.

The second reason behind the group's invisibility is that the types of activities *ostensibly* sought out through Uni_cock often run counter to university regulations and British law.[10] Bearing in mind the fact that the majority of group members are either students of, or are employed, by the university, exposure means not only criminal prosecution but also the loss of jobs, places on degree courses and professional reputations. Security is a recurring theme amongst the membership and invisibility serves to hide the group's activities and avoid monitoring from university officials or the police:

> 11:29: Hi Guys, Library's shut and there is security hanging around [computing department], so I'm heading into [local recreation ground] if anyone's interested ?? Pls ??

Additionally, the fact that the venues suggested by the membership are often near one of the university's computing hubs suggests that many of the members use the university network to send and receive messages. With strict regulations governing the use of the university network, there is a risk of exposure involved when accessing the gay websites via the Midchester computer systems. Due to the 'innocent' hosting company that makes up the first part of the Uni_cock URL, the site appears to avoid detection. While filters are in place to restrict university students from accessing pornographic material, the innocuous address that directs members to the Uni_cock homepage appears to slip past the university server, and group emails sent and received via the university server go undetected. To refer once more to De Certeau's categorisation, the URL for the website reiterates Uni_cock's position as a 'tactical' rather than 'strategic' site of queer identification.

The final reason behind such invisibility relates to both the stigma historically attached to cottaging and the prevailing rhetoric of gay assimilationist politics, which conflates homosexual activities with a specific identity. Uni_cock members who express and act out homoerotic desires, but who 'fail' to maintain a corresponding identity may well feel insecure about using a website that is well advertised and therefore well known. The group is hosted by an international web service accessed the world over by millions of users. The service is not considered to be gay identified (unlike Gaydar) or explicitly linked with sex of any kind. As such, the relationship between sexual acts and sexual identity is reduced dramatically by basing the group within such an 'ordinary' virtual space. In many ways, this is a reflection of the type of sexual activity sought out through Uni_cock. Both the group and the activity are constructed, maintained and performed within spaces

10 As I shall demonstrate later, Uni_cock is as much a fantasy space as it is a site for arranging genuine 'offline' meets and while the original intention behind the site was to facilitate casual sex in and around the university, it would seem that many of the group members do not engage in cottaging beyond their involvement online.

that are not typically thought of as gay and are, therefore, coded as 'normal' i.e. heterosexual. As I shall discuss later, the covert nature of the group and the activity sought is integral to understanding how Uni_cock functions as a queer space.

Having (eventually) found Uni_cock, browsers are invited to join the group (the only means of accessing the messages, pornography and membership database). If they choose to do so, a profile is created, which automatically includes the user's chosen nickname, email address, and details of the his membership to other groups hosted by the web service. Recently the owner of the group – 'Fitboy' – requested that members also include details of location and gender on their profiles. However, this request was made in light of a security risk, brought to the group's attention by the hosting company and following this request, some (but by no means all) members updated their profiles and included information regarding age and gender. Nevertheless there remains a marked difference between the way in which profiles are used on Gaydar and the role they play at Uni_cock. Indeed, profiles in the latter space appear to be almost redundant, leading us to assume that, if the user profiles on gay dating sites act as representations of the self, within the cybercottage, they appear to be little more than a hindrance. Or, to put it another way, if Gaydar is an environment in which subjectivity comes into being through the textuality of the profile, Uni_cock is a space that promotes activities which appear to have less investment in an attendant subjectivity. In this respect Uni_cock represents a departure from the 'activity = identity' equation integral to metropolitan gay male subculture and points instead to the abundance of homosexualities that continue to co-exist alongside the recognisable and politically acceptable metropolitan gay identity today, but which remain hidden, out of view, and marginalised.

Tatchell (1999: 37) reminds us that 'individuals' have not always described themselves 'according to their sexual orientation' and that 'the notion of 'the homosexual' as a distinct category of person has not been around forever.' At Uni_cock gay *sex* – the search for it, the requests for it and the recording of it – is ever-present, but the gay *man* – as an identity – is conspicuous in his absence. This is not to say that gay men do not use the cybercottage – as we shall see later, they clearly do – but rather that throughout all their profiles, posts and comments, members of Uni_cock perform a decoupling of same-sex desire from a specific identification.

Content analysis of the 100 postings posted to the group during the research period confirms this detachment of sex from identity. Almost 20% (n = 19) of messages contained details of the poster's physical attributes, while only 5% mentioned personality traits. Correlatively, of the nine posts that mentioned the poster's choice of sexual partner/s only one mentioned non-physical traits ('like minded people'), the others being concerned with physical attributes and age (for example, 'young guys'; 'fit young lads'; 'Lads 18–27ish'). In contrast to the lack of personality indicators, the postings often focussed on the type of sexual activities sought. Details of specific sex-acts were evident in 40% of postings. The most commonly sought activities were masturbation (22%) and oral sex (18%) ('suck/wank fun'). Despite the 40-year gap, this is in line with Humphries' (1970:

76–7) findings. In a further 30% of the postings general references were made to sexual activity ('bog meet'; 'toilet sex'; 'action'; 'cock fun'). This absence of personality indicators not only suggests that anonymous action is sought by members of Uni_cock (in line with traditional cottaging narratives) but also that action is the *only* function of the mailing list (relationships or friendships are never sought nor suggested).

Don't mention the G-word: Uni_cock and the language of invisibility

Additionally, the language used within postings and profiles demonstrates that the act of self-identification (the nexus of contemporary gay male subjectivity) is carefully avoided at Uni_cock. The term 'gay', which signifies the fastening of desire to identity, is rarely used either in messages or on the group website:

> 11:18: hi all any guys up for being sucked off later today – drop me a line only to happy to suck a nice hot cock off this afternoon.
> 14:59: Hi lads, I will be around for 1/2 hour or so … if anybody wants to join me.
> 15:12: Hi Lads, A quick not[e] to see if anybody fancies some seriuos [sic] action … ONLY young fit lads pls!
> 17:25: Hi … !! You sound good man! I'm looking for some wank fun!!
> 09:48: Hi guys I live in … and am a total wank addict (2–3 a day), … Always looking for some spunky cock fun with lads … I'm very st8 actuing [sic] bi

From 'Lads' to 'guys' to 'boys' and 'men', at Uni_cock the object of desire is undoubtedly male and postings are firmly focussed on the search for sex with men. But rarely is this form of sexual behaviour aligned with a gay or bisexual identity. Having found no use of the word 'gay' in the 100 posts analysed, I widened my search to include all 514 messages posted to the group since its formation. Not one mentioned the word 'gay', though six mentioned gay profile websites (namely Gaydar and Gay.com), and one mentioned a gay porn website. Only one member used the abbreviation 'GWM' to indicate both his sexuality and his race in his posting while three further posts included a reference to bisexuality and one post identified the member as married and therefore heterosexually identified.

The most frequent use of the word 'gay' was within the 'Interests' section of the member profiles. This section is controlled by the hosting service – *not the user* – and automatically lists the names of other groups that each member subscribes to via the service. A total of 12 profiles out of 124 mentioned the word 'gay' within their respective 'Interests' section. These included 'Gay Male UK' (9 entries), 'Gays in the Military' (1 entry), Gay, Lesbian and Bisexual' (2 entries) and 'Gay Men' (2 entries)[11]. The user has no authority over this section and, short of cancelling his membership to other web-groups hosted by the service, he is unable to alter the content of this list.

This information contradicts the rest of the profile content, where there is any. Where users have *chosen* to include details in their profiles, and therefore where they have a choice over language use, there seems to be a concerted effort not to mention the 'G' word or, by extension any kind of sexual identity. For example, the following quotations come from the 'about me' section of various profiles where users are invited to include personal information about themselves:

> Hobbies: Meeting sexy men to have fun with ;-)
> Hobbies: Sports gear, suited business men. lve [sic] sucking and expect nothing back in return – just want a nice cock to suck
> Hobbies: horny sex with hot guys
> Hobbies: Builder, blue collar, tattoed [sic]? Yummy! Forces/999 welcome too... big, strong, horny guys... Bisexual, married, unattached.

Such descriptions stand in stark contrast to the Gaydar profile, and its offline equivalent, the contact advert. One need only look to contemporaneous examples of the latter to see that many men begin their advertisements through an act of self-identification. By no means all of the contact adverts appearing in *Gay Times* (for instance) include a specific reference to sexual identity, but there remain a substantial number of adverts that do explicitly mention self-identify as gay or bisexual:

> 'Chunky gay male, 45 with a GSOH, seeks a slim younger guy for fun times'
> 'Belfast bi-guy 32, stocky-build, seeks discrete genuine non-scene like-minded guy (21–35) for friendship and possible one-to-one'
> 'Manchester, gay male 25, professional, good-looking fun-loving, an everyday sort of guy, seeking similar (21–30). Photo please.'[12]

It is this act of self-identification that is lacking within the self-descriptions found in Uni_cock profiles. Sex and identity are torn asunder and this separation is reflected in the mission statement on the group homepage:

> LADS AT MIDCHESTER UNIVERSITY THAT LIKE OTHER LADS!!! If Your bored, on campus and Up for a bit of Safe Fun!!! Then this is the group for you.

---

11 Whilst there are a total of 14 entries, two profiles include more than one 'gay' interest.

12 Adverts were taken from editions of *Gay Times* randomly sampled between the period December 1994 and January 2004.

Sex here is positioned as a 'fun' pastime, something to engage in when 'bored, on campus'. The term 'lads' acts as a keystone, carrying with it connotations of class, gender, sexuality and age. Within a British context (and we should remember the local specificity of the cybercottge), the term 'Lad' specifically signifies a young working-class heterosexual male[13] and while the 'lads' who populate Uni_cock may not, in reality, embody this identity, the strategic use of the male moniker suggests both the type of class-based masculinity desired by users in this space and, as a consequence, the performance of that same class-based masculinity that users should employ in their postings in order to 'fit in' and 'succeed' on the site. This reliance on the working-class male identifier is in keeping with historical accounts of cottaging, cruising and queer sex in the 19th and early 20th century, where 'the love of working-class men was an important part of the English homosexual subculture' (Whisnant, 2003: 133).

The youthful connotation of 'lads' serves to reiterate the sense of sexual play I alluded to above. As the saying goes, 'boys will be boys', and in a queering of this nostalgic phrase[14], what these boys do is have no strings sex 'for a laugh' as it were. What these lads *don't* do is align this sexual 'fun' with any kind of sexual subjectivity. This 'failure' to identify is reconfirmed through the double use of the word 'lads'. If we accept that the 'lad' is an (eroticised) figure of working-class masculinity, then we must also concede that this figure has historically been positioned (rightly or wrongly) as marginal to an avowedly middle-class homosexual identity (see Weeks, 1991; Chauncey, 1994; Wishnant, 2003; and Kaye, 2004). So while *homosexuality* continues to require an investment (be that psychological, political, economic, social or cultural) in a specific (middle-class) identity, the anonymity of the cottage means that some forms of *homosexual*

13 From the 1960s sitcom *The Likely Lads* (Clement and Le Frenais, 1964), through to the *Lads Army* and *Bad Lads Army* reality TV series (ITV, 2002 and 2004), British popular culture has long identified the figure of the 'lad' with a specifically working-class heterosexual masculinity. Both the term – and its connotations – have been appropriated by gay sub-culture with recent dating/sex/networking websites ladslads.com and fitlads.com employing the 'lad' motif as an erotic signifier of 'working-class masculinity. Fitlads, a popular club night in London in the mid-noughties extended this further, offering a strict dress code of contemporary working-class youth attire and a backroom sex environment dubbed 'Chav Alley'. The 'lad' has also been deployed within gay porn narratives where class difference (most often a difference between the characters on screen and the presumed audience) is positioned as central to the erotic economy of the text. British porn producers, Triga Films, offer several examples of this, with titles such as *British Bad Lads*, *Dads & Lads Night In*, *Soccer Lads*, *Marine Lads* and *Barrack Lads*, being just five of them.

14 A phrase which is highly problematic when considered from the perspective of gender equality and gender politics. 'Boys will be boys' has historically been used as an excuse for young (and old) men to behave in ways that would be unacceptable for women. It is the quintessential 'get out of jail' card for hetero-patriarchal society and provides allowances for inappropriate and otherwise unacceptable behaviour on the basis of the perpetrator's gender.

practice have escaped this 'naming'. To rework Foucault's well-known claim, if the homosexual became a 'species' in the 19th century, then today, the cottage continues to remain a site of 'temporary aberration[s]'.[15]

The political consequences of such anonymity and freedom from identity may sound tantalising for anyone invested in queer responses to gay identity politics. Cruising, cottaging and public sex have previously been celebrated as acts of sexual liberation and sexual rebellion against both heterosexual and homosexual 'norms' (see Rechy, 1978; Walters, 1980; Bell, 1997; Califia, 2000). But as well as acknowledging the fact that such rebellion is not without real risks[16], queer celebrations of the cottage are not unproblematic. Not least because, as the analysis of the Uni_cock membership demonstrates, the cybercottage includes those who identity as heterosexual, and remains an outlet for men who have (or feel that they have) no other means of expressing their queer identities. From this perspective the cottage is perhaps more of a prison than a playground. Unlike their gay counterparts, several heterosexual members of Uni_cock maintain a stable sexual identity – namely heterosexuality – within their profiles. Three members stated that they were married in their profiles, while five listed interests that can be bracketed together as non-homosexual in terms of content.[17] Whether online or offline, the cottage remains a site of furtive opportunism for those who otherwise cannot forego normative sexual identities.

Yet, as illustrated above, it is clear that non-heterosexually-identified men do use the cybercottage. To write Uni_cock off as a virtual cottage for straight men too scared to admit their queerness would be to write off obvious indicators that gay men *do* make up a considerable percentage of the membership and that some members identify themselves as gay in other online spaces. Earlier I discussed the 'Interests' section of member profiles, and to this we must add the fact that several members include hyperlinks to Gaydar and other gay-identified profile sites in posts and listings. It certainly is the case that alongside the 'closeted' members of Uni_cock, gay men also frequent the cybercottage.

This conclusion mirrors the extensive research carried out by Scott *et al.* (1998, np) in which it was found that that an overwhelming majority of cruisers and cottagers were men with a 'confident gay identity', the rest maintaining a

15 I am, of course, referring to *The History of Sexuality Vol. 1*, in which Foucault writes that 'the sodomite was a temporary aberration; the homosexual was now a species', thereby indicating the creation of the homosexual as a person though medical discourse in the 19th century (Foucault, 1976: 43).

16 The international database of cruising grounds located at www.squirt.org, provides an example of this disparity between concept and practice. Alongside details of each cruising ground and cottage, the website includes details of homophobic attacks that have been reported at specific sites visitors to the website.

17 These include Bukkake (which is generally considered to be a heterosexual activity); UK swingers; Older men for younger women; Extra-marital affairs; Straight and Lesbian (for male consumers).

'confident bisexual identity'. These findings run counter to the 'classic stereotype of ill-informed marginalized MESMEN'[18] and demonstrates that men who identify as gay actively use cottaging sites for sex. Sinfield (1998: 7) provides a response to the stereotype that this research undermines when he notes that 'for those who have felt themselves to be interested in same-sex passion but somewhat to one side of the metropolitan identities, gay has been a constraint'. In the face of the 'inevitable reification of gay men', a consequence of the Western homo/hetero binary, Dowsett *et al.* (2008: 124) argue that 'men whose understandings of their sexual interests precede gay liberation and who may not see any connection with the late modern notion of 'gay' struggle to find their place under this new, homogenous identity.

As I demonstrated earlier, the cybercottage remains somewhat asynchronous with the notion of 'gay' as we understand it today. Indeed for some it has always been antithetical to the concept of an 'out' gay male identity. Early gay newspapers and magazines were quick to identify cottaging as being firmly outside of the emerging gay lifestyle and comments such as 'soliciting in public lavatories is perhaps the greatest blight on the homophile community' are typical of the gay print media's response to such activity (Weeks, 1990: 180). Given this disparity between the prevailing definition of 'gay' and perceptions (mistaken though they might be) of those who cottage, the absence of the 'G-word' at Uni_cock is perhaps unsurprising. The question, we must therefore consider is this: if the cybercottage is not gay, might it be (cyber)*queer*?

Cyberspace = queer space? Uni_cock and the philosophy of 'meet, beat and retreat'

In much the same way that 'queer' was seized upon in the early 1990s by those dismayed by what they saw as the inadequate liberal reformism of mainstream gay agendas, the label 'cyberqueer' has been utilised by many commentators writing from a non-heterosexual position, who consciously seek an alternative discursive, cultural and political space to that which is currently on offer. The term has successfully allowed the likes of Macrae (1997), Stone (1998), Plant (1997) and Lin (2006) to conceptualise cyberspace outside of heteronormative parameters. Wakeford (1997: 30) explores what she terms as the 'uneasy amalgam' of these two terms in order to provide a foundation for critical studies of non-heterosexual cyberspaces. Identifying the term queer as a method of approaching 'all non-normative sexualities as identities' (ibid) she discusses the impact of adding the prefix 'cyber' to this sexually dissident position. This includes using the term as a site of resistance, since too often discussions of technology and technological

18 MESMEN stands for 'man who has sex with men', within this context, an individual who uses PSEs but does not identify as gay or bisexual and/or is not out of the closet regarding his sexuality.

practice have marginalised or erased notions of sexuality. Wakeford goes on to identify the specific relationship between space and sexuality that is emphasised within cyberqueer writing before inevitably addressing the issue of identity, and more specifically the formation of identities that are organised through sexuality and manifested in virtual worlds.

Responding to the (over)use of 'cyberqueer' Morton (1999) attacks queer theory, which he regards as a middle-class academic enterprise that ignores questions of cultural privilege and material inequality. For him, cyberspace is the ideal environment for proponents of queer theory and queer identities, operating as it does as a series of infinite environments whereby those with the means to play can immerse themselves in a realm seemingly divorced from reality. In such spaces, the nostalgic re-visioning, which Morton sees as inherent in all virtual realities, (and which is present within the discourse of Uni_cock), illustrates the 'ahistoricity' of both the queer experience (295) and cyberspace (304). This ahistoricity, necessary for the perpetuation of postmodern thought, is the product of a 'post-al'[19] queer theory that privileges desire over need, the signifier over the signified, exchange value over use value and performance over concept (295). In opposition to the Left-wing liberal politics of an Enlightenment-inspired gay and lesbian movement, Morton sees the new queer subject as being one concerned only with the 'localizing of cultural phenomena' (ibid), driven only by desire and not rational thought. As a result of this, highly individual, anti-communitarian queer subjects (and the texts that they produce) can never speak for anyone else:

> The queer subject is deprived of the possibility not only of speaking for (others or even itself) but also of speaking in the name of: it cannot speak in the name of any principle, such as social justice. (301)

This inability to organise, conceptualise or politicise on a collective level is what, according to Morton, the queer subject revels in: an idealism that runs counter to the historical materialism inherent in the terms 'lesbian and gay' (295). Morton sees the queer as the perfect subject for cyberspace, an illusory world that foregrounds the textual and in which performance is pre-eminent (304). According to Morton's logic, cyberspace performs the same trick as queer theory: it seeks to delude the subject into believing that his desire-based existence is a radical political stance against both normative ideology and the 'compromised' stable left, whilst all the time compelling him to conform to the ideology of late capitalism and indulge in commodity fetishism.

Morton's criticism can easily be levelled at Uni_cock, which, it could be argued, is indeed 'a bourgeois designer space in which privileged Western or

19 The term 'post-al' is used by Morton (1999) as a means of identifying the contemporary situation of cultural theory and the wider debates surrounding dissident identities. The 'post-al' queer is postmodern, poststructuralist, post-AIDS, post-identity, post-community, and (perhaps most importantly for Morton) post-political.

Westernized subjects fantasize that instead of being chosen by history, they choose their own histories' (ibid). The majority of Uni_cock's members are operating within the middle-class confines of a British university. The material requirements of a computer terminal, modem and constant Internet connection are afforded by their positions within the university. These positions continue to be obtained via an education system that reflects economic, social and racial inequalities in contemporary Britain. The lack of engagement with gay identity politics can be seen as a new defence for remaining in the closet, while the lack of interest in anything other than sex reveals a startling level of apathy amongst the group. Uni_cock members, like Morton's cybersex participants and Nintendo-bomber pilots, are situated in a virtual space 'supposedly disconnected from actuality, putting them beyond social responsibility' (305). And, like the other ahistorical queer projects that Morton refers to, the cybercottage both predates the emergence of a self-defining gay subject and postdates the sedimentation of gay liberation into a single homogenous identity.

Uni_cock also reflects other traits that Morton identifies as being central to the cyberqueer experience. For example, the group fosters the belief that desire should be privileged over need; Uni_cock is a website for the opportunistic as members wander in and out as solitary figures who seek only one goal: the immediate and selfish satisfaction of sexual desire. Unlike Gaydar, no one chats at Uni_cock. No one gossips or swaps stories. No one talks about what they are studying or what their interests are (save for sexual fetishes). Uni_cock is not a community, it has no interest in nurturing feelings of belonging. Like its physical parallel, where 'men's motivations are unitary and unambiguous' (Flowers *et al.*, 2000: 74), the cybercottage is about sex and nothing else: its ethos is 'meet, beat and retreat'.

Uni_cock also promotes the 'localizing of cultural phenomena' (Morton, 1999: 205), another device regularly employed within queer theory. As mentioned at the start of this chapter, cybercottages are notoriously difficult to find and publicity is rarely undertaken. In opposition to the globalising nature of gay identity politics and gay culture (Gaydar, for instance, has become an international brand, sponsoring events as far away as Australia), the cybercottage, in line with Castell's (1996: 370) theory of 'customized cottages', represents a cluster of local identities and sexualities that resist not only the abuses of heteronormative power but also the rhetoric of gay assimilation[20]. Echoing my earlier discussion of PSEs as 'tactical' sites, Johnson (2007: 533) writes that '[p]ublic lavatories are essentially 'troublesome' landscapes because they comprise highly contested spaces' and that 'the long-standing appropriation of toilets by men for the purpose of sex (as a `safe haven') disrupts and resists continued attempts to de(homo)sexualize these'. Uni_cock defies heteronormative power when it defies university regulations, and the

20 I am reminded of the preface to Duberman's Stonewall (1994: 5), where the author declares that 'Stonewall is the emblematic event in modern lesbian and gay history' and thereby unproblematically levels the playing field of sexual dissidence, creating a benchmark against which all articulations of homosexuality should be measured.

agents of those regulations (officials, security guards, the police) by appropriating, sexualising and queering university space for their own needs.

It also undermines both the liberal politics of assimilation personified by Stonewall and the direct-action campaigns of *OutRage!*. Neither group (twin but divergent inheritors of the legacy of the GLF) can be seen to advocate public expressions of sex. Regardless of the fact that, in some ways, cottaging represents a radical appropriation of gendered and heteronormative spaces, its covert nature, lack of engagement with politics and historical reputation has ensured that while 'kissing strangers in public may be a political act' 'sucking them off [remains] bad public relations' (Hoffman, 1996: 350). Given the 'adolescent' tone of (mis)behaviour and the refusal to 'play by the rules' of a more respectable metropolitan gay subculture, one might be driven to conclude that the men populating cybercottages are choosing to be cyberqueer because they are, in fact, *bored* with being gay.

This may sound strange, but in explaining this claim, I want to point out that most Uni_cock members are in their twenties or younger and this generation of gay men have grown up – and into – their sexuality during a time when gay men (and to a lesser extent, women) have become an increasingly visible part of British society (Bersani, 1995: 11). The last 25 years has seen the cultural climate in Britain simultaneously validate (some forms of) homosexuality and maintain anxieties regarding the 'dangers' gay men pose (dangers that have most regularly coalesced around the spectre of HIV/AIDS). Responding to this first point – that of validation – Simpson (1999: 7) comments that today's gay culture has in turn become 'safe' and 'reassuringly similar, wherever you go'. His retort demonstrates his concern with this homogenising of sexually dissident cultures. While growing up gay today continues to be an uphill struggle, the proliferation of more positive representations[21] of happy gay men inevitably colours the view of the generation entering university today.

In Chapters 2 and 3 I spoke in detail of this rise in both legitimacy and anxiety. Bearing this in mind, I believe it is possible to see how a space that removes gay sex from the twin spheres of anxiety and conformity, and which relocates it in a discourse of uncomplicated satisfaction, might be of distinct appeal for young gay men today. What I am arguing for here is the recognition that, in creating and maintaining cybercottages such as Uni_cock, some men are investing in 'public spheres … where the fantastic can flourish' (Hoffman, ibid: 341) and where sex is no longer governed by a politics of assimilation that purports to liberate gay men, or overshadowed by the 'viral veil' (ibid) cast over gay men by HIV/AIDS.

---

21 For a discussion of gay representation in the mainstream Anglo-American media, see Gross, 2002 and Pullen 2004.

Fear, fantasy and the great dark man: Performing masculinity in the cybercottage

This scenario can be better understood through a consideration of digital spaces as sites of imaginary play, and the political potential of ludic existences on the Web have been explored by several scholars (Bassett, 1995; Weinstein and Weinstein, 2000; and Armstrong, 2004 to name just three). While Uni_cock functions as a contact point for men who wish to meet offline, it simultaneously operates as a site of queer *fantasy* in which members are players in an unfolding, disjointed narrative of 'deviant' sex. By refusing to identify as gay within the cybercottage group members (many of whom, we must remember, can and do identify as gay in other spheres of their lives) engage in a *consensual performance* of queer desire. By this I mean that the cybercottage is not 'just' a place to arrange 'real' assignations, but also operates as a virtual space in which narratives of desire can be formed within an overarching framework of a particular sexual fantasy. This fantasy pervades gay and queer cultures and is present in much of the pornography, art, literature and film produced by sexually dissident subjects and communities (Bersani, 1995). It is the fantasy of 'capturing' heterosexual masculinity, of a coupling with the bearer of power, of what Quentin Crisp (1985: 62) named 'the myth of the great dark man'. This fantasy, which Crisp describes as haunting 'the dreams of pathological homosexuals' (ibid) centres on (what he at least) sees as the queer ideal; that of going with a *real* man and not another homosexual.

Of course, as Crisp points out, such an ideal is always illusory:

> [The] problem that confronts homosexuals is that they set out to win the love of a 'real' man. If they succeed, they fail. A man who 'goes with' other men is not what they would call a real man. (ibid)

Despite the inevitable collapse of this fantasy at the point at which it is realised, the queering of heterosexual masculinity remains a powerful motif within gay and queer sub-cultures. Bersani (ibid: 63) identifies this fantasy when he writes that:

> In his desires, the gay man always runs the risk of identifying with culturally dominant images of misogynist maleness. For the sexual drives of gay men do, after all, extend beyond the rather narrow circle of other politically correct gay men.

Registering this desire for heterosexual masculinity allows us to further understand Uni_cock's 'failure' (or perhaps refusal) to be gay. Not only does the cybercottage facilitate sexual encounters that fall outside of the metropolitan model, it provides a space in which members can invest in this fantasy of 'the great dark man'. In doing so, moreover, they are simultaneously investing in older forms of homosexuality and traditional locales of homosexual activity. Knowingly or not, a nostalgia for the cottage emerges: at Uni_cock the subject revisits old haunts through new technologies. Furthermore, this nostalgia operates as a resistance to the sanitising effects of societal acceptance. In her discussion of sex and city spaces, Califia (2000: 217) writes that:

> Most people won't admit that the legitimized pleasures available outside the sex-zone … may be less prized or enjoyable than the illicit delights consumers hope to obtain when they enter this black market.

The reason for this denial lies in the unspoken belief that 'all members of society are supposed to possess automatically the legitimate pleasures, which are in turn supposed to be sufficient to keep any "decent, sane" person happy' (ibid). This is particularly interesting when we consider the case of gay men. Prior to the decriminalisation of homosexuality in 1967, the homosexual was not considered to be a member of society; he had no rights and he was not a citizen. As such, there were *no* 'legitimate pleasures' and there were no legitimate spaces in which such pleasures could be *openly* validated. The gay man's only option was to seek pleasure within the sex-zones of the city. These zones included the parks and lay-bys as identified by Califia, but also the homosocial spaces of locker rooms, toilets, prisons and dormitories. Homosexual sex *was* public sex[22].

The advent of gay liberation means that legitimate pleasures and legitimate spaces have since been afforded to (some) gay men. Califia (ibid: 219) is quick to point out that gay men are the only sexual minority to have established legitimate enclaves within urban spaces. These 'ghettos' (San Francisco's Castro district, New York's Chelsea and Greenwich Village, London's Soho and Vauxhall, areas and Sydney's Oxford Street) are accepted by the city at a social, cultural and institutional level. Cottaging, existing as it does both outside of the ghetto and before the formation of such enclaves, has a history of tacit acceptance and recognition amongst queers living in homophobic contexts. As Leap (1996: 75) notes:

> Gay high school and college students list graffiti-based comments [in public toilets] about gay meeting places and other issues among the sources of information orienting them to gay culture during the earliest phases … of their coming-out process.

Metropolitan gay subculture increasingly insists that legitimate pleasures in legitimate spaces should be enough to satisfy the gay man. This belief is widely supported, as Brown (2001: 50) acknowledges when he remarks that '[t]he law and societal norms demand that the proper place for expressions of (homo)sexual

22 It could be argued that prior to the decriminalisation of homosexuality, there were private member's clubs and private relationships that were homosexual. However, it could also be argued that such spaces and relationships were not legitimate, nor were they stable or openly identified as homosexual.

desire is in 'private'. While cottaging has ostensibly been rejected by gay culture in an effort to rid itself of stereotypes and criticisms, its spaces, replete with its (homo)sexualised graffiti, continue to serve as both signifiers of previous queer activity and a promise of yet more to come. The cottage has fallen even further out of favour, a sacrifice made in the drive towards assimilation but paradoxically, this has only served to increase its erotic appeal, at least for some.

Califia (ibid: 225) identifies this paradox, writing that 'one strategy for dealing with oppression is to eroticize certain signs which symbolize it and transform them into signs imbued with meaning supplied by the minority'. The public toilet is one such symbol of oppression and contained within its walls is a history of queer desire, covert negotiation, fear and entrapment. The cracked tiles and filthy porcelain, scuffed concrete and scribbled walls all operate as signifiers of pre-liberation homosexuality, a time of agent provocateurs and watch queens, of silent fumblings in lunch hours and guilty pleasures stolen on the way to and from work.

It is via this paradox, and the cultural milieu that young gay men find themselves in today that the fantastical element of the cybercottage can perhaps be best understood. In the cybercottage members (at least those who elsewhere identify as gay or participate in gay subculture) can imagine that the man they are 'meeting' is the great dark man of their own sexual fantasies, fantasies that extend beyond the confines of the gay village and which continue to resonate deeply with a subculture that has an 'unnatural' interest in its oppressors.

Queer carnality?

Bearing all this in mind, can Uni_cock – a site which appears to operate in direct opposition to Gaydar – be understood as a site of similar cybercarnal experience? The members of Uni_cock have no truck with gay identity, with visibility or with subjectivity. They do everything they possibly can to eschew it. Only one posting out of the sample analysed in the case study alluded to the term 'gay', and nothing at Uni_cock would seem to promote sexual identity in the way that Gaydar does. Faced with these facts can Uni_cock also be cybercarnal?

In response to this I would argue that if Gaydar imagines itself as a community first and foremost, Uni_cock positions itself as a conduit for the satisfaction of carnal desires. In doing so the emphasis on physical descriptions means that while the construction of identity is consciously avoided within the cybercottage, members *do* construct virtual bodies at Uni_cock. These bodies are rendered visible via the postings members make to the group. For example:

> im a indian teen lad. im 5ft8, slim, dark hair and eyes, smoth [sic] chest, hairy legs, 6" cut cock.
>
> It's [Name deleted] here, 23, 6' tall, slim and fit and a nice juicy 8½ inches of cock!

> [N]eed to spunk in someone's mouth nice cock, hairy chest, toned body.

This focus on physical descriptors within the cybercottage (as opposed to personality traits) echoes earlier studies of cruising locales where 'sexual partners are represented purely in terms of sexual anatomy (i.e. cock, hole)' and where this 'somatic focus structures sexual activity' (Flowers *et al.*, 2000: 74). The focus on representing bodies – or rather specific parts of bodies – not only suggests that anonymous action is sought by members of Uni_cock (in line with traditional cottaging narratives) but also that sexual action is the *only* function of the mailing list (relationships or friendships are never sought nor suggested). Uni_cock is a space where the male body is constructed solely as a carnal body – a body of desire – a body to consume and be consumed.

I will briefly return to Kappeler's work here in order to explore the cybercarnal dimension of the cybercottage in more detail. Kappeler's (1986) discussion of pornographic representation (which I outlined in Chapter 3) begins with an analysis of a newspaper article detailing the prosecution of white South African farmer, van Rooyen, for the torture and murder of Thomas Kasire, a black worker in his employment. During van Rooyen's trial, photographs taken during the torture were produced as evidence. Reporting on the trial, *The Guardian* commented that without the photographic evidence Kasire's murderer would not have been convicted. Kappeler complicates the newspaper's understanding of the photographic evidence, claiming that the images are in fact integral to and cannot be separated from the physical torture:

> The coincidence of this kind of violence and its representation is no accident. It is no curiosity in the domain of representation. The pictures are not documentary evidence, snapped by a journalist or observer by chance in the right place at the right time. The pictures are compositions, deliberate representations, conforming to a genre. (ibid: 6)

Representation of the crime moves beyond documentation and becomes a part of that which it purports to (re)present – the murder of Thomas Kasire. The victim was caught by his torturers and he was similarly captured by the camera: 'Thomas Kasire lives on in his representation, though Thomas Kasire is dead' (ibid: 10). For Kappeler, there is no difference between the torture photos of Kasire and pornographic images. Problematising the argument that pornographic *fiction* is inherently different from the photographing of *real* murder, she concludes that as Kasire lives on in the photographs, 'the fiction [of the image, of pornography] continues its existence in reality' (ibid). Thus the connection between pornographic representation and the torture photos – indeed with all representation – is established. The object of representation is turned into a fiction, only existing within the representation, and is made real by that representation.

The political implications of such a statement do not need spelling out. Indeed, such a political perspective can be extended far beyond the parameters of both photography and pornography. While the content and consent of the postings at Uni_cock are far removed from the torture photos of Kappeler's discussion, the structure of representation remains the same. As illustrated above, representations of the body at Uni_cock are always pornographic. This mode of representation is not a new phenomenon but rather draws on what we might call 'traditional' cottaging narratives, namely the sexual graffiti commonly found in public toilets used for sex between men. Graffiti has historically been integral to cottaging and is both a signifier that sexual acts have occurred/are likely to occur in this space and a part of that sexual act. In this respect, and if we follow Kappeler's fundamental line of argument, the graffiti-style postings of Uni_cock can be understood as operating in the same way as the camera – as both recorder of information *and* complicit in the formation of that information.

Writing on the toilet wall of the cottage (whether that cottage is digitally or physically manifested) is not just documentation, nor is it simply advertising (though doubtless it is an advertisement), it is a part of the cottaging experience; it cannot be separated from the act that it precipitates or that it memorialises. Hence the postings and images of Uni_cock allow users to construct and engage in erotic encounters without physical contact; messages can be strung together to form unique sexual narratives, which can then be juxtaposed with (often professional) pornographic images and video clips (uploaded by members) to create visual representations of the text on the screen. Users do not have to meet in the semi-public space of the cottage to encounter one another's bodies. Representation ensures that the 'fictional' body of the other is always available, always willing, always sexually responsive. Indeed one could argue that the 'real' body of the cybercottager is dead, it no longer exists beyond the representation; as his body is discursively produced and inscribed upon the 'walls' of Uni_cock, his real body seems redundant, irrelevant, meaningless. Echoing Kasire, the body created by the virtual cottage is subject to two processes of consumption; the physical meet in which the (real) subject is consumed, and the fantasy space in which the virtual body is consumed.

If pornographic representation, one element of the cybercarnal can be found at Uni_cock, what of the techniques of surveillance that remain integral to cybercarnality? As the pornographic body is discursively produced at Uni_cock, so such techniques manifest themselves firstly in terms of the postings – through the editing of specific information in postings and images – and secondly through the group's relationship with its offline environment – the public and semi-public spaces of Midchester university. While the former can be aligned with the processes of self-identification and self-surveillance previously discussed within the context of Gaydar, the latter warrants further explanation.

'Watching' Uni_cock: Practices of surveillance in the cybercottage

> For most of us part of the attraction of cottaging is the danger of being caught which gets the adrenalin pumping and heightens the enjoyment of the sex act itself – and do not forget that many sex acts are illegal. (Gay Cottaging GB, online)

By its very nature, cottaging has a specific relationship with structures of surveillance. As the quotation above demonstrates, the fear of surveillance is part of its attraction, adding to the thrill of the erotic encounter. Additionally, the pleasures of watching (for) others in PSEs, surveying them, measuring them up to detect their potential interest and willingness, is part and parcel of public sexual cultures (Humphries, 1970; Flowers *et al.*, 2000). The postings to Uni_cock make regular reference to external surveillance, most often in the form of cleaners and security guards, and there is little doubt that the possibility of getting caught out greatly increases the appeal of having sex in a public convenience for members of the web-group. Other cottaging websites are a testimony to the thrill of the cat and mouse chase that exists between the individual and State.[23] Within the cybercottage, space is continually reconfigured as external forces either close down locales or turn them into 'dead' sites through regular patrolling and exemplary prosecutions.

From this perspective, the cybercarnal operates as a *defence* against such surveillance techniques. Communicating through their discursively produced bodies, men are negotiating new sites of erotic display and activity via digitally produced environments. Reading the discussions of over-zealous cleaning attendants patrolling their 'patch' and local police forces organising operations to identify men using cruising grounds, one begins to see why cottaging has previously been articulated as politically subversive. Rechy (1978: 28–32) reconfigures public sexual culture as a uniting force, bringing disparate men together momentarily to forge intense and politically powerful connections:

> The promiscuous homosexual is a sexual revolutionary … To the sexhunt he brings a sense of choreography, ritual and mystery – sex-cruising with an electrified instinct that sends and receives messages of orgy at any moment, any place. … Knowing that each second his freedom may be ripped away arbitrarily, he lives fully at the brink. Promiscuity is his righteous form of revolution.

Earlier, I warned against celebrating Uni_cock, and by extension all cottaging, as a consciously political activity. Given the lack of political discussion on these websites, to make such a claim runs the risk of seeing something that is

23 'Cocktales' the stories written by members of Squirt.org, the international cruising website, regularly include details regarding surveillance and escaping surveillance as a distinct erotic motif in their narratives.

simply not there. Having a brief entanglement in the library toilets may be fun, erotic, satisfying, daring and kinky, but in itself it isn't political. However, re-contextualising cottaging within a discussion of cybercarnality does provide us with an opportunity to step beyond the specific sex acts engaged in and interact with the wider relationship between gay men and surveillance.

While the State has repeatedly attempted to identify and control homosexual males, (see Chapter 3 for discussion) gay men themselves have been preoccupied with surveillance techniques as they try to identify each other – primarily for sexual contact. It is no surprise that Britain's most popular gay male space is named after a form of queer surveillance[24]. Men have been watching each other for as long as they have desired each other. Within cyberspace, cruising is reconfigured as websites become shop windows and profiles become advertisements, invitations and promises. And while the membership of Uni_cock eschews profiles, much of their time is spent watching one another. It is interesting to note that postings discuss individuals who have been spotted both in PSEs and in 'regular' spaces:

> there is a cute guy i keep making eye contact with in the library but all he does is smile and look a away shyly tall-ish, dark kinda short hair, post grad i think, mostly on level 4, cute ears if thats you, get back :o)

Similarly stories that appear on the international cruising website, Squirt.org, often focus on the process of identification that the author goes through prior to engaging in the sex act:

> As I drove into the park, I sensed something strange. First, there were plenty of parked cars, second, I didn't recognize most of the cars, and third there were a number of men standing outside their vehicles … I sat on the hood of my car sucking on a cigarette and checking out the guys. Let's see, six cars, and three men standing in darkness. By chance a car circled the lot and I caught a glimpse of a couple of guys in the headlights. (Squirt, online)

Cottaging may not be an activity that has developed or proliferated as a direct result of digital ICTs (as I will argue is the case for barebacking subcultures in the following chapter), but the opportunities afforded by such spaces for the articulation of cottaging stories, fantasies and offers of sex allow us to identify both the pleasure and fear of surveillance integral to public sex acts. As such Uni_cock and other cottaging websites are heavily invested in a discourse of cybercarnality. The cybercarnal articulates both the pleasure of the cottaging experience – the surveillance of the erotic other - and a means of identifying and advertising the self, via a fragmentation and erotic coding of the virtually constructed body.

Cybercarnality, within this context is an acknowledgement of the *lack* of division between the offline and the online. The virtual bodies described at Uni_

24 The term 'Gaydar' refers to a gay man's supposed ability to spot other gay men.

cock may well be fictions – that is, they may not be the same as the body of the user who constructs and speaks through them – but the virtual body is still subject to the systems of classification, hierarchies of taste, and discourses of legitimacy that operate offline. And as has been shown above, representation problematises the very notion of reality, as fiction 'continues its existence in reality' (Kappeler, 1986: 10). Furthermore, cybercarnality also allows us to recognise how online space is informing our understanding of our own corporeal bodies.

Conclusion: Loitering with intent?

To repeat myself, let us not fall into the trap of believing that the members of Uni_cock – gay or straight – are having sex in the university toilets in order to make a political statement. The fantasy of working-class heterosexual masculinity that pervades the cybercottage is politically problematic to say the least. It runs counter to gay identity politics, which in seeking recognition, citizenship and acceptance on its own terms, draws on the anti-oppressive, anti-patriarchal discourses of feminism. As Bersani (1995: 63) identifies, such fantasising reveals 'a more or less secret sympathy with heterosexual male misogyny' and this sympathy 'carries with it the narcissistically gratifying reward of confirming our membership in (and not simply our erotic appetite for) the privileged male society' (ibid: 64). Cottaging is not an example of conscious political action, but it is an illustration of how the very concept of a public sexual culture not only flouts legal and societal rules but also reveals to us the fact that the everyday spaces of our lives are shaped by a heterosexist ideology, while simultaneously undermining that ideology. Baker (1985: 32), a self-confessed cottager, argues that:

> Cottaging isn't a social evil; it isn't a political gesture; it isn't oppressive; it isn't liberating. Cottaging is simply one way of seeking a sexual adventure.

Be this as it may, such sexual adventure does not go unjudged within contemporary mainstream culture. As such, we might heed Campbell's (2004: 190) assertion that 'when one's pleasures are coded (or stigmatised) as non-normative, then engaging in those pleasures becomes, in itself a political act'. Young gay men are on the receiving end of a sexual identity increasingly devoid of sexuality; pornography has become an educational tool and sex has been invaded by medical discourse.[25] The global dominance of a metropolitan gay male identity, seen in the growth of the gay media industry and the huge increase in the representation of that identity within the mainstream media leaves little or no space for the articulation of other less politically correct(able) homosexualities.

It is within this cultural context that web-groups like Uni_cock should be understood. Uni_cock is perhaps most coherent when interpreted as a space in

25 These two points shall be taken up in Chapter 6.

which a specific type of homosexual activity can be articulated. In doing so the queer potential of new media communication systems is realised. The decentralised system of information allows the cyberqueer to play along the faultlines that separate the hetero from the homo and fantasy from reality. In doing so it not only problematises the essentialist idea of difference but also reveals the political potential the Internet holds for dissident sexualities. This inevitably subverts the codes and conventions that govern the space we move through offline too. If on Gaydar gay subjectivity is created, manipulated, and re-orientated back out towards the user, at Uni_cock, the potential for queering the spaces of our offline lives is realised via our online involvements.

Chapter 6
Bareback Sex Online: Knowledge, Desire and the Gay Male Body

Taking stock almost twenty years after the first HIV diagnosis in Britain, Watney (2000) explored the impact HIV/AIDS has had on British gay culture and pointed to the integral role that gay print media played in raising awareness of the virus amongst gay men during the 1980s and 1990s:

> BOYZ is … the most impressive gay publication in relation to safer sex. Indeed, it is perhaps the only gay paper in Britain which evidently has a clear and consistent policy on HIV prevention issues, presenting HIV as a very important question which is constantly addressed, but as a reminder rather than with a sledge-hammer, always around but never obtrusively. (Watney, 2000: 77)

Having followed the epidemic since its inception, Watney was able to draw on a rich history of HIV/AIDS interventions, awareness campaigns, developments and battles in order to assess how far we had come and how much more work needed to be done in the fight against the virus. It was in *Imagine Hope* that he suggested changes might be occurring in the relationship between gay men and HIV:

> In the same way as material circumstances in which gay identity is acquired, developed and lived over the course of a lifetime change, so gay identity may alter and vary in relation to perceptions of risk from HIV. This is an especially important question in countries such as Britain, where the epidemic is most prevalent among gay men, while being disproportionately small by international standards. (Watney, 2000: 66–67)

Watney did not have to wait long to see his prophecy come true. In the same year that *Imagine Hope* was published both the mainstream and the gay press in Britain reported on a new sexual practice occurring within the gay community. Responding to an interview published by the *Pink Paper* in March 2000, in which broadcaster Nigel Wrench 'confessed' to having had anonymous unprotected sex since testing positive for HIV, tabloids and broadsheets alike ran exposés on 'the barebacking phenomenon'. These stories reported that some gay men seemed to be disregarding safe sex advice and actively seeking out unprotected sex (and even HIV infection). Ever the moral guardian of the British public, *The Mail on Sunday*

(19th March 2000: 15) defied copyright laws and reprinted Wrench's interview, as a warning to middle England that once more, the queers were revolting:

> [W]e feel his [Wrench's] views should be made public because they illustrate the debate which could result in radical and controversial changes in the laws that govern public behaviour in this country.

Unsurprisingly, the story was hijacked by those seeking to strengthen the case against proposed changes to the public sex laws.[1] Overlooking the fact that barebacking and public sex have relatively little in common, both *The Mail on Sunday* and *The Guardian* linked this change in sexual behaviour to the (re)emergence of a public (homo)sexual culture in Britain (see Wells, 2000: 2).

While the mainstream press seized the opportunity to once more pathologise homosexuality as deviant, the gay press focussed on putting as much distance as possible between the 'reckless' barebacker and the rest of the gay community. Mathew Hudson, editor of the popular gay magazine, *Boyz*, condemned Wrench and his ilk for risking the lives (not to mention the political endeavours, AIDS funding and mainstream acceptance) of 'normal' gay men. In an editorial reminiscent of the Larry Kramer speech quoted in Chapter 5, he asked, 'I thought if you cared about someone, you'd want to do your best to protect them, not put their lives at risk – or your own' (Hudson, quoted in Wells, ibid).

This response illustrates several interesting points about the political state of the gay press in contemporary Britain[2]. Chief among these is its unwillingness (perhaps even its inability) to acknowledge the fact that barebacking confirms Watney's assertion that, for some, gay identity is indeed altering and varying 'in relation to perceptions of risk from HIV'. Talking about choosing unprotected sex is fraught with difficulties in contemporary gay subculture. Admitting to engaging in such practices has for a long time been virtually taboo. This chapter explores how, within the context of this discursive 'absence', those who choose to engage in this form of 'unprotected anal intercourse' have exploited the Web in order to create discursive spaces that allow for the articulation of previously unmentionable desires, fantasies, questions, critiques and fetishes.

I employ a textual analysis of two websites that cater to the emerging bareback subculture in order to investigate how sexual identities are formed and negotiated in these spaces, how relevant information is disseminated within the subculture, and how such spaces serve to validate sexual practices that are elsewhere condemned as suicidal or murderous. I also discuss how new safer sex strategies outside of the condom code are being formulated by those who choose to bareback. Finally,

---

1 See Chapter 5 for a more detailed discussion of these changes.

2 Not least the fact that even within the context of barebacking, the metropolitan rhetoric of monogamy is upheld and maintained ('caring for someone'). This ties in with the discussion of the changing political ideology of the gay press set out in Chapter 2, and discussions of non-metropolitan practices in Chapter 5.

I explore how the arguments made for sexual choice are held in tension with the economic means by which such discursive spaces – and therefore such arguments – are forged.

Barebacking is a controversial issue, of that there is little doubt. Adam (2005: 334) states that '"barebacking" in recent years has often come to be treated in the gay and mainstream press as something of a scandal, and has sent researchers into the field in search of new impairments and pathologies to explain this ostensibly irrational behaviour'. It is not my intention here to pathologise, judge or condemn those who practice or promote barebacking, but neither do I wish to celebrate or elevate barebacking to the status of a queer sexual practice par excellence. In attempting to avoid being judgemental I am in a small minority, since, as implied by Adam, much of the literature on barebacking has opted to demonise it. Those who condemn barebacking as dangerous regularly identify the risk not only to the individual but also to gay culture and its struggle for acceptance. Key figures in this camp have included Signorile (1997), Rotello (1997) and Kramer (2004). Fall identified the negative link between gay politics and barebacking when he asked:

> Why should we expect lesbians, who receive comparatively scant support from gay men, to continue to make the tremendous efforts many of them have made around HIV if it appears that we are actively courting the virus? (Fall, date unknown, online)

Framing bareback sex as a danger to the fragile relationship between lesbian and gay men illustrates the political hinterland of many bareback critics who continue to identify with the collectivist mentality of gay civil rights work. Fall's criticism is that barebacking jeopardises political alliances and as such is anti-communitarian: barebacking should be sacrificed for the greater (political) good.

Opposing such commentators and scholars are self-styled sex radicals such as Gendin (1997), Valenzuela (1999) and O'Hara (1998) who have celebrated bareback sex as an act of queer transgression. To them, bareback sex is a political act that takes power back from the 'condom Nazis' of gay men's health agencies, who they feel are guilty of sanitising gay male sexuality to the point of extinction. Beswick (2000, online) quotes Shelbi, an advocate of barebacking to demonstrate the political dimension of this sexual practice:

> It's sad that at this point in history, we're actually perceiving sperm as a bad and evil thing. We're very much in a 'middle-ages' in that respect. … The topic of exchanging fluids has become so negatively impacted, that we've allowed the radical 'condom Nazis' to rule our private lives, snooping in on our sex-club interactions and attempting to pass laws that would make sex without condoms illegal.

Doubtless both sides of the bareback debate have valid points to argue, and the political implications of barebacking should not be overlooked. However, the politics of barebacking have come to overshadow the realities of bareback sex, the discourses spoken by barebackers and the spaces of communication that they have created. This oversight must be addressed and by investigating the online spaces constructed and inhabited by those who choose to bareback I hope to demonstrate not only the important role that digital communication plays in a discussion of bareback sex, but also how an analysis of such spaces can help us to understand how gay men are grappling with HIV/AIDS in the 21st century.

The barebacking 'problem': Gay culture's response to unprotected sex

While the Wrench story in 2000 caused a flurry of moralising copy, critical editorials and angry letters, for the most part the discussion of barebacking in the British gay press in the intervening years has been relatively quiet. On the health awareness front, a few organisations in Britain (including Gay Men Fighting AIDS (GMFA) and the George House Trust (GHT)) have acknowledged the need to allocate resources to barebacking, and facilitate an open and honest debate about choice within the context of safer sex campaigns. But while the gay press served as a prime site for safer sex information during the 1980s and 1990s, today it struggles to provide a stable and lasting forum for the rational discussion of barebacking, even within the context of developing safer sex strategies in response to barebacking. There has for a long time been an awareness that condom use may change depending on context and as early as 2001 advertising was appearing in the British gay press that acknowledged this reality. Often these adverts alluded to such 'failures' to use a condom as occurring within the context of monogamous relationships.[3] Interestingly, the term 'barebacking' was not used. GMFA has perhaps been the most pro-active in acknowledging the fact that 'most gay men with HIV fuck without a condom at some point' (*QX International* – GMFA advert, Nov. 2001). The same organisation faced severe criticism when they addressed the issue of barebacking directly in a 2004 advertisement. Published in *Boyz*, *The Pink Paper* and *QX Magazine* this moderate advert[4] tested the limits of British gay male subculture and found them impervious. Complaints were lodged with the Advertising Standards Authority (ASA) against the advert for promoting unsafe sex and although the ASA rejected the complaints, the outrage that some felt at barebacking being addressed directly was telling. This response is also deeply ironic considering that the advert, planned and written by the GMFA's Positive

3 See, for example, the advertisement for Westminster Primary Care Group (and funded by GSK HIV care), that appeared in *QX International* (Feb. 2002, issue 368: np), which depicted a gay couple within the context of an advert about unprotected sex, but which did not mention 'bareback' sex.

4 Unlike much of the recent HIV/AIDS advertising that employs pornographic motifs, the GMFA advert consisted of a cartoon image of two men wearing the front and rear end of a pantomime horse.

campaign group, was designed to challenge the media's response to people who choose to bareback:

> The group decided to tackle the issue after recognising that the debate in gay, positive and mainstream media was often reactionary and ill-informed. (MetroM8 f*ctsheet, 2000, online)

It is understandable, though nevertheless problematic, that the gay press has been reluctant to pursue a line of open discussion with the barebacking community. As the London Gay Men's HIV Prevention Partnership commented:

> Barebacking, until recently, has been something of taboo subject, of course as a result of the cast-iron 'wear a condom every time' safer-sex message – the orthodoxy most gay men have lived with during the 80s and 90s. (MetroM8 f*ctsheet, 2000, online)

As discussed in Chapter 2, the gay press spent a large part of the 1980s and 1990s raising awareness about HIV/AIDS and countering claims from the religious Right that the virus was God's answer to homosexuality and that gay men were the perpetrators and not the victims of the disease. Many have commented that HIV/AIDS has been the single most powerful force in terms of uniting les/bi/gay people (Weeks, 1990; Schwartzberg, 1996; Rofes, 1998) and while the mainstream press in Britain oscillated between stories that suggested AIDS was a myth and reports that 'the gays' were going to infect 'us' all, the gay press became the mouthpiece for AIDS activism. Watney personified this activist element within the gay press and as 'AIDS-watchdog' he wrote a regular column in *Gay News/Times* for almost fifteen years, reporting on new drug regimes, modes of transmission and services.

Perhaps most importantly though, and a long time before the 'tombstone and lilies' images of the British government advertising campaign, the gay press was instrumental in publicising what has since become understood as the 'condom code' – the use of condoms during penetrative anal sex. It was through the combined efforts of the gay press and community grassroots awareness organisations that the condom code became normalised behaviour within the gay community. As discussed in Chapter 2, it was not the government but the gay press that the gay community turned to for information and instruction:

> gay men are likely to delegate responsibility for reliable information and policy on HIV/AIDS issues to community-based institutions which are understood, rightly or wrongly, to be part of the wider gay community. Hence the significance of the role of the gay press, for example, or gay television shows. (Watney, 2000: 69)

The gay press remains integral not only to the dissemination of safe sex information but also to the continual re-negotiation of acceptable and unacceptable sexual practices within gay male culture. Russell (2005: 156) provides a psychodynamic reading of this governance role, concluding that the (re)organisation of gay sexuality means that 'gay men can only identify as the good gay citizen of HIV prevention to the degree that they can alienate themselves from the transgressive jouissance of unprotected sex which is its necessary accompaniment'. Not only has the press, together with HIV/AIDS organisations, been responsible for maintaining the boundaries of gay sexuality, the gay community and gay identity, it has also been responsible for marginalising dissent and criticism of condom use, in order to promote the idea that the British gay community is one that is '100% safe – 100% of the time' (see Watney, 1996 and Dean, 2009).

Adam (2005: 334) notes that at the height of the HIV/AIDS crisis, homosexuality was 'refashioned into a model for good citizenship' and became 'tamed, responsible, and governed by the safe sex ethic'. This refashioning and subsequent representation of the gay community as one united by, and conforming to, the condom code inevitably marginalised some members of the gay community. It also altered people's perception of transmission. Sero-converting after the introduction of the condom code increasingly became understood as the result of tragic accidents ('the condom split'), heat of the moment relapses ('he was so hot, I couldn't resist') or failures in education ('I never knew I could get it the first time'). When, during the 1990s, gay men were still testing positive – despite ten years of HIV/AIDS prevention work – drugs and alcohol (as opposed to choice) were brought into the discussion as reasons for rising rates. This ultimately led to the commercial gay scene being slammed by Signorile (1997) for creating contexts that increased the risk of viral transmission.

It was in this same article, that Signorile labelled powerful new antiretroviral drugs 'protease dis-inhibitors' suggesting that the successes of such drugs were inadvertently responsible for many men abandoning the condom code and having unsafe sex.[5] In Britain, drug and alcohol awareness campaigns were launched by HIV agencies in an effort to stem the rising number of new transmissions[6]. Believing these transmissions to be 'accidental' i.e. unplanned breaches of protection, organisations such as Positively Healthy linked transmission rates to drug and alcohol use (Figure 6.1). For a percentage of the sero-converting population, such a belief was indeed correct and research identifying the link between recreational drug use and unsafe sex has been well documented (see Elford, 2006).

5 Elford (2006) notes that while the success highly active antiretroviral therapies ('HAART') may have been a contributing factor in the large increases in high-risk sexual behaviour among gay men since 1996, this trend has now levelled off. Furthermore, this levelling may in part be due to the affordances the Internet provides HIV positive (and negative men) for sero-sorting.

6 The work of the Terrence Higgins Trust since around this time is perhaps the most notable example of this in the UK context.

Figure 6.1 A 2004 advert produced by the lifeormeth.com drugs awareness resource for gay men. The organisation has worked with Positively Healthy to try and reduce drug-induced lapses in safer sex behaviour[7]

7 I would like to thank the owners of lifeormeth.com for their permission to use this image here.

Stories of drug-induced relapses, of condoms splitting and of plain old-fashioned ignorance, however, have only ever made up a percentage of new HIV diagnoses. What many health professionals have struggled to comprehend (or rather, what the framework of HIV prevention work has been unable to accommodate) is the fact that there has always been a percentage of gay men who, having received the advice, the opinions and the free condoms on offer, have actively *chosen* to have unprotected intercourse. These men have weighed up the risks against the benefits and made a conscious decision not to use condoms.

Defining barebacking

As intentional unprotected sex between men became more widely recognised, the definitions of such acts within the field of HIV care and prevention struggled to account for the conscious decision-making processes involved in bareback scenarios. The 5th annual CHAPS conference in 2002 grappled with the subject of barebacking with Mark Maguire, head of HIV health promotion at Camden and Islington Health Authority defining bareback sex as, 'non-negotiated unprotected sex where one of the partners is HIV positive and does not know, or care, about the status of his partner' (quoted in Carter 2002, online). This definition was the first of its kind within such a context[8] and it was the first time that barebacking had been publicly discussed at CHAPS[9]. As a definition, Maguire's statement served to underline a number of assumptions regarding bareback sex, commonly held at the time, and identified potential problems HIV practitioners might have in connecting with the bareback scene[10]. In particular it demonstrated both the moral underpinnings and ideological blind spots of the existing discursive framework of HIV prevention. Let me be clear, I am not suggesting that in defining barebacking in this way Maguire was being singularly prejudiced or discriminatory. In acknowledging the existence of barebacking his statement signalled the recognition of barebackers and bareback subculture, something which had hitherto been absent from CHAPS. Rather, the discursive framework of HIV prevention work has forestalled any recognition of unprotected sex as a personal choice.

---

8 The CHAPS conference is an important event within the field of HIV health promotion work aimed at gay men. The first conference was held in 1997 and since then CHAPS has become a cornerstone within HIV prevention work (see Terrence Higgins Trust – information resources, online).

9 With the exception of the GMFA's 'controversial' advertising campaign relatively little work had been done in terms of designing and implementing campaigns aimed at the barebacking community. Maguire's definition appears to be the first time that barebacking was raised as an issue at the CHAPS conference: his definition was an important landmark in the recognition of barebackers.

10 For a discussion of how research into HIV transmission has been affected by issues of personal–moral judgement (assumed or otherwise) see Coxon (1996: 4–5).

I would like to dwell on Maguire's definition for a moment in order to tease out some of the problems HIV professionals have had in coming to terms with bareback subculture. The definition talks of bareback sex as being 'non-negotiated' and this term is a complicated one, suggesting a spectrum of 'deviant' behaviour, from anonymous casual sex through to coercive sex (rape, for instance is non-negotiated sex), and power-imbalances within sexual scenes (one or more actor might be incapable of rational negotiation). The term also carries with it a negatively-charged meaning in HIV terminology. Risk negotiation became a key term during the mid-nineties when British awareness campaigns utilised it within advertising aimed at increasing awareness, responsibility and safer sex activities amongst young gay men; negotiation, in the British context at least, is therefore good – non-negotiation is consequently bad. Thus bareback sex, being non-negotiated according to the CHAPS definition must be wrong; it is already negatively-weighted. However, as I shall demonstrate later, aside from giving rise to the question 'is negotiation of unprotected sex (i.e. vocally choosing to have unprotected sex) in some way more appropriate than assumptions based on non-disclosure', this assertion is misinformed and inaccurate.

Secondly, the CHAPS definition suggests that bareback sex must include an HIV positive partner. Admittedly, the context of this definition demands that the focus of the discussion be on the virus. It is also true that many barebackers *do* identify as HIV positive and presume that their sexual partners are also positive. Furthermore, bug-chasing and gift-giving (both practices that actively seek to transmit the HIV virus) are often included under the generic heading 'bareback': if you go online to find a bug-chaser, the first places to check out are the user profiles on bareback websites. However, this does not mean that HIV is central to all bareback experiences. Indeed there is a percentage of the bareback community who either do not know their sero-status or presume that they are either positive or negative. Owing to the discourse of HIV prevention (which emphasises regular testing for sexually active non-monogamous gay men) the definition struggles to recognise the multiplicity of different HIV statuses, both confirmed and unconfirmed (i.e. known negative, known positive, presumed negative, presumed positive, unknown) that operate within the bareback community. Neither does it acknowledge the fact that bareback sex does not have to involve an HIV positive partner.

Moving on, the phrase 'does not know or care, about the status of his partner' is problematic when trying to form non-judgemental and objective approaches to bareback subculture. The lack of 'care' twinned with the unknown status of the partner tacitly identifies the HIV positive individual as both the 'problem' and the individual 'responsible' for reducing sexual risk for others (see Flowers and Church, 2002 and Adam, 2005 for further discussion). Finally, the definition also aligns barebacking with a particular sexual lifestyle, namely the promiscuous hedonistic lifestyle labelled the 'circuit lifestyle' by Signorile (1997, ibid). The phrase 'does not know or care' implies that barebacking is both careless and hedonistic, a practice involving promiscuous anonymous sex between uncaring and unthinking individuals. It is true that the anonymous and casual nature of sexual encounters, such as those discussed in Chapter 5, preclude any discussion of sero-status. Within the context of a sauna, sex-club or public toilet, sexual partners rarely talk about their sexual histories. One could argue that, by contrast, long-term monogamous partners discuss their sexual histories and often go through the HIV testing process together[11] (Flowers and Church, 2002). But aligning barebacking *only* with casual sex serves to obscure the reality of barebacking; unprotected sex is still unprotected sex whether you are in a committed relationship or not. What I shall term the *practical*[12] risks are still the same.

Rather than accurately defining what bareback sex is then, this definition is perhaps most useful when viewed as an illustration of the difficulties that many health professionals have faced when discussing bareback sex. Due to the pervasive nature of HIV/AIDS discourse within gay male subculture, bareback sex (being a form of gay sex) must negotiate the issue of the virus. Yet a discursive space in which this negotiation can take place has rarely been available. Stephen Gendin, co-founder of Sex Panic and vice-president of *Poz* Magazine, acknowledged this discursive need at the 1997 Sex Panic Summit in San Diego when he posed the following questions:

> Why is it important for me to get fucked without a condom – and I can't tell when somebody's fucking me whether they're using a condom or not, I can't feel a difference but its really important to me – but its not important to me when I am fucking someone to use a condom and believe me I can feel the difference between those two things. […] I can't answer these questions for myself and society hasn't given me the tools to answer those kinds of questions. (Geddin, 1997, Online)

Being able to articulate sexual choices that operate independently of the condom code and which consciously reject aspects of conventional HIV/AIDS awareness discourse has been fraught with difficulties since the adoption of condoms and the advent of safer sex campaigning. In creating a space in which they can speak, gay men who choose to bareback have become involved in the construction of a new lexicon through which to speak. And, somewhat paradoxically, the virus has remained central to this lexicon, though in ways that radically differ from contemporary discourses of metropolitan gay male sexuality. As has been the case throughout this book, understanding offline contexts and histories are essential for a full understanding of online environments and the two websites I want to

11 See Flowers and Church (2002) for an overview of HIV testing – and rationales behind testing – by gay men.

12 In using the term 'practical risk', I am drawing a distinction between the risk involved in unprotected sex as a practice – as a specific sexual behaviour – and the host of other factors that are brought into play, including relationship status, HIV status and sexual habits.

analyse in the rest of this chapter need to be located in this wider framework of controversy that surrounds barebacking.

Creating a space for barebacking

Type 'bareback' into a search engine and the result will include thousands of hyperlinks to websites ostensibly catering to the bareback community. Reflecting the fact that sex is one of the most commonly searched for subjects on the Internet, the majority of these entries are for pornographic websites offering images and video feeds depicting bareback sex. More often than not, these appear alongside other images and videos of fetish sex, signalling that, for many, bareback sex is deviant and – for that reason – thrilling.

However, alongside the purely pornographic are links to websites that, whilst often featuring some pornographic content, provide a space for bareback subculture to flourish. The web spaces chosen for inclusion in this chapter both contain elements of the pornographic. But in offering a variety of services and membership levels, these spaces are more than just porn sites, and this separates them out from the vast majority of websites that show up in search engine results. They provide environments in which gay men interested in this sexual practice can interact with one another (as opposed to the isolated experience of browsing a pornographic website and downloading hardcore data). Often the objective of such interaction is to meet up, but there are occasions where advice is sought, or where the *fantasy* of bareback sex is ultimately the goal. In this respect bareback websites share common traits with other 'deviant' spaces such as the cyber-cottage discussed in Chapter 5. Whatever the type of interaction, in each instance it can be said that gay men are using these digital spaces to interact with barebacking – as an identity, a sexual choice and lifestyle – in ways that have largely been unimaginable within the context of offline media.

That the Internet has been taken up as the preferred method of communication by this disenfranchised group is of little surprise. I mentioned the work of Lin (2006), Mitra and Gajjala (2008) and Gray (2009) in Chapter 5 as just three examples of recent work that charted the digital interventions made on the 'queer margins'. In their study of two marginalised scientific communities Mukerji and Simon (1998) discuss the importance that the Internet holds for groups who have been discredited and/or rejected by wider society. Having been similarly marginalised by critical voices in the gay press, barebackers use the Internet as their primary discursive space. Grov (2006: 991) notes that, via the Internet, '[i]ndividuals with specialised sexual interests may develop a sense of community that may reduce some isolation and shame'. In contrast to the scientific communities of Mukerji and Simon's study, barebackers have not fallen out of favour or *become* stigmatised. Barebacking, as an identity, a practice and a subculture has been *formed* as a result of such stigma and condemnation. Barebacking is a *product* of the particular moral accent that the gay press adopted within their responses to the HIV/AIDS epidemic. I shall return to this point shortly.

Bareback subculture is also a product of the Internet: it has not existed outside of digital ICTs. Obviously, the practice of prophylactic-free anal sex between men is neither confined to virtual environments, nor confined to this country, or indeed this century. Men have been 'going Greek' since, well, before the ancient Greeks[13]. The difference between these historical acts and the new practice of barebacking lies in the precise cultural and historical context.

And at this point, perhaps as a response to the one provided by the CHAPS conference, I feel I should provide my own definition of bareback sex. Therefore let me clarify: for a man to bareback he must firstly engage in anal sex with another man without condoms but within the context of HIV/AIDS *and* contemporary Western gay male subculture, though HIV as a biological entity need not be present in the encounter and neither man may identify as being a part of that subculture. Secondly, to bareback is to tacitly acknowledge the central role digital media technologies play within the pursuit, negotiation and performance of this kind of sex. For while unprotected anal sex can and does occur outside of digital interventions, bareback subculture is heavily dependent on access to digital media technologies. My definition accepts that the Internet 'might be *productive* (not just reflective) of emerging sexual cultures' (Dowsett *et al.*, 2008: 122), and identifies the digital 'tools' that men who seek bareback sex have been able to utilise in order to communicate, negotiate and sustain a sexual culture. Bareback subculture demonstrates the potential for digital media to both open up spaces for the disenfranchised to speak and a method by which the disenfranchised can construct an identity through which they can speak.

The relationship between men who bareback and digital ICTs has been touched upon by several scholars (see Elford, 2006; Elford *et al.*, 2007; Grov *et al.*, 2007; Berg, 2008; and Dean, 2009). Some of the earliest research on bareback subculture (Malinger, 1998; Scarce, 1999; Halkitis *et al.*, 2003) highlighted the importance of using various forms of new media technologies as a means of sourcing interview cohorts from the barebacking community and this seems logical given the fact that these studies often concluded that:

> [p]articipants, regardless of barebacking behaviour, believe … that use of the Internet facilitate[s] the barebacking phenomenon among gay and bisexual men. (Halkitis *et al.*, 2003: 354)

As early as 1997, Sheon and Plant were claiming that 'the barebacking phenomenon has been most extensively debated on the web' and that the 'anonymity of the web' allows 'forbidden desires' to be articulated within a relatively safe forum (3). Two

13 The term 'going Greek' refers to the act of anal sex between men, but also between men and women (though the term is less commonly used in cross-gender anal-genital encounters).

years, later, Scarce (1999, online) noted that the bareback community 'flourishes in privates houses and especially on the Internet', citing the freedom from 'stigma attached to openly soliciting unsafe sex' as being an attractive facet of new media. More recently, Grov *et al.* (2007: 533) have stated that 'the Internet has played an important role among self-identified barebackers' and that 'barebackers spen[d] more time on the Internet engaged in a variety of activities' especially looking for sexual partners. Indeed, the Internet appears to be both the primary method of communication for bareback subculture and an important mode of communication for those writing about bareback sex[14].

The two websites analysed here, BarebackJack.com and Bareback.com, have been chosen both for their similarities and for their differences. That is to say, both websites are American-based but seek to serve an international community of barebackers[15]. Bareback.com has a dedicated forum for British barebackers, while the homepages listed at BarebackJack.com indicate that the site is popular with British barebackers. In both cases full access is dependent on membership level. While much of each website is freely accessible, subscription brings access to a range of additional services. At BarebackJack.com this includes access to the chat room ('Jack's Lounge') and the ability to browse and download pornographic images and videos. Members can also link their own homepage (or external web space) to the website, along with a description of that space, or indeed themselves. Bareback.com membership allows users to browse, message and build profiles, as well as accessing the chat rooms, pornographic material, and a private email account. Both websites also gain revenue from third-party companies who advertise access to bareback pornography and/or sell bareback video and DVD titles.

In this respect there are definite similarities between the two websites. As with Gaydar and Uni_cock they are also representative of other, (less populated) websites that cater for similar needs. They can also be understood as representing the differences found across bareback web spaces; the form and content of each site is significantly different from the other, and acknowledging these differences (as opposed to writing all such spaces off as the same) is the key to understanding how bareback subculture negotiates not only sex, but HIV online.

14 Many of the sources cited in this chapter are web-based texts that have only been published online.

15 At the time of researching this chapter there was a British-based website that ostensibly catered to the British bareback community and was therefore initially considered for inclusion in this study. However, at the time of selection, the site was under-populated and often strayed from the bareback mantra of 'sex without condoms'. For instance, erotic stories posted by the Webmaster included condom use. For these reasons, 'international' sites (that happened to be based in the United States) were chosen.

BarebackJack.com: Kitsch critique and a 'healthy combo platter'

Claiming to be the longest-running online space dedicated to the subject, BarebackJack.com has been providing information, social comment and pornography to the emergent bareback subculture since 1998. While the site has undergone a number of design changes during its lifetime, the aesthetic is reminiscent of a 1950's American diner.[16] Having entered the site, users are offered a 'menu' of different options (the 'healthy combo platter', 'smorg-ass-board' and 'hot spicy links') depending on membership status. 'Vintage' pornographic images are juxtaposed with cartoon-style illustrations reminiscent of this era, and the official discourse of the site plays on the discursive style of this period:

> Mmm Mmmm! All sorts of yummy treats can be had when you go for our Homepages. We give you meat and potatoes from around the world (and the men they're attached to), each one with its own home-style flavor [sic] as individual as the guys who cooked 'em. (BarebackJack.com, online)

The design of BarebackJack.com is notably different to many gay sex websites, and the decision to adopt the kitsch aesthetic style of 50's Americana runs deeper than a question of design taste. In one of the mini-essays posted by the Webmaster, the style of the website is specifically addressed:

> The mid-century style is more than just retro. It represents a unique period in our culture … a period of post-war prosperity, the first baby boom, the atom bomb, the space race, the jet age, massive social, economical, and population growth … and all the exuberance and optimism that went along with those times. … I wanted it to represent the exuberance we feel when we liberate ourselves from the 80's mindset by choosing to refuse condoms. (BarebackJack.com – Jack's Perspective, online)

Moving beyond its aesthetic appeal then, Jack, the Webmaster, draws parallels between this period of economic and technological growth and the choice to bareback. In doing so, he recontextualises barebacking, placing his discussions within a time that existed prior to the advent of HIV/AIDS (indeed, prior to the formation of a gay community). This reference to what is commonly understood as a period of Western optimism, growth and advancement is integral to the way in which the twin issues of bareback sex and the condom code are explored within this space: both are woven into the fabric of the website.

For example, while it might at first appear that this space presents a halcyon dream of 'days gone by', of a time before viruses and safer sex campaigns and moralising, (which, one could argue, is akin to sticking one's head in the sand and

16 The initial analysis of BarebackJack.com and Bareback.com began in 2004. Since this time both websites have been updated.

ignoring the current epidemic), a detailed reading reveals that the design of this space allows for the development of a sophisticated critique of the condom code. Central to this critique is the way in which time frames – historical periods – are juxtaposed. For although the content of the health information pages is contemporary, including discussions of HIV, crystal meth and safe sex, the style and mode of presentation places these discussions outside of contemporary urban gay culture. For example there is no reference to a particular gay scene, and no suggestion of a particular 'type' of gay subculture. If anything the 1950s theme suggests a heterosexual masculinity – a time when men were still 'men'. This collision of contemporary content with historical form is highly effective in extracting the user from the network of discourses that have shaped gay male sexuality since the early 1980s. In doing so, HIV is 'cut off' from gay sex and at BarebackJack.com the mode of discourse not only 'ignores' contemporary urban gay male culture, but also changes the relationship between gay male sex and the virus.

This is not to suggest that at BarebackJack.com HIV is ignored. As the mission statement demonstrates, quite the opposite is true:

> We believe that men can enjoy hot, unprotected sex best if they are informed about the risks involved and what they can do to minimize those risks to themselves and others. We're the only bareback site on the internet that refuses to sweep HIV under the carpet. (BarebackJack.com – health, online)

BarebackJack.com prides itself on being first and foremost a health information website. Many of the articles discuss HIV, and there are no claims as to the fallacy of the virus or the end of AIDS. But the severing effect created by the tension between content and form allows bareback sex to escape the rhetoric of the condom code. By placing bareback sex outside of contemporary gay culture Jack is able to argue for what he sees as the universal *naturalness* of bareback sex, and remind users that HIV is an *intrusion* into gay sex not integral to it. BarebackJack.com thus offers a discursive space in which societal norms become skewed and where what we understand as the 'truth' about the world we live in is questioned. Jack creates a space in which the browser is invited to re-think their relationship to sex:

> it seems rather appropriate to the bareback set to reinvestigate this style. … As gay men who bareback, we also know the forgotten pleasures of no-barrier sex, and feel comfortable carrying on this natural tradition. (BarebackJack.com – Jack's Perspective, online)

The aesthetics of the website simultaneously look back to this period of optimism and suggest that through this looking back gay men can (re)discover bareback sex in the future. This manoeuvre carries with it wider ramifications when we consider the percentage of gay men populating the gay scenes of the UK and the USA who have come of sexual age under the shadow of HIV. Strub (1999, online) notes that a 'generation of gay men was defined by AIDS' and whilst young gay men today are not 'immersed … in the immediacy and the urgency of the epidemic' their sexual identities are still shaped by the virus; it has become a bodiless spectre[17] at the centre of gay culture. Considering Sinfield's statement identified in Chapter 2 regarding British gay culture's relationship to AIDS, and the disparity between the lived experience of HIV and the spectre of AIDS, the discovery of 'real' gay sex is perhaps even more tangible – and tempting for British gay culture: to put it bluntly, in Britain the fear of death from AIDS has (thankfully) not been matched by a corresponding body count.

BarebackJack.com does not offer a fantasy of an HIV-free world, but it does offer the opportunity to think, talk and have gay sex outside of discourses that silence bareback sex practitioners. The web facilitates the problematising of truths and assumptions such as those mentioned above. As Fletcher (2004) of Manchester's George House Trust states 'gay men are encountering the Internet as a comparatively liberating zone in which to engage in these [bareback] debates and encounters'[18] and at BarebackJack.com the unspeakable gets spoken and new truths are explored and validated. Such practices serve to highlight the contrived nature of the official discourses on HIV, not to mention the process of assumption that often surrounds such truths. For example consider the following statement, made by Jack in response to a letter entitled 'Neg/Poz coupling':

> In the hysteria over HIV and AIDS, many people (including healthcare professionals) have apparently forgotten that one person in a sexual encounter must have the virus in order to transmit it. (BarebackJack.com – letters, online)

While HIV agencies acknowledge the need for the virus to be present in order for it to be transmitted, popular discourse, such as that found in the gay press, serves to further mythologise HIV, transforming it from a virus into a behavioural or moral effect. Against this discursive backdrop, and in response to the CHAPS definition of barebacking and the assumptions of cultural commentators such as Signorile and Rotello, BarebackJack.com provides a forum in which unprotected sex can be interrogated using the situated truth of the barebacking community. As such, it offers a counter-discourse to prevailing hegemonies.

Having distanced HIV from gay sex and argued that bareback sex is normal and not an aberration, HIV is re-introduced within a framework of *relevant* safer sexual health advice. In contrast to the stereotype of the ill-informed, psychologically impaired barebacker who fails to face up to his sexual responsibilities, BarebackJack.com demands that users engage with this new framework from the outset. In order to enter the site, browsers must answer the question 'safer sex begins with?' by clicking on the correct answer. The answers available include a

---

17 I call HIV a bodiless spectre because for many gay men today HIV is not personified in the death of friends, lovers or celebrities as it was in the early days of the epidemic.

18 Quoted during an email exchange between Fletcher and the author (April 2004).

cartoon image of a brain and that of a condom, suggesting that safe sex is always about making rational decisions rather than simply following a doctrine. By asking this question, and demanding that users answer it before gaining access to the website, BarebackJack.com creates a space outside of the condom code in which gay men can re-establish their own sexual autonomy.

In doing so, the website echoes Adam's (2005: 344) assertion that barebackers operate as neoliberal actors invested in a discourse of self-governing freedom of choice:

> it [bareback subculture] combines together notions of informed consent, contractual interaction, free market choice, and responsibility that create a platform for constructing unprotected sex as a 'responsible' choice among adult men.

While BarebackJack.com does not position unprotected sex as a politically subversive activity (as perhaps the sex radicals mentioned above would), the very existence of this space serves to critique the unquestioning adherence to the 'rules' of safer sex perpetuated by gay culture. Breaking the rules of safer sex then, is positioned not as 'radical' act of 'queer' defiance, but rather as an issue of *individual choice*. At BarebackJack.com, gay men are positioned as 'rational, adult, contract-making individuals in a free market of options' (ibid) and barebacking is situated as an issue of 'personal choice … attributing responsibility *back* to the individual' (Grov, 2006: 993). Employing this neoliberal discourse, BarebackJack.com presents itself as a sexual health website for the man who has *chosen* to bareback and in doing so it seeks to educate him about safer sex *outside* of the dominant discourse of HIV/AIDS awareness. It offers a range of relevant sexual health advice tailored to the needs of barebackers and health awareness is taken seriously, but so is the fact that relying on the condom code will only alienate the barebacking community further. While admitting that HIV – as a topic – may well be skirted around by other websites, here the bareback community is offered practical information on HIV transmission, ways of reducing risk and cold hard facts (i.e. 'there is no cure for HIV') *relevant* to their own sexual choices.

This tailoring of appropriate health advice can be seen in the Webmaster's discussion of recreational drug use. Here he makes a distinction between barebackers and 'tweakers' (drug users) and in many ways, the website echoes the messages sent out in campaigns by GMFA and THT that target drug use on the commercial gay scene. But BarebackJack.com comes into its own when it re-contextualises these messages so that they once again become relevant to the barebacking community:

> Condom use and/or honest discussion about HIV status is infrequent in these venues, [inhabited by tweakers] Being in control of yourself and your actions is your best weapon against HIV transmission. (BarebackJack.com – health, online)

Again, the neoliberal rhetoric can be seen in Jack's discourse, where the individual is responsible for his 'actions' and for 'being in control'. It should also be noted that although the website provides useful information on HIV, in this space bareback sex and HIV do not go hand in hand, as implied by the CHAPS definition. In a response to a letter entitled 'are there negative barebackers like me?' Jack identifies himself as both a barebacker and HIV negative. He goes on to say:

> I cannot stress enough that barebacking is NOT about passing the virus along to others. Barebacking IS about getting the maximum level of pleasure out of fucking. (ibid)

Jack's negative status heavily influences the site content and HIV is positioned as something to engage with as an issue but not as an aim. The Webmaster's HIV status is particularly pertinent here as he uses his website to communicate not only his desires, but also his choices and responsibilities: Jack is an HIV negative barebacker who wishes to remain negative. In concluding his response to the letter he states that 'I have been selective in deciding who I'll fuck and under which circumstances, I have managed so far to remain negative'.

This would at first seem poor advice; adopting a strategy of harm reduction based solely upon assumption is both ignorant and irresponsible. However, within the context of the website we learn that BarebackJack.com is not promoting a 'moderation = safe sex' model of HIV prevention but is reminding the addressee that sex, like any other area of life, is about judgement, taking responsibility and identifying the risks involved. BarebackJack.com is not advocating sexual moderation as a solution to HIV, and neither does this model form the bedrock of most contemporary HIV strategies. But it should be noted that the call for gay men to form mutually monogamous relationships (and the consequent political lobbying for the right to marriage), together with the adoption of HIV/AIDS as a reason why such coupling should be promoted, continues to pervade the rhetoric of writers like Andrew Sullivan and organisations such as the Log Cabin Republicans and Torch[19]. At BarebackJack.com, Jack offers users the opportunity to separate sexual choice from moral judgement. The surreal juxtaposition of frank sexual discussion and kitsch 1950's domesticity not only reveals sex to be contrived and discursively structured, it also validates alternative sexual health messages that find no avenue for discussion elsewhere in contemporary gay culture.

In seeking to (re)educate gay men about their sexual choices and corresponding sexual risks, and in providing a space in which barebackers can renegotiate their relationship with their sexuality, BarebackJack.com is invested in the same neoliberal rhetoric that Adam (2005) identifies in his Canadian-based study. But

---

19 Torch is a specialist group affiliated to Britain's Conservative Party, which seeks to represent the party to the gay community in the UK. In many respects they are similar to the Log Cabin Republicans of the USA, a grass-roots organisation for within the Republican Party that promote gay and lesbian issues.

BarebackJack.com appears to go further than Adam's research participants by offering a neoliberal critique of contemporary discourses surrounding gay male sexuality. This is not to suggest that the website condemns conventional safer sex strategies, or indeed the use of condoms. Such condemnation would be counter to the neoliberal rhetoric of choice; Jack has no problems with gay men using condoms in sex – it's just that *it's not for him*. But in creating a space where alternatives to using condoms can be explored, and where 'raw sex' can be considered in a non-judgemental context, BarebackJack.com posits gay men as individual sexual actors within a free market of sexual practice. Of course, viewing barebacking as a choice implies that such actors are making informed decisions and free to use a variety of strategies in order to make such decisions. BarebackJack.com offers a wealth of information to its members and appears to subscribe to this notion of informed choice. However, as I shall discuss later, these strategies find their limit point within the context of bareback pornography, and the means by which the website generates finance problematises this neoliberal approach.

Bareback.com – who's afraid of the big bad bug?

In contrast to BarebackJack.com, Bareback.com ostensibly fails to engage in rational discourse. If BarebackJack.com is the equivalent of a market place for rational debate and the exchange of ideas, Bareback.com more closely resembles an SM playroom, (replete with leather accoutrements and explicit language) that appears to offer little to no reasoned discussion. Measured argument and ironic design are dismissed at Bareback.com as members are commanded to 'get down and dirty' and take part in an orgy, throwing caution to the wind in search for the ultimate sexual high. The mission statement of Bareback.com illustrates both the differences between this space and BarebackJack.com and what the typical attitude fostered and championed on the site:

> Welcome to the new Bareback.com. We are the premiere home for all you studs who crave the feeling only raw sex can provide. Who's afraid of the big, bad bug? Not our little piggies. We'll huff and we'll puff and we'll blow your Dick Down! Chase those bugs all over town like the horny toad you are. Get dangerous and seek out new perversions and new fetishes. (Bareback.com – mission statement, online)

The pastel colours and yesteryear cartoons of BarebackJack.com are substituted for black backgrounds and metallic-effect fonts at Bareback.com and this 'backroom aesthetic' has become typical within the design of websites dedicated to pornography and in particular, fetish sex. While the aesthetics could not be more different, the metaphorical use is the same; the site design reflects the content and attitudes promoted at Bareback.com. Banners, consisting of slogans set against collages of hardcore pornography, urge users to 'leave the Trojans at home' and 'just bring your bone' and promote bareback sex, 'No glove? Good, then get ready for hot love.' In contrast to the rational discussion of BarebackJack.com, where users are asked to *question* their dependence on the condom code, at Bareback.com users are *commanded* to forget their former belief in, and adherence, to the prophylactic in order to pursue the ultimate sexual fetish and (within gay subculture) the ultimate taboo.

This fetishising of 'raw' sex, absent within the discourse of BarebackJack.com, is central to the discussions at Bareback.com, where unprotected sex is positioned as a kink, a perversion, and most importantly, as something *new*. This attitude towards 'risky' sex echoes Rotello's claim that barebacking serves to glamorise unsafe sex and that, 'the popularization of that term seems to indicate a shift from describing unprotected sex as unsafe sex, to describing it as sexy and alluring. (quoted in Mallinger, 1998, online). Considering the mission statement of Bareback.com, it would appear that Rotello's assertion is correct. The advent of the term 'barebacking' has re-cast the previously untouchable as both thrilling and rebellious. Rotello is highly critical of this re-articulation of condom-less sex but appears unwilling to engage with the issue of why a bareback subculture has emerged. In particular, he overlooks the highly plausible contention that it was the very discourses of the condom code and safer sex that *produced* the practices and subculture he rails against. The late Eric Rofes (1998) was more willing to engage with such an argument and his work has served to re-evaluate the effectiveness of the condom code within contemporary gay culture. Rofes saw the 'state of emergency' reaction to AIDS in the 1980s as being an effective short-term response to the epidemic, but questioned its effectiveness in long-term gay men's health work:

> If we created this narrative of gay heroism in the 1980s, fabricating politically useful explanations for the decline in new infections in order to win public sympathy and gain funding for AIDS services, we should not be surprised that it has come around to confront us just a few years later. … the heroic narrative of the first decade of AIDS couldn't help but be transfigured into a demonic narrative in the second decade. (Rofes, 1998: 201)

Rofes was commenting on the North American perspective but similar voices can be heard this side of the Atlantic. Reaney (2000, online) has argued that as a result of 'the cast-iron "wear a condom every time" safer-sex message' barebacking has been positioned as a 'taboo subject' within the community most affected by HIV in the UK. This, he claims, has been criticised by HIV positive gay men who feel that the 'black or white' nature of the safer-sex message obscures the particular circumstances of their lives'. Meanwhile, Russell (2005: 156) states that 'the very notion of transgressive barebacking is a product of prohibitive HIV prevention itself' and that,

> transgressive barebackers are the disruptive participants of HIV prevention – the outcome prevention does not want to own but which is the required manifestation of the transgressive desire which retrospectively necessitates prohibition in the first place.

Neither Rofes, Reaney or Russell seek to dismantle the condom code, nor do their arguments suggest that barebacking is inherently 'better' or 'queerer' or 'liberating' (as perhaps Gendins and other pro-bareback spokespeople would). But such arguments allow us to see how and why an interest in bareback sex has grown in popularity. Thus, while appearing to be the antithesis of HIV prevention programs, barebacking is in fact the illegitimate child of the condom code, and on websites such as Bareback.com, this child revels in his newfound freedom, sticking two fingers up to the culture that created him.

The metaphor of the child is pertinent here, not least because Bareback.com plunders childhood narratives in order to convey a sense of playful libidinality, which frames discussions of bareback sex in this space. To refer to the mission statement once more, the fairytale of the *Three Little Pigs* is appropriated and turned upside down, as the 'wolf' of this morality tale becomes the HIV virus and the pigs become the members of the site.[20] In asking 'who's afraid of the big bad bug?' the site draws on the well-known song from Disney's 1933 animation of the fairytale. Convention would suggest that only those foolish and arrogant enough would say 'no, not I', the moral of the story being that the world is full of danger and one must spend time, money and patience in order to be safe. Yet at Bareback.com the arrogant 'no' of the first two piggies (those who ultimately get eaten by the wolf in some versions of the story) is celebrated and upheld. In response to the question, 'who's afraid of the big bad bug' the site answers 'not our little piggies' for they will 'huff and puff and blow your dick down'. Bracketing off opinions and criticisms to such a response, this retort is the key to understanding how HIV and bareback sex are discussed in this space. The reversal of power relations, which lies at the heart of this re-narrativising of the fairy-tale, acts as a metaphor for how the website negotiates the virus. Gay men's fears regarding HIV ('the bug') is equated with a child's fear of the fictional wolf character and, while HIV is not positioned as a fallacy on the site, the central position that it has arguably occupied within discourses of gay male sexuality over the last twenty-five years is destabilised and here called into question.

Indeed this reworking of the story goes even further as not only is the feared 'HIV-as-Wolf' figure rendered impotent, it is then attacked and hunted down:

20 For those unfamiliar with contemporary meanings of the term 'pig' in gay male subculture, a 'pig' – or 'sex-pig' – refers to someone who enjoys a range of sexual activities generally considered to be at the more extreme end of the sexual spectrum. These activities may include forms of BDSM together with leather-play, group sex and sex sessions lasting several hours, recreational drug use, urination, fisting, role-play, sex-toys and a host of other activities.

'chase those bugs all over town'. This is clearly a reference to 'bug-chasing' (actively seeking HIV infection) and while the website is not dedicated to promoting HIV transmission, in this instance at least, there does appear to be a sense that (putting aside other questions surrounding this practice) bug-chasing disavows the censorial role HIV has played in gay men's sex lives. 'Real' men don't worry about HIV according to Bareback.com, and here they can reclaim their sexuality outside of the dominant 'parental' discourses of HIV prevention. As the homepage states, 'Don't tell your mommy, but it's just about time to meet the boy toy of your dreams'.

Michael, the Webmaster, continues this discursive style throughout the website. In the introduction to the forum he writes:

> Welcome to the Bareback.com community home page. Prepare to take your first step out of the condom closet. … Being mean or lecturing any members of the community is not allowed. Health class was in high school – we have grown up! Rubbers are for women and children on a rainy day – not for a little piggy's bedroom! (Bareback.com – forums, online)[21]

If the mission statement sounds like childish rebellion or 'acting out', here we see how the invocation of the child is in fact something far more thought provoking. In utilising childhood motifs (fairy-tale characters, references to 'mommy' and high school for instance) Michael isn't suggesting a regression back to an infantile stage (such a move would arguably support the misguided assumption that barebacking involves forgetting or denying HIV), but is rather advocating *growth*. Gay men are here positioned as being 'childish' for allowing themselves to be restrained by the fear of HIV and governed by the 'AIDS Nazis' of gay culture. This supports Dean's (2009: 52) claim that within bareback subculture condoms make 'masculinity vulnerable to doubt or derision'. At Bareback.com, Michael offers a space in which he believes gay men can escape this 'vulnerability' and become sexually mature.

To many this will seem both absurd and dangerous; stating that barebackers need to come out of the 'condom closet' suggests that bareback sex is in some sense more gay, more queerly correct, than adhering to the condom code. Let me be clear, this is not a position that I either endorse or support. However, it is possible to plot a course through recent critiques of HIV prevention (and specifically the proscription of bareback sex) in order to see why Michael makes this assertion, irrespective of whether we agree with him or not. Reaney (2000, online) asserts that the taboo over barebacking 'hinders [HIV positive gay men's]

21 Aside from being slang for condom, the term 'rubber' in this context also means Wellington boots. I am indebted to my American friends and colleagues for enlightening me regarding this fact. What is particularly interesting is that when explaining the meaning of this phrase each person independently remarked that they hadn't heard the term used within the context of footwear since childhood.

ability to rationalise their desire for bareback sex' and when commenting on the closure of a bareback chat room on a gay dating site, Taylor (1999, online) states that 'our health is our own individual responsibility and these guys have the right to risk their lives if they choose to'. He then goes on to make the point that 'queers should know better than most how futile it is to try and repress unconventional or unpopular sexual practices'.

Bareback.com's use of childhood motifs can be seen as a response to these measures and attacks. It is also interesting to note that, as with BarebackJack.com, time frames are central to this environment. While BarebackJack.com involves a collision of contemporary content with historical design, Bareback.com involves a return to childhood in order to critique the unquestioning belief in the condom code and critique what some feel has become a restrictive framework of gay male sexuality.

But the manipulation of time is not the only similarity between the two spaces; although Bareback.com ostensibly rejects the 'lectures' of the former website, the Webmaster does offer a similar advice column for members and non-members of Bareback.com. The language of Michael's responses differs from Jack's but interestingly, the content suggests a similar political viewpoint. Most notably, Michael employs a critique of the condom code in order to validate the right to *choose* bareback sex. In a response to a user who questions the risks involved in bareback sex the Webmaster begins by stating that 'no sex act is completely safe. Condoms break, people get caught up in the moment, Shit happens. So you need to get over the idea of safe sex'. He then continues by arguing that 'yes, barebacking feels much better. It is the most intimate act of love that can exist between two men. And, despite what Bareback Nazis say there are ways to make it safer without wrapping your crank in latex' (Bareback.com – ask Mike, online).

Michael then goes on to list numerous suggestions for *safer* barebacking, including monogamy, but also the use of lubricant to avoid bleeding, partner selection and the avoidance of semen exchange. These suggestions echo the prevention campaigns prevalent in Britain since the mid-nineties but with one important difference.[22] These messages are articulated in a space in which choosing to bareback is not met with condemnation and social exclusion and is not seen as 'second-best' (in terms of safety) to wearing a condom. Michael appears to be acutely aware of this fact and uses it to his advantage here. Having stated that 'no sex act is completely safe' he comments that, while 'breeders [straight people] always preach sa[f]e sex, they seem to have a lot of babies and abortions which

22 Britain's Health Education Authority ran advertising campaigns to raise awareness of condom use and safer sex throughout the 1990s. One example, from *Gay Times* (February, 1995) specifically focuses on the types of lubricant that should be used during anal sex. *Attitude* (April, 1997) carried a sexual health supplement sponsored by GlaxoWellcome, which included a safer-sex scale of no-risk to high risk activities and advice on safer fisting and other forms of penetrative sex. More recently in *QX Magazine* (issue 461, December 2003) GMFA ran an advertisement entitled 'use more lube' to promote safer anal sex.

means they don't always practice what they preach' (Bareback.com – ask Mike, online).

This is but one of example of how the Webmaster aligns safer sex campaigning and the 'Bareback Nazis' with heterosexuality. As quoted above, at Bareback.com condoms are considered the domain of heterosexual sex ('rubbers are for women') and this 'straightening out' of contemporary safe sex campaigns pervades the advice column. This contrasts the polemics of BarebackJack.com, where Jack critiques the gay community as a whole:

> It is by exercising responsibility that we can help break down the wall of fear that has others in our gay community and beyond addressing us as reckless, emotionally flawed, or suicidal. (BarebackJack.com – Jack's perspective, online)

While BarebackJack.com does not point a finger at any particular group, Bareback.com seeks to support the idea that safe sex rhetoric is in fact homophobic anti-sex discourse. Michael uses his advice column to not only (re)educate bareback subculture but also to attack the hypocrisy of heteronormative (and homonormative) society's commandment that gay men adhere to the strictures of the condom code.

Indeed it is surprising just how often that heterosexual sex and heteronormative lifestyles crop up in Michael's writings. In his response to another letter (this time on the subject of 'how can I tell someone is telling the truth about their HIV status?') he compares HIV infection with pregnancy:

> Do you have any idea how many girls have gotten pregnant because their boyfriends promised them they would marry them 'if anything happens? Do you know how many boyfriends actually stayed around after breeding the bitches? (Bareback.com – ask Mike, online).

This illustrates an important difference between the two spaces in terms of their understanding of barebacking. Jack appears to see barebacking as specifically a homosexual activity, arguing for the rights of gay men to freedom and choice over how they handle their sexual lives. Michael, on the other hand, chooses to align barebacking with heterosexual sex. To put it another way, for the Webmaster, the act of barebacking and the act of procreative sex are parallel activities.[23] Not only do they involve unprotected sex, but they also carry risks – be they of contracting HIV or getting pregnant: 'wake up people!! There is no such thing as safe sex!! It's all a little dangerous!! That's part of what makes it fun!' (Bareback.com – ask Mike, online).

---

23 Dean (2009) offers an interesting discussion regarding how bareback subculture draws on 'breeding' culture in order to fashion its own response to HIV.

Hetero-patriarchy is located as the stuffy parent that must be rebelled against, but at the same time, and somewhat paradoxically, barebacking is paralleled with heterosexual sex or, more specifically, a stereotypically masculine, adolescent and rebellious attitude to heterosexual sex. This paralleling is maintained via the deployment of misogynistic discourses commonly found within the macho language of teenage heterosexual boys. Drawing on the archetypal binary of the virgin and the whore, women are positioned as either 'mommies' – stay-at-home, passive subordinates (as seen in the mission statement) – or as 'bitches' – sexually-promiscuous animal-women who are 'punished' through pregnancy for their sexual freedom. While utterly repulsive, the misogyny of the site is an important trope and must be acknowledged here, not least because the invocation of anti-feminist, chauvinistic discourse serves to attach a well-worn set of power relations based on gender difference to a context in which both partners (all partners) are male.

This invocation occurs at the point where pregnancy and HIV are positioned not only as similar risks, but also as the risk or 'problem' for the passive partner only, be that a woman or a 'bottom' (the 'receiver' within the anal-genital act). This is not to suggest that the passive partner is overtly feminised by the Webmaster; there is no use of feminine pronouns to describe the 'bottom', and the stereotype of the butch penetrating the femme is notably absent on the website.[24] But through the deployment of hegemonic masculinity, the alignment of pregnancy and HIV infection as a problem for s/he who is penetrated means that the 'passive' partner becomes feminised, objectified and, ultimately, de-humanised. For example, when responding to a reader's enquiry about the sero-conversion of his ('passive') boyfriend during group bareback sex, Michael writes:

> What the fuck is wrong with you!! He's your boyfriend! He's your bottom. He's your property. If you want to lend him out to random guys that is your right, but not before you mark your territory first. If you want him POZ and he wants to be POZ it is your fucking responsibility to make him POZ. (Bareback.com – ask Mike, online)

Bracketing off the issue of conscious sero-conversion[25], the objectification of the passive partner borrows from the dominant ideology of hegemonic masculinity where the feminisation of the Other is used specifically to masculinise the Self. In

24 Indeed, both Dowsett *et al.* (2008) and Dean (2009) note how the 'bottom' is regularly masculinised in bareback sex and writings on bareback sex, through the deployment of what might be called a rhetoric of 'taking it like a man'.

25 In researching and writing this chapter I have chosen not to explore the sub-cultural phenomenon of gift-giving and bug-chasing, which I have previously indicated involves the conscious transmission of the HIV virus via unprotected sex. While these two identities exist as a sub-section of the barebacking world (barebacking being the context in which such identities are formed), it is beyond the scope and remit of this chapter to undertake an analysis of this controversial and complex behaviour. Such activities have been written

doing so, the homosexual sex act – an act that ostensibly works against notions of gendered difference – is (re)read via dominant understandings of heteronormative gender relations. Michael is speaking 'man-to-man' to the correspondent about how to control and manage his 'property'. Suggesting that there is a 'responsibility' to be the person who transmits the virus to his boyfriend, the Webmaster draws on hegemonic ideals of masculinity; the correspondent has a duty to his boyfriend, it is his job, his task, to do what needs to be done, he must (literally) be up to the job. While less obvious, HIV is once again aligned with pregnancy: the active partner has a responsibility to impregnate his (HIV positive) semen into his passive partner in the same way that the heterosexual male must penetrate the woman in order to continue the blood line. This base, animalistic need to penetrate and claim ownership is identified by Michael when he writes that the correspondent must 'mark' his 'territory' before he allows any other man to penetrate his boyfriend. This process of objectification and identification (namely of responsibility) (somewhat bizarrely) serves to frame the homosexual act (barebacking) within a quintessentially heteronormative structure of understanding.

So while both websites claim the right of gay men to have bareback sex, the method by which this right is justified varies. In the former we see Jack working from the perspective of a fully formed gay male identity; in the latter, Michael emulates a rebellious (straight) teenager who acts tough in front of his audience in an attempt to prove that 'real men' don't wear condoms. If BarebackJack.com is a platform upon which gay men can congregate and discuss barebacking, Bareback.com is a 'closed-off' space that shuns rational debate in favour of an altogether more hedonistic, and ideologically dubious, approach to unprotected sex.

Arguing for barebacking – approaches used by BarebackJack.com and Bareback.com

So far in this chapter I have sought to examine how the Web has been used by men whose sexual desires, identities and practices are marginalised by mainstream gay culture. Similar to the cyber-cottage discussed in Chapter 5, the two barebacking websites interrogated here must be understood as responses to a lack of valid discursive, cultural and physical space in which such practices can be discussed, considered and negotiated in 'mainstream' gay culture. Any discussion of barebacking must entail an acknowledgement of how integral digital technologies are to this emerging sub-culture, and the central role that the Web plays in maintaining a validating that culture.

At BarebackJack.com we find the Webmaster engaged in a project of rational debate and open discussion that finds no outlet within the gay print media. Responding to the attacks launched by the gay press and by spokespeople within

about recently and I would direct interested parties to Rofes (1998) and Signorile (2002) for more specific discussions of these twin activities.

gay culture, BarebackJack.com provides a site for discussion, and an environment in which strategies for safer unsafe sex can be developed and disseminated. Unlike the CHAPS definition, 'raw' sex at BarebackJack.com does not necessarily involve HIV transmission, or indeed the risk of HIV transmission. HIV is not positioned as an object of desire, a myth to be overcome or a side issue to be ignored. Instead the virus is positioned as central to *discussions* of barebacking but not to gay male sexuality itself. Through his website, Jack is able to play with language and design in order to sever the link between the virus and gay male sex. This allows him to explore sexual practices that continue to be demonised within gay culture, in a non-judgemental manner. As a result, the Webmaster is able to promote new sexual health strategies appropriate to a group of men who have *already* chosen not to use condoms.

By contrast, Bareback.com would appear to confirm the very worst fears of the British newspaper mentioned above, which breached copyright law in order to warn the public of this dangerous new practice. For while BarebackJack.com offers its users constructive advice regarding safer barebacking, Bareback.com seems, on the surface, to play into the hands of its worst critics, offering a sanctuary to those who wish to pretend that HIV is either a fictional virus, or something akin to the common cold. No doubt it is the ease with which this site is open to such superficial readings that has allowed many commentators to reach the conclusion that barebackers are suicidal and deluded individuals with no real understanding of the virus or the risks involved in this sexual behaviour. However, as I have demonstrated, a closer inspection of the discourse employed in such a space reveals that the Webmaster and his followers are engaged in similar processes of sexual critique. They also seek to uncouple gay male sex from discourses of HIV and conventional safer sex promotion, via the deployment of childhood motifs and language reminiscent of adolescent rebellion. Through these methods, Bareback.com advocates 'growth' within gay mens' perception of sex, risk and identity and argues for an awareness, but not an irrational fear, of the virus. Instead Bareback.com promotes an understanding of risk on par with heterosexual risk – namely pregnancy. While such a strategy can easily be criticised for ignoring the realities of living with HIV, it does serve to underscore the fact that considerations of risk – and responsibility – are central to all sexual acts.

Despite their differences in approach, language and style, it would appear then that the two spaces encountered here do share similarities. Both seek to provide a space in which barebacking is able to be discussed, in which HIV is not swept under the carpet but addressed as a negotiable risk, and where gay male sexuality can be re-organised in a manner that does not place HIV at the centre of gay male sexual culture. I am reminded of an acquaintance whose ex-boyfriend used to occasionally demand that they wore condoms during sex. This demand, it turned out, always came after the boyfriend had read an article in the press about HIV/AIDS. Both partners were monogamous, and did not engage in group sex or 'threesomes', both had (repeatedly) tested negative for the virus, and neither doubted the other's fidelity. Both were highly-educated, intelligent and balanced individuals. Yet this request was repeatedly made. Why? I would argue that while this guy knew he wasn't at risk of infection, the culture in which he was invested in, British gay male subculture, has aligned (or been co-erced into aligning) certain sexual practices with HIV transmission, irrespective of sero-status.

This response can be considered an effect of what Russell (2005: 147) calls the 'the grossly anxiety-inducing shadow of the AIDS epidemic' and bareback websites must be understood within this context of fear and anxiety over an ever-present virus, which, paradoxically, might often be absent. As my definition above illustrates, it is precisely this context that is responsible for the creation of barebacking. Dean (2009: 54–55) writes of the 'state of permanent terror' that HIV has induced amongst gay men and that barebacking can be seen as a response to this anxiety. Viewing barebacking from this perspective is not to suggest for a moment that the many millions of pounds and millions of person-hours that have gone in to promoting safer sex amongst gay men has been wasted. On the contrary. Nor is it to suggest that charities such as THT or GMFA or the raft of other HIV agencies and voluntary groups are to 'blame' for the rise of barebacking. I mentioned previously that bareback sex and bareback culture can be viewed as the illegitimate child of such hard work and good deeds – and it is indeed illegitimate, for no-one could have predicted that the successes of such campaigning would have paved the way for this new turn in gay male sexual history.

There is, however, an important difference between the two websites that lies in the relative openness and inclusiveness of each space. At BarebackJack.com, assimilation into mainstream gay culture may not be a priority for the Webmaster but a validation of barebacking as a legitimate sexual act *is*. In seeking such validation, Jack builds bridges with the wider gay community. The website's health pages are supported by hyperlinks to progressive gay male health websites, articles on drug abuse, sexual health and other relevant topics. One such example would be 'BarebackJack.com Headline News', a section of the main website that details recent news items occurring at a national and international level, relevant to barebackers. In the past this news has included information on new HIV testing ('new "bloodless" HIV test is accurate, less invasive'), new research into HIV transmission ('HIV-Neg Tops found to be at greater risk for catching HIV than previously believed') and also on other political matters ('Citizen's rights at stake as USDOJ tosses out Constitution in war on porn!').

Such examples indicate Jack's desire to link discussions of barebacking to wider issues surrounding freedom of speech, HIV testing and HIV infection. This is further reflected in the list of URLs provided at the end of the news bulletin, pointing not towards other barebacking websites, but to health websites, HIV websites and websites set up to defend civil liberties. While the specific focus of the bulletin is on the implication of each news item for bareback subculture, the need to integrate with existing health care agencies, with the wider gay male community and with society at large, becomes apparent. For instance, following the bulletin item on new HIV screening methods, Jack universalises the call for regular testing, arguing that:

> Public health is EVERYONE'S concern! It is our basic human responsibility to contain and help eradicate HIV and other STD's. If you do not know your HIV status or you only 'think' you know, GET TESTED! (BarebackJack.com – health, online)

This move towards integration is an important element of the website, and at BarebackJack.com, the barebacker is positioned as a gay man who barebacks; his sexual identity is not confined to his preference for unprotected sex. As such, the website does not hold on to claims that barebacking is deviant, but instead validates bareback sex, placing it as an option on par with the rest of gay male subculture.

Bareback.com, by comparison, appears to revel in its outsider status. 'Perversions' and new fetishes are actively promoted within the website, where the promotion of barebacking is maintained within the context of deviance. At Bareback.com to bareback is to be perverse and to be consumed by its culture. There are links to other websites at Bareback.com but these are not of the kind found at BarebackJack.com. Fetish as opposed to health websites are the norm on the links page of the site and this is just one example of how Bareback.com appears to inhabit the space created for it by both mainstream and gay culture. Both cultures identify the barebacker as deviant and at Bareback.com, this deviance is celebrated. In doing so, the website forms an online 'ghetto' and closes in on itself. Michael, the Webmaster, has no interest in forming a network of alternative relevant information for the barebacking community. He does not engage in discussions with leading HIV agencies, and his website does not seek to counter the 'myths' of the 'bareback Nazis'. Indeed, this phrase alone epitomises the separatist mentality of Bareback.com, which sees itself as the last outpost of sexual experimentalism in a world of gay homogeneity.

The investment in a rhetoric of adolescent rebellion, together with the site's explicit and 'immature' misogyny, seems to suggest that its main concern is with maintaining its 'outlaw' status and flaunting it in the face of its critics. But we might also think of Bareback.com as mobilising a 'reverse discourse' (Foucault, 1976: 101) and the website certainly employs the deviant status of barebackers in ways that allows it to speak back to the mainstream. It is through the mobilisation of a reverse discourse that bareback sex is positioned as both natural and correct, and indeed pre-eminently central to homosexual desire and practice. Similarly, semen, which for the last twenty years has been coded as a harbinger of disease, is invested with an almost mystical quality in this environment. During a discussion entitled 'what does it feel like to have a guy cum in your ass' on the Bareback.com community board, respondents identified a transcendental quality within the act of semen exchange:

> You can't really feel him cumming. But the experience is psychological.

> When you are getting fucked really good by a man, you should feel the energy of his body flowing into yours.
>
> Feelings when he is cumming is like you cumming … only more intense. Talk about fire works. Then the satisfaction cums over both of you and you just lay with each other enjoying what has just happened … true communication m2m.
>
> The ultimate feelings are those when he says 'I am cumming'. Knowing you are taking his sperm deep inside your body, holding it for several hours, feeling it as it moves around inside you. (Bareback.com – forum, online)

This belief in transcendence can also be traced in the discussions of gay male sexuality at BarebackJack.com,

> Bareback fucking is not a new thing. It's really the *normal* way people fuck. Has been for a hundred centuries. … What the politically correct generation has accomplished by this redefinition process [in coining the term bareback] is to cast new and less-favorable connotations onto the oldest form of pleasure known to man. (BarebackJack.com – letters, online)

And later,

> As gay men who bareback, we also know the forgotten pleasures of no-barrier sex, and feel comfortable carrying on his natural tradition. (ibid)

Thus, while the websites do differ greatly in their approach to bareback sex, both position bareback sex as an opportunity to reconnect gay men with their own bodies. In response to what Michael terms the 'condom Nazis', these two sites help to negotiate what they perceive to be a 'liberation' of the gay male body.

There were several reasons why I chose to look at these two websites. Not least is the fact that at the time of my initial research these were two of the most popular sites dedicated to barebacking and attracted more visitors and members than any such similar site. However, along with their popularity, it was their differences that intrigued me and I wanted to demonstrate how, in dealing with the criticism that barebacking has faced in mainstream gay culture, these two websites respond according to two very different trajectories. It is difficult to remain neutral in the face of such divergent responses. I admit that BarebackJack.com's commitment to opening up discussions about barebacking is an attitude that I personally find far more politically progressive, healthier and useful than the gruff adolescent posturing to be found at Bareback.com. Maintaining a dialogue between barebackers and the mainstream (whoever we choose to identify in that category) is imperative and sites such as BarebackJack.com may well provide spaces for such dialogue to be forged. However, as I shall demonstrate in the concluding section of this chapter, the cost of such a dialogue, framed within contemporary discourses of gay male digital culture, may well be higher than anticipated and contradictions between the ethos of such spaces and the way in which they are financed serves to further extend and complicate understandings of barebacking culture online.

BarebackJack.com and the politics of porn

As I have already mentioned, BarebackJack.com promotes itself first and foremost as a sexual health website. As with many health awareness websites (particularly those concerned with HIV), information is free to all users. But generosity can only go so far and, like many other barebacking websites, BarebackJack.com is partially funded through the sale of pornography, either directly (in the form of videos and DVDs) or indirectly (in the form of site membership, which allows access to online porn galleries and stories). Mirroring the content and remit of the website, the majority of this pornography depicts bareback sex and BarebackJack.com promotes video sales via the annual bareback porn awards, hosted by the website. Dean (2009: 52) identifies how 'pornographic representation is central to bareback subculture because it offers a form of witnessing' and such representation acts (like the Kasire murder photos discussed in Chapter 5) as more than just a recording of an event – bareback pornography is a part of the bareback scene.

Thus it is unsurprising to find that BarebackJack.com is also involved in pornographic film production and distribution and is tied to Desert Mirages Media, a relatively new Arizona-based gay porn studio. The site also serves as a recruitment ground for new bareback performers and a link to a microsite[26] provides an opportunity to apply directly to BarebackJack.com Productions. It is on this microsite that the limits of BarebackJack.com's ethos of openness and honesty are ultimately revealed:

> There are many reasons why we will not ask you about your HIV status in your application or on the set. We also do not permit discussion of HIV among our actors. (BarebackJack.com Productions, online)

According to State law it is illegal for prospective employers to ask potential employees about their HIV status[27]. This is undoubtedly a positive piece of legislation in the fight against discrimination based on HIV status and has been just

---

26 This microsite was live throughout 2004, the period in which the initial research for the case study was collected. Since then, the microsite has been sporadically offline, and it is currently unclear whether BarebackJack Productions is either recruiting, or indeed still continuing to produce bareback pornography. Having said that, BarebackJack.com continues to be heavily involved in the distribution, publicising and evaluation of bareback pornography and the argument made here remains relevant to online barebacking subculture.

27 There is similar anti-discrimination legislation in Britain.

one of the battles successfully fought and won by AIDS awareness campaigners on both sides of the Atlantic. To ask applicants their HIV status within the context of employment would be counter to current employment law. However, feeling that more justification is needed for this censorship, Jack goes on to (correctly) state that even a negative test result immediately before application is no guarantee of negative status at the time of performing.[28] Additionally, he states that there are no guarantees that actors either know or are inclined to be honest about their HIV status and at first glance this statement appears to echo the discourse of health awareness offered on the main website; each individual is responsible for his own sexual health and cannot rely on others to take on that responsibility.

Yet while these facts are medically and legally accurate, they also serve to reveal a central contradiction between the discourse of the main site and the advert for performers, a contradiction that highlights an underlying tension between the commercial and non-commercial aspects of BarebackJack.com. For example, having given legal and medical reasons behind the censorship of HIV status during the application process, Jack advises applicants to 'assume that the actor(s) you might be partnered with for the video are probably HIV positive'. Again, this advice is arguably correct[29] and safe sex campaigns in both Britain and America have operated along similar lines in the recent past[30]. Jack isn't *wrong* in promoting this strategy. But in acknowledging this we must also acknowledge that there is no suggestion of how to minimise the risk of HIV infection during bareback sex, no hyperlink to the health section of the main website and no discussion of risk negotiation. Of course, risk has been conceptualised as integral to bareback subculture. Dean (2009: 66) talks of 'embracing risk' in order to bypass the kinds of 'superegoistic health imperatives' that I mentioned in my discussion of self-surveillance in Chapter 3.

But such arguments (which I find difficult to uphold[31]) are open to contradiction. Elsewhere Jack himself validates the open discussion of HIV status as a key resource within safer barebacking, (namely within the main website discussed

28 HIV is generally regarded as having an 'incubation period' of up to three months (though cases where a positive result is generated up to six months after exposure are known) and actors would have to avoid sexual contact between (re)testing and filming.

29 In the same way that the assumption that anyone (be they an actor or just a casual partner) is negative is incorrect.

30 A recent (2009) advertising campaign run by Terrence Higgins Trust and aimed at London's gay community explicitly addresses the (false) assumptions people may make about their partner's HIV status, and encourages both condom use and discussion of sero-status in casual sexual encounters.

31 While Dean (2009) does make an important contribution to the discussion of barebacking, I take issue with his claims on a number of counts. Specifically, within the context of my discussion here, is the notion that to bareback is to circumvent practices of self-regulation and self-surveillance within a culture of risk. Responding to this, I would argue that the intense focus on working out, maintaining a particular body shape and performing a specific type of masculinity that bareback subculture and bareback

above). Risk negotiation is his *response* to the condom code. As such, the advice given in advertisement for bareback porn performers conflicts with the rhetoric of the main website; assuming HIV status (whether that be positive or negative) is never suggested in the health discourse of BarebackJack.com. In fact, BarebackJack.com's porn enterprise operates outside of – and in opposition to – the progressive framework of safer bareback practice promoted on the main website. This opposition lies in the fact that while HIV status is addressed within the advertisement, it is side-lined as an issue – it is not only off-topic but *off-limits*: in the words of Jack:

> We do not permit discussions of HIV among our actors. (BarebackJack.com Productions, online)

Such censorship contradicts BarebackJack.com's health pages and the commercial side of the operation, the method by which the health pages are funded, offer a starkly different and altogether more problematic attitude towards sexual health and HIV risk. These differences serve to enforce an awkward division between the performer and the consumer of bareback pornography. To put it another way, at BarebackJack.com the performer engages in unsafe sexual acts in an environment of censorship for the consumption and sexual enjoyment of the consumer, who is actively encouraged to adopt an entirely different attitude towards barebacking and HIV risk. While this, on its own, is a highly problematic dichotomy[32] it would seem that such a division proves highly difficult to maintain considering the fact that this advertisement forms part of the BarebackJack.com enterprise; it is from the community of consumers that the company hopes to recruit actors. In doing so, the self-governing consumer-subject is transformed into the censored performer.

In my discussion of cybcercarnality, in Chapter 3, I mentioned how the 'pornographication' of sexual health campaigns targeted at gay men, and the inclusion of pornographic material, has served to blur the boundaries between consumer and performer, and between pornography and education. Yet the conflicting discourses of BarebackJack.com run counter to this slippage, where a distinct separation between performer and consumer is fostered. BarebackJack.

pornography so often appears to demand are examples of the types of self-regulation that Dean claims barebackers escape through raw sex.

32 Elsewhere I have discussed the increasing porosity of categories such as 'consumer', 'producer' and 'performer' within digital pornography. Digital media technologies have provided the means by which the boundaries between these already loose and unstable categories have become further eroded. See Mowlabocus, 2009. O'Toole (1999) similarly identifies the fact that media technologies of production and distribution have meant that the line between performer and consumer has become even more blurred. From Reader's Wives, to amateur porn websites, to sexually explicit user profiles and homepages, to camera phones, the punter is interacting with pornography in ways that allow him/her to not only watch, but be watched, to perform and to be recorded.

com's recruitment site not only fails to provide a hyperlink to the health pages but also promotes an understanding of HIV that is antithetical to the main website. One might assume that individuals interested in becoming performers will already have visited the main website and will be fully versed in safer bareback practices. But this argument falls apart when we acknowledge the fact that anyone who has read, considered and taken on board the advice set out on the health pages will realise the dangers of barebacking in such a censorious environment.

BarebackJack.com's enterprise relies on separating out the performer from the official discourse of the website. It relies on excluding him from the various methods of negotiation, risk reduction and open dialogue, which are central to the notion of safer barebacking promoted on the main website. In doing so it provides the circumstances in which non-negotiated unsafe sex (often with several partners) can take place, with minimum legal risk to the production company and, of course with maximum profit. The commercial underpinnings of such spaces must be read within the context of cybercarnality and earlier (in Chapter 3) I demonstrated the preoccupation gay men appear to have with the construction of bodies in digital spaces. This construction, I contend, has also been subject to a process of consumption: the user profile constructs the gay male body only to then subject it to the fragmenting system of the search engine through which it is served up for consumption; the textual bodies of Uni_cock are always available for consumption by the invisible Other. A discourse of cybercarnality reveals the same central contradiction within bareback subculture. The gay male body is simultaneously 'liberated' via bareback sex and, paradoxically, commodified as the fetishising – and by extension, the promotion – of unsafe sexual practices threaten the body of the bareback performer, for the satisfaction of the (paying) consumer. One might even go so far as to claim that bareback pornography generates revenue out of the eroticism of risk, fear, infection and death.

This claim requires further substantiation and I shall briefly unpack this argument a little here. While it may be the case that barebacking and HIV do not go hand-in-hand within the main site, *representing* barebacking cannot be separated from *representing* HIV. Although barebackers such as Jack continue to argue for the separation of gay sex from the virus[33], and while this can be understood on some levels as a response to the policing of gay male sexuality, bareback pornography is a different matter. Barebacking may have developed as a response to HIV but bareback pornography has developed through the *eroticising* of HIV infection; the erotic appeal of bareback pornography comes specifically from transgressing the boundaries of safer sex: from literally risking lives.

I am not suggesting that bareback pornography is produced or promoted on the basis of sero-conversion – to my knowledge there are currently no commercial 'bug-chasing' titles available. Aside from the potential legal ramifications of such

33 Jack goes to great lengths in his discussion of barebacking to highlight an intrinsic difference between himself, gift-givers and bug-chasers (those who actively seek to infect/be infected by the virus).

a text, proving its 'authenticity' would be impossible. This is not to say that the *potential* for transmission is absent: it is in fact central to the erotic economy of bareback porn. Like all porn, bareback pornography relies on witnessing something taboo, something that shouldn't be seen. But in bareback porn, it is through the attendant discourses of HIV that the audience firstly comprehends and secondly gains satisfaction from the text.

The individual barebacker may form an argument in defence of barebacking (his decision to bareback being based on his dislike of condoms, of feelings of greater intimacy and pleasure, of a transcendental connection with his sexual partners), but bareback pornography, by virtue of being a *representation* of sex, can never make such an argument. The audience can enjoy watching raw sex, but the appeal can never be the same as the appeal that the barebacker claims as his reason for having raw sex. An audience can never experience the transcendental bond 'BB' practitioners claim to enjoy, nor can pornography ever deliver the sense of intimacy, passion and ecstasy that skin-2-skin sex allegedly offers. Which leaves us wondering exactly what the appeal of bareback porn is?

And considering that the only visual difference is the lack of a condom during the penetrative act, we must conclude that *risk* namely the risk of HIV transmission, is the primary erotic appeal of such pornography. As Dean (2009: 105) notes, 'unlike "pre-condom" gay porn produced during the 1970s and early 1980s, bareback porn is far from oblivious to HIV'. This marries with my ongoing assertion regarding the centrality of HIV to bareback subculture (even if HIV is not biologically present). If we accept that such risks of infection are integral to bareback pornography, and we also acknowledge the separation of performer and consumer that BarebackJack.com imposes, we must conclude that bareback subculture, whilst ostensibly concerned with reconnecting gay men with their bodies, is also deeply rooted within a much wider process of representation premised on objectifying that body; on turning a body into an object by exposing it to dangers for the erotic satisfaction of the paying consumer.

Conclusion

Bareback sex, the culture that surrounds it and the pornography made off of the back of it are provocative and challenging subjects to write about. When I first began researching this chapter I regularly found myself being asked what my position was on the issue. Instantly politicising this sexual practice (as if there were no alternative), colleagues, friends and health professionals demanded I take sides and identify myself as either for or against what was either a morally reprehensible act of utter selfishness or a sexually liberating act of queer defiance depending on where you stood. At the time (around 2004) almost no-one I spoke to offline admitted to barebacking. The Right-wing journalist and commentator, Andrew Sullivan, was famously 'exposed' as being the man behind the 'Rawmusclglutes' profile, hosted by barebackcity.com in 2001 and more recently Tim Dean (2009) 'outed' himself as a barebacker in his book *Unlimited Intimacy*. But barebacking remains something that comparatively few gay men are willing to openly admit to today on the gay scene.

Yet it remains a fact that while bareback sex between men may still be relatively taboo, bareback pornography has become an increasingly tolerated aspect of our subculture. At a think-tank seminar on bareback pornography, run by the Terrence Higgins Trust in 2008, one porn producer (who only made 'condom-porn') claimed that sales of his titles had fallen drastically since the rise of bareback pornography. XTube, the porn version of YouTube returns over 10,000 results on a search for 'bareback' sex and in the UK, gay sex shops now stock a wide range of bareback titles catering to a variety of tastes. While many of us may not be willing to talk about (un)safe sexual practices, it seems we're happy to pay to watch others take the risks.

Condemning barebacking has never been a productive course of action and I hope that this chapter has steered clear of this, though I freely admit I have critiqued and problematised elements of online bareback subculture. Anyone who thinks that raw sex can be stuffed back into the closet and hidden away is dangerously naïve, acting as ignorantly as those who choose to believe that HIV doesn't really exist. HIV exists and so does barebacking. Neither, it seems, is going to be disappearing any time soon. This chapter has demonstrated how gay men are using digitally-created and maintained spaces in order to form a voice and speak up about their right to, desire of and preference for bareback sex. These voices, no matter how contrary they may be to some, need to be listened to and demand serious attention and understanding. At the same time, the economic structure that lies behind the online barebacking scene is fraught with tensions between sexual liberation and commercial gain. I hope I have been able to negotiate this rocky terrain and illustrate some of the challenges, contradictions and problems that websites such as BarebackJack.com and Bareback.com face in both maintaining and funding their line of argument.

Finally I hope I have demonstrated, once more, the impact that digital forms of communication, particularly the Internet, have had on contemporary gay male subculture. This is particularly visible within the context of barebacking not least because whereas cybercottaging and Gaydar both have their offline predecessors, barebacking exists, in part, because of digital ICTs and it is only as a result of spaces such as those websites discussed here, that a subculture of barebackers has been able to be formed and maintained. It is therefore unsurprising that such a subculture is deeply invested in the themes identified in cybercarnality in Chapter 3.

Chapter 7

Digital Cruising: Mobile and Locative Technologies in Gay Male Subculture

While carrying out research for the other case studies presented in this book, I became increasingly aware of a range of practices some gay men were engaging in while 'on the move'. Stories of using Bluetooth to 'cruise' on public transport started to reach me around 2005 and more recently I've witnessed an increasing interest in gay social networking applications designed to be used on mobile devices such as Apple's iPhone. It will probably come as no surprise that this chapter consists of the most recent research undertaken for this project. In the introduction to this book I expressed the need to see the case studies presented here as historically situated – a series of snapshots taken across a ten year period, which represent aspects of gay male digital culture at specific points in its emergence and development. This chapter represents the most recent snapshot and seeks to identify shifts that have occurred within gay subculture as a result of both recent technological developments and recent appropriations of 'older' digital technologies. If, in 2001 when I first started my research, Gaydar was the hot topic that men were talking about on the scene, then the host of technologies, practices and behaviours that I explore in this chapter are, perhaps, set to become the contemporary equivalent.

This chapter focuses on issues of movement, space and access as they present themselves within gay men's digital culture towards the end of the first decade of the 21st century. In doing so, my discussion builds upon and acknowledges the findings in earlier chapters of this book and uses them to begin exploring how gay men's use of digital technologies has begun to alter, develop and respond to the increasingly mobile experience of such technologies. Unlike the previous chapters, this discussion is not organised around a specific case study and while I refer to specific websites, applications and practices in what follows, I have chosen to move away from the representational model (that I've adopted in Chapters 4–6), and instead offer a broader discussion that takes in a wider range of technologies, techno-practices and techno-spaces. In doing so, I hope to provide a multifaceted discussion of these emerging practices and demonstrate how they connect with other aspects of gay men's everyday experiences.

In 2004, Herring (34) offered a prophecy for the future of digital culture, suggesting that:

> Increasing technological integration, combined with assimilation of day-to-day uses and the corresponding need to ensure the trustworthiness of one's interlocutors, will continue to make the internet a simpler, safer, and – for better or for worse – less fascinating communication environment.

At the end of the first decade of the 21st century this prophecy appears to have been borne out. New technologies (such as mobile Internet and mobile communication devices), twinned with new applications and services (such as Twitter and Facebook) have served to further integrate computer-mediated communication into our everyday lives, and we increasingly experience such communication within mundane and 'ordinary' contexts. The Internet – and Internet-based practices – have become objects and acts that we engage in and with, often while doing other things. Indeed, the communication practices generated by digital technologies might now in fact be understood as mundane and ordinary themselves. It is towards such mundane acts of communication that I turn my attention here and it is the 'everyday' aspects of gay men's lives that I have at the forefront of my mind in this chapter.

Using material taken from semi-structured interviews with twelve gay men, promotional material from commercial networking services and posts made to forums on cruising websites, I want to construct a critical reading of emergent forms, which collectively I label 'digital cruising', in order to consider how issues of space, identification and connectivity pervade these new practices. The analysis is split into two sections. In the first, I will consider how mobile forms of digital communication are serving to create 'hybrid spaces' that reconfigure the spaces and places gay men move through and in which they encounter one another. Leading on from this, I explore the content and meaning of those digital encounters and, responding to Miller's (2009) notion of 'phatic culture', I argue for a re-evaluation of 'pervasive communication' (Kindberg and Jones, 2007: 2). This re-evaluation acknowledges the specific relationship that gay people have with issues of 'placelessness' (Knopp, 2004) and of movement and migration.

Background

While there is little to nothing of note written about Bluetooth and mobile web deployment among gay men (the latter being a relatively new concept in Britain), the use of Bluetooth (in particular) by heterosexual men and women has been repeatedly acknowledged in the international press. Use among men and women living in Islamic states such as Qatar, Dubai, the UAE and Saudi Arabia is well documented and stories proliferate in the global news media. These often focus on men who drive around sending Bluetooth messages and photos to nearby 'discoverable' mobile phones that have female or feminine sounding usernames. Sullivan (2006) documented one such case in Saudi Arabia:

> Thobaity, 23, pushed a button on his cellphone and activated Bluetooth, a short-range wireless function that is standard on most new cellphones. Within seconds, the girl's Bluetooth screen name popped up on his cell's glowing display. He laughed: She called herself 'Spoiled,' which matched the flashy Daddy's Girl car. Excited, flustered, using his left hand to steer, he clicked on her name and sent her a text message with his phone number.

Three years later, in the same country, Mazen Abdul-Jawad was found guilty of 'promoting vice' and sentenced to five years imprisonment and 1,000 lashes following a televised interview in which the Saudi citizen 'boasted' of having had sex with numerous women. In the interview he described how he had used Bluetooth to meet and correspond with his sexual partners. Strict religious laws governing contact between genders in many Gulf States have forced men and women to become resourceful in their dating and courtship practices. The ubiquity of Bluetooth-enabled mobiles provides a popular method of circumventing the Mutaween – the name given to the religious police, whose job it is to ensure that 'moral laws' are upheld – especially those that involve gender and gender difference.

I have come across stories of how Bluetooth outwits the strict segregation in place in a Starbucks in Abha, Saudi Arabia (Bielski, 2009), and of young women conversing with men in the shopping malls of Dubai using short-range technologies, in spite of cultural taboos that forbid unsupervised interactions between single men and *any* women other than family members (Hiel, 2007). In Italy, sites such as Bluetooth.it have helped to support and popularise burgeoning 'toothing communities' (*Townsville Bulletin*, 2006) and a report in the British press claimed that British men and women were integrating Bluetooth into their dating practices (*News of the World*, 16th April 2006).

Meanwhile, back in the Middle East, posts on international cruising forums and gay websites have mentioned using Bluetooth to find potential gay sex partners in hotels and other public spaces. With the crime of 'sodomy' carrying a maximum sentence of death by stoning, sex between men is forbidden under Shari'a law and gay men operate in many of the Gulf States under the shadow of such oppression. Like their heterosexual counterparts, these men are also appropriating a technology that was originally conceived as being purely for sharing data between known devices, in order to evade detection and almost certain punishment.

Such use chimes with Bilandzic *et al.*'s (2009: 1517) assertion that 'users often materialize a specific communication technology for rather unexpected purposes that the respective medium was not intentionally designed for' and the relationship between mobile ICTs and sexual practice is beginning to be documented within scholarly circles. Hearn (2008:42) has written of the 'increasing technical possibilities for many-to-many 'social software' and 'new sexual affordances' for mutual identification', citing the 'Yenta' Jewish dating service, which uses web and phone technologies for matchmaking purposes as an example. Meanwhile, Bell's (2006) work on 'dogging' identifies the intrinsic role that Internet and mobile phone technologies play within this heterosexual public sex subculture. However, while anecdotal evidence, commercial enterprises and the popular press suggest that Bluetooth is being used by gay men for social and sexual purposes, the process of researching this phenomena proved to be somewhat more challenging. Sourcing interview participants for this chapter was a long and protracted process and initial requests for participation were met with refusals – normally on the grounds that they 'didn't really get it'.

Having recognised early on that such practices were 'underground' and not as visible as, for instance having a Gaydar profile was, I was unsurprised to find recruitment a challenge. However, through the course of wider research into gay men's use of digital media when travelling, I was able to interview twelve gay men, around half of whom had used Bluetooth to cruise other men. Some of the twelve had also migrated onto newer web-based platforms, which I consider later in this chapter, and all incorporated mobile phones into their dating/cruising activities. Having indicated that the interview would cover a range of technologies and a range of use-contexts, I asked each interviewee towards the end of the interview if they had ever used Bluetooth or another mobile-based service to locate or identify or search for other gay men – irrespective of the reason. Most of the interviewees had heard of such practices although usage varied across the cohort.

An additional challenge to researching these phenomena lies in the fact that such practices are fragile and precarious in their nature. Some of the practices that my respondents identified rely on participants being physically near one another, while others rely on a level of attentiveness on both sides of the communicative act. As more than one participant identified, such attentiveness was regularly challenged as these techno-practices were conceived of as 'something to do while waiting', or 'something that killed time'. I shall return to this in more detail later as the transitory nature of the communication is a defining element of its practice.

These issues regarding knowledge, attentiveness and network fragility were summed up by one interviewee, who had recently started using Grindr[1], a mobile Internet application designed for the iPhone,

> this Grindr profile, this Grindr application on the iPhone its just, its opened up a new world really erm … if you're bored, waiting at a bus stop, load it up 'hi how you doing?' and then – I'm not sure of the etiquette. But people seem to send short messages 'you alright?' and then they just go and that's it. It's a bit of chat,

1 Grindr is a mobile 'app' developed for the iPhone and designed as a gay social networking tool. The service provides men with the opportunity to create a profile (not dissimilar, though smaller than a Gaydar profile), which is then visible on the Grindr database. The key to the service's success, however, is in the locative power of the iPhone. Using the device's GPS and WiFi/3G capabilities, Grindr not only displays users who are online, but it also records their current distance from the browser. A more extensive discussion of this type of application follows later in this chapter.

> chat chat and then they might disappear … there seems to be a lot of cut outs, but you can exchange pictures. (Philip, 33)

Having only recently subscribed to the service, Philip expressed uncertainty regarding precisely how users interacted with each other and what the correct 'etiquette' was. Phillip, who had used the Internet extensively in order to construct a sense of self, and to meet other gay men when coming out, had a good working knowledge of both Gaydar and Gay.com, and understood the sub-cultural rules of engagement that operated on these 'static' websites. Having recently deleted his profile on Gaydar, he now found himself in the position of being a newbie once more, needing to negotiate the terrain of this new mobile networking service. He commented that he had already begun to employ certain rules in order to assess the veracity of a profile:

> I think there's a lot of fake profiles, there's a lot of beautiful people on there and I don't think they're genuine profiles, so some of the pictures are too perfect. … It's more realistic if they've got, if they've taken a picture with the iphone [gestures to suggest taking a picture in the mirror using a mobile phone] so you think 'oh they've taken it' it may not be them but at least you know its an iphone picture and its not touched up and a fake profile. (Phillip, 33)

The practices I want to consider here are varied and operate across a variety of mobile digital platforms. They share in common the fact that, to different extents, they depend on users moving through physical space and this dependence creates complex and myriad relationships with different types of space. This focus on rearticulating space through digital interventions builds on and extends recent work on mobile phone use, mobile Internet uptake, laptop use and mobile gaming (see Bull, 2004; Garcia-Montes *et al.*, 2006; Daliot-Bul, 2007; Bittman *et al.*, 2009; Bassett, 2009). Much of this work has developed in response to mobile phone ubiquity, or a perceived 'unshackling' of the Internet (from fixed landlines, desktops and Ethernet connection points), or the mobilising of web access via Wi-Fi, WiMax and 3G networks. Of course these different technological developments cannot be fully separated, and the mobile web was preceded by the global uptake of the mobile phone, to the point where it is now 'an important location for contemporary culture and its reproductions and variation' (Goggin, 2009: 231).

I shall label the practices that I'm analysing in this chapter, 'digital cruising' and in doing so, I want to highlight both the methods by which these communicative acts take place (the digital), and the rich sub-cultural history that such acts draw upon (cruising). One might argue that browsing profiles on Gaydar or posting messages in a cybercottage might also be acts of digital cruising, and the phrase 'online cruising' has certainly been used to describe such acts. However, in using the term 'digital cruising', I want to underline a specific difference between these 'earlier' forms of net-enabled interaction and newer forms of communicative practice. This difference – and the reason why I specifically employ the term here – relates to the *mobility* of the latter – the live, 'on the go', opportunistic and serendipitous facet of digital cruising. As one interviewee commented, 'with Gaydar you've got to sit there, you've got to turn the computer on and send a message'. By contrast digital cruising is seen as being much more simple; 'I mean it's pretty easy'.

Digital cruising can thus be conceived of as a constellation of communicative acts that take place between men via any one of a number of mobile interfaces, as they move through the physical spaces of their everyday life. In doing so digital cruising echoes the claim made by Bilandzic *et al.* (2009: 1517), that users of mobile technologies may form 'their own set of distinct social practices around the ICT of mobile telephony' and that such practices may have little to do with the intended utility of the technology. Digital cruising also realises Barton's (2009: 93) claim that the mobile device 'enables physical, communicative and thereby social mobility' and 'dramatically reinserts specific location into digital space'. As such, digital cruising might be considered to be one iteration of 'a new genre of computing: interaction-in-the-wild' (94).

In line with conventional understandings of cruising, such acts do not necessarily signal more than an acknowledgement, perhaps an appreciation, of the queer other. Nevertheless cruising remains a powerful and recognisable trope within gay male culture. As I have already discussed elsewhere in this book, gay/queer cultures have a complex relationship with issues of visibility (see also Healy, 1996 and Tattelman, 1999) and cruising is an integral part of that relationship. Male homosexuality was legalised in Britain less than fifty years ago and prior to this time, homosexual relationships were not only invalid, they were unlawful. The lack of recognition historically afforded homosexual relationships and identities has meant that gay men have had to be resourceful. If straight culture has bound itself up in convention, gay people long ago learned to rely on *opportunity*. While writing up this chapter, a link popped up in my Twitter feed. The content of the linked webpage seemed so serendipitous I am compelled to quote extensively from it here, not least because the sentiment it expresses some of the themes and arguments expressed in this chapter:

> If you are a Jew like me (love you Mum!), you will know the importance of Passover. Once a year, my family gets together to dip apples in honey, eat matzo ball soup and fight with the relatives … We do it each year because it's a tradition—something our forefathers did before us and their forefathers before them … Which brings me, inevitably, to cruising … You know what that is. You are standing against a wall minding your own business and some bloke smiles or winks at you from across the way. You check him out and then he walks away. You follow him to where he ducks into a side street and voila—you are in the middle of a hot anonymous sexual encounter. … This is as much a tradition in the gay community as Passover is in the Jewish one. Years and years of oppression had lead to the divine necessity to get our cocks out in public areas and fornicate with one another. Sure, it can get ugly, and it doesn't always lead to revelation but it's part of the fabric and history of gaydom. It has allowed

> our forefathers to get their rocks off when there was simply nowhere else to do it, and it has created some of the most fabulous sessions of beachside sex our community could dare hope for. So let's protect it, as a fundamental right—just like religious freedom. The freedom for gay men to fornicate in pre-designated areas is a God-given right. One as important as a matzo ball, and, in some cases (but not all) just as tasty. (Buckingham, 2009: online)

Cam Buckingham, the author of this quotation was writing in response to claims that residents in the Canal Street area of Manchester (a major gay village in the UK) were complaining of men cruising out on 'their' streets. Such expressions of 'public' distaste, complaint and outcry serve to remind us of the politics of public space and, particularly, of the fact that such space is more often than not coded as heterosexual, or rather, heteronormative. Buckingham not only identifies the opportunism and public-ness of cruising, he also alludes to its historical place within gay male subculture, unashamedly celebrating cruising as a part of our culture.

The practices I document in this chapter do not necessarily result in sexual contact but irrespective of whether digital cruising leads to sex or not, Buckingham's argument remains relevant to a discussion of this techno-practice because it identifies the political dimension inherent in looking at another man in public and positions cruising as a part of the 'fabric' of gay subculture. Thus digital cruising relies on the 'existing social norms' established within gay cruising culture in the same way that other techno-practices, such as 'beeping'[2] rely on established conventions found in other cultural contexts (Donner, 2007: np).

Cruising (like Cottaging) is always 'tactical' (De Certeau, 1984: xix), not only because it regularly takes place within contexts that are avowedly heterosexist, but also because the notion of looking at another man is fraught with anxieties in Western culture (see Chapter 3). Cruising opens up transitory spaces that articulate homosexual desires and identifications and I want to suggest that digital cruising approaches this queering of space through the creation of 'hybrid spaces', which rely on and exploit the tension between physical and digital environments. In this respect cruising can be thought of as a response to the sense of 'placelessness' queer people contend with in societies that privilege, and normalise heterosexuality:

> We [queer people] are keenly aware of the hybrid nature of our existences, and of the highly contingent nature of both our power and the constraints on it. Hence our ambivalent relationships to place and identity, and our affection for placelessness and movement. (Knopp, 2004: 129)

---

2 'Beeping' is the practice of phoning someone's mobile phone and hanging up before the receiver picks up the call. The motivations for engaging in this practice of intentionally missed calling are varied and depend on context, as well as relationship between caller and receiver (see Donner, 2007 for a comprehensive discussion).

My use of the term 'hybrid space' refers to the work of Adriana de Souza e Silva, whose definition I draw on in order to develop a critical framework through which we can comprehend digital cruising. I shall begin this analysis here with an extended quotation taken from one of the research interviews.

> I've used Bluetooth. I've been cruised with Bluetooth actually. … I was on the tube in Madrid … and I'd got on at the far end [of the line] Some lad got on, he was really cute, he was South-American … Anyway then the train filled up a bit and my phone went and it was a Bluetooth message and it was a picture of him. So I kinda saw him through the people, and the train is getting busier and busier and busier as the train is heading in to the centre of Madrid and he was checking whether I had checked it and then he smiled at me to make sure I'd made the connection between [him and the message] but actually, he must have been broadcasting to the entire [carriage] … unless he picked my phone out?
>
> Anyway, at each stop he sent a more and more graphic picture to me, made it very clear what he was interested in and what he wanted me to do to him, and then when I got off the train he got off the train and he called me by name, because of course my phone had my name on it. It was quite odd to have a stranger who'd gone from being a total random stranger, to having seen the intimate side of him, calling out my name. And then I went and had sex with him and it was really nice. (Frank, 41)

It transpired that this form of 'Bluejacking'[3] was something that Frank's sexual partner (let's call him Ernesto) engaged in on a regular basis. The metro line chosen is important for two reasons. Firstly, it cuts through Chueca, the heart of Madrid's gay district. Anyone familiar with gay Europe will know that Spain's capital has a thriving gay scene and is something of a mecca for European bear culture.[4] Much of the scene is based in and around Chueca, a formerly rundown district near downtown Madrid. Travelling Line 5 (the name of line on which the above interaction took place) provides Ernesto with the best opportunity to connect with men who might be interested in sex with him as they travel to, from and around this gay epicentre.

Secondly, the choice of line is important because Ernesto uses it to commute between his home and the two low-paid jobs he is forced to work. As an illegal immigrant, Ernesto faces few employment options and needs to stay off the

---

3 'Bluejacking' is a term used to describe the appropriation of Bluetooth technology to send short messages, often to strangers, as one passes nearby. Bluejacking can be social or antisocial, friendly or malevolent. The message, often stored as a business card often includes a greeting (such as 'hi, you've been bluejacked'). I have also witnessed pornographic images being sent in this manner too. More details can be found on the Bluejacking online resource, bluejackq.com (online).

4 For more information about bear culture in Spain, visit Mad.bear.org (online).

radar as far as possible. He works as a waiter and as a kitchen porter in two different locations and uses the metro system to move between them. Line 5 is not so much a destination for Ernesto but a structuring device within his daily life – an unavoidable journey that he has to take as he shuttles between his shared accommodation and two work sites. As Frank recalled in interview:

> He [Ernesto] got on the tube two hours before he had to work – he worked in a hotel, it was quite convenient – and then he'd pick someone up and he'd shag them, either at their place or at the hotel, and then he'd go to work.

Line 5 is thus positioned as both the quotidian *and* the erotic, offering a site of potential sexual adventure within the context of (migrant) flows of labour. Through his digital cruising, and the sending of explicit photos and text, Ernesto performs Rechy's sexual outlaw (1978) both in response to and as a result of the monotonous commute he is forced to undertake day in and day out. My interviewee, clearly fascinated at how Ernesto had picked him up, recalled the details of the messages as such:

> The first one was a picture of him on the train [taken in real time] to say 'this is me', the next one was him on the beach with his pants on, the next one was him on the Playa, naked, and then there was one of him in his bathroom, … and there was one of him being shagged by someone, and the final one was a question mark. He'd planned it – he knew what he was doing – that was his mode.

Frank explained that Ernesto didn't feel welcome in the bars and clubs of Madrid, owing to his ethnicity. Alongside issues of racism (though arguably the two are interlinked in multiple ways) was the issue of economics, and Ernesto found the drinks and door charge of many of Madrid's gay bars and clubs too expensive. So it was to more 'underground' spaces – namely the subway system – that he turned when he wanted to meet men.

Technologies harnessed within the daily commute serve to construct new uses for, and new meanings of space (Caronia, 2005) and can extend the sense of private space during periods of travel (see Sheller and Urry, 2003 and Bull, 2007). Scholars such as Ito *et al.* (2008) and Hampton *et al.* (2009) have identified the creation of private spaces and 'bubbles' of privacy through mobile communication technologies. But while some commuters may be using mobile technologies to escape their physical environment, or to individualise it through the creation of personal soundscapes, others are engaging with their fellow passengers, winking, flirting, chatting and possibly (though not always) arranging to meet up, either on the train or at the end of the journey. Evidence of this can be found on the popular cruising website, Squirt.org, where posts to local forums[5] identify the use of Bluetooth to cruise for sex on commuter trains,

> Bi guy on 7am train from [home location] to [work location] every morning … BLUETOOTH … BI GUY COCKSUCKER .. why not have some fun … normally in 4 carriages (at the front).
>
> Train to London around 7:30/8 tomorrow am. Bluetooth will be on to see who's around!
>
> I'll be at [name of service station] today from 11am for about an hour, looking for some fun. I'll have my Bluetooth on in the toilet with an obvious title. Please message me via Bluetooth to arrange it. Hope to see you..

During another interview, one respondent summed up the experience of using Bluetooth for social – and sexual – purposes when he recalled the hour-long train commute he used to make every weekday. When I asked him if he'd ever come across Bluetooth being used for cruising, his response was enthusiastic to say the least:

> Oh god yeah, yeah … it was the most amazing thing. It was the safest way [to communicate], anonymous and erm and very short-span [meaning it didn't last very long] … people would make contacts [address book entries] and the contacts would be 'hi how are you' so when you go on Bluetooth and you are discoverable and you are accepting these things you see these people – and some of their names are funny of course – and you can send contacts to that person, which would be 'hi how are you' no content but this'd be in the title. So you'd be on the train and it was brilliant, so on the train and it was about a year's time that it was happening, and it was fantastic and it was free and erm, almost everybody has a phone. (Craig, 38)

The interviewee went on to recall an experience in which he had met a guy using Bluetooth, and, following a relatively innocent start, the communication had become more flirtatious until finally, when the train pulled in to its destination, the pair left the station together and had sex in a semi-public location nearby. The entire communicative process (though not the sex[6]) took place in full view of other

---

5 'Local' in the sense that each forum is identified as pertaining to a physical location such as a city or county.

6 In this instance the interviewee did not engage in 'public sex' at the site of the communication (namely a train). However, he later spoke extensively about an extended interaction that he had with a fellow commuter, whom he first began communicating with via mobile phone screens (text as opposed to voice calls). This interaction, which spanned

passengers on a packed commuter train and neither participant knew the other when they began 'chatting'.

Craig also discussed the 'pursuit' element of his Bluetooth experiences, explaining that 'you'd try and figure out who it is [in the carriage] is it a man is it a woman? Gay, Straight? It was fascinating'. This ties in with Kindberg and Jones' (2007: 3) argument that Bluetooth is a '*partially embodied* medium', located 'somewhere between the wholly embodied medium of a face-to-face conversation, and the wholly disembodied medium of an Internet chat between physically dissociated strangers'.

Along with a shift in embodiment, I would argue that such practices serve to create new 'layers' of communicative space and push us to consider new understandings of the spaces we move through. The appropriation of this techno-practice suggests that men are finding ways of communicating sexual desires within contexts that would not otherwise provide for such negotiation.

Adriana de Souza e Silva (2006: 262) identifies and argues for a new category of space, defining it as follows:

> Hybrid spaces are mobile spaces, created by the constant movement of users who carry portable devices continuously connected to the Internet and to other users.

Hybrid space recognises the increasingly mobile nature of the Internet (and, I would add, other forms of digital communication) but offers a different understanding of such mobility to those encapsulated in terms such as 'augmented reality' and 'augmented space', (where digital information such as maps, advertising or signposting are layered over material spaces) or 'mixed realty' (which generally signals a blurring and slippage between digital and physical spaces). Of chief concern here is the fact that 'a hybrid space is *not* constructed by technology. It is built by the connection of mobility and communication and materialised by social networks developed simultaneously in physical and digital spaces' (265–6*)*. In this respect, hybrid space rearticulates pre-existing relationships between space, subject and technology. Bratton (2009: 92) argues that through mobile technologies 'foundational, even primal conditions are now reanimated (layering effects, invisible information made visible, physical computation, collapsed distances, remote control etc.) that cannot be reduced to a new digital sheen on an old analogue world'. Hybrid spaces continue to 'reanimate' the material world through mobile interfaces and the networks maintained through them. To quote de Souza once more:

> Mobile technology users take the nomadic concept one step further, because not only their paths are mobile but also the nodes. With the fixed Internet, and

---

several months, concluded in a sexual act taking place amidst a packed commuter train one morning.

> fixed landlines, computers and telephones were primarily connected to places. Conversely cell phones represent movable connection points accompanying their users' movements in physical spaces. (2006: 267)

Unlike other forms of digital space, hybrid spaces cannot be constructed in advance. They are not something to 'go to' and the space is never fully fixed. Instead, hybrid spaces are fragile, maintained through precarious networks that come into being only to 'melt' away and be re-formed in different places, through different 'nodes'. Kindberg and Jones (2007: 12) assert that 'as Bluetooth users move around urban places, they typically know less about the changing presences [other people] nearby' and we might understand such places as 'passings', which Knopp (2004: 129) describes as 'fluid and ephemeral, always contingent and always in the process of becoming'. Garcia-Montes *et al.* (2006: 78) suggest that mobile phones create a 'new kind of subject' who acts as 'a sort of node in a web of social relationships that is woven and unwoven according to quite variable and diverse circumstances'. The same can be said for hybrid space, which is conceptualised by its *potential* to contain networks and connections between the nodes that flow into and through it – like commuters getting on and off a train:

> In this movement, not only the nodes of the network become mobile, but also the paths through which they move are critical to the configuration of the network. (de Souza e Silva, 2006: 267)

The connections created by digital cruising often exist for a matter of minutes, sometimes even seconds. It is therefore not only physical space that determines the creation of hybrid space and the mobile network, it is also *time*; such as the time it takes for the metro to travel from stop-to-stop, or for a user to get distracted by work or other duties, or for the network to be interrupted by signal drop-outs.

This is as true for web-based digital cruising as it is for Bluetooth-enabled contact. While the former provides for far greater coverage and reach, a focus on the local continued to come to the fore during interviews. And despite the constant web connection that the latest 3G handsets provide users, the fragility of these communications was also noted:

> I mean on Grindr a lot of gay guys are really flaky and I just think 'do you want to meet or don't you want to meet?' because if you don't I won't be asking again but they sort of like, show a bit of interest and like then they fizzle out, its like hot cold, hot cold all the time. (Phillip)

Grindr, along with similar services such as Purpll and Boy Ahoy, is available through Apple's iPhone and iPod Touch series and these 'gay social networking' tools have attracted well over a million users to date. In all three cases, the GPS and Internet capabilities of the hardware are harnessed, allowing users to not only view profiles, but also to identify how near the corresponding individual is to their current location. These applications draw on established modes of interaction within gay male digital culture. Each service requires the user to build a profile, through which they are represented to other subscribers, and my earlier analysis of user profiles applies equally well to these 'mobile' profiles. I shall not repeat the points I've made elsewhere other than to remark that similar issues regarding the types of bodies represented, the forms of masculinity performed, and the language with which users describe themselves are apparent on these 'Apps'.

However, while these services may look similar to conventional dating/sex websites, they maintain a far closer relationship with the spaces through which users move. The basic premise is that not only can users look at profiles, they can also find out how close the corresponding men are. Using GPS technology, the services track members' whereabouts and display this information alongside their profile:

> Whether he's Mr. Right or Mr. Tonight, your man is hanging out on Grindr, a killer location-based social networking tool for the iPhone or iPod Touch. (Grindr, online)

In what is perhaps the most direct digital iteration of the term 'Gaydar' – the original use of the term as opposed to the website – these applications 'scan' the local area and allow the user to not only see who else nearby is subscribed to the service, but also provide the means for instant communication. Dean (2009: 175) laments the loss of cruising culture's 'publicness', which he blames on the isolating experience of online cruising. While services such as Grindr also prioritise the individual, placing him behind an (albeit smaller) screen, digital cruising can and does occur 'on the street' and may serve to reintegrate gay men back into public space in a manner that accommodates Dean's ambition. In contrast to the solitary experience of checking out profiles on a desktop PC then, we might best understand digital cruising practices as an attempt to revitalise what Dean regards as an 'indispensible component of urban gay life' (177).

As Boy Ahoy states in its advertising material 'in a bar hanging out or just chilling at home? Just pick up your iPhone and see who's around' (Macworld, online). Such networking tools rely not only on the physical spaces through which users move, but also the 'quality' of that space – who is nearby at any one time, who is moving through that bar, or club, or train or service station. Indeed, it is the movement *through* physical space that provides the most enjoyment. As one blogger comments in relation to Purpll 'it's fun to just see who is on and gay *around* you' (Purpll, online, author's emphasis).

Time and again interviewees were only interested in who was physically close-by, and who was passing by. In other words, many interviewees engaged in these practices because they allowed them to see who else nearby was gay or 'into men'. During one interview, 'Daniel' pulled out his iPhone and began scanning the local area using Grindr. 'Look!' he said, pointing to one of the profiles listed, 'He's 5 metres away! He could be in my flat!' Daniel's astonishment that Grindr had located another gay man in such close proximity also seemed to compound his feeling that his private space wasn't really that private. Earlier in the interview he bemoaned the lack of privacy his flat offered him, it being overlooked by several neighbouring buildings. Daniel appeared unnerved as he studied his own Grindr profile, commenting that not only could people physically see him, he was now also visible via this digital interface. Of course on one level Daniel was aware of this, the whole point of Grindr is to see and *be seen*. But on another level, he seemed anxious at the thought that Grindr might be contributing to the publicising of his private life through the hybridising of his everyday space. Bassett (2009, 43) recently asserted the need to recognise 'how pockets of game space and game time … contribute to the increasingly complex fabric of everyday life, particularly everyday life as it is lived in public'. In that moment, Grindr revealed to Daniel not only the complexity, but also the increasingly public and hybridised nature, of the spaces he occupied on a daily basis.

In another interview, Christopher commented on an incident that had happened the previous evening, when using one of these services,

> Last night it went a bit funny and all these people just popped up and they were all like no feet away from me … yes, they were all in my room! And then [it turned out] they were all in Canada, Alberta Canada so I'd been like teleported over there!

Of course Christopher did not believe he had been teleported to Alberta, but the language that he uses to describe this software error perhaps reveals less about the accuracy of the service and more about the levels of 'physical' investment that digital cruising requires of the user. I shall return to the theme of space later in this chapter but now I wish to turn my attention from how men connect to one another, to what it is they're saying to one another (or not, as the case maybe) when they maintain a sense of 'connected presence' in public space.

'Alright Mate ;-)': Reclaiming phatic communion through digital cruising

Many of the descriptions of digital cruising that I encountered during my research included mention of people 'disappearing' from the network, signal cut-outs, breaks in the service and users being 'flaky'. Meanwhile the participants themselves commented that digital cruising was an activity that didn't require much investment or commitment. Interviewees suggested that such activity was something to do when 'you've got nothing to do' or 'whilst you're doing something else'. Digital cruising also seems to rely on relatively small amounts of information being transmitted (especially in the case of Bluejacking). 'Alright mate?' and 'how's it going?' seem to be popular messages to send. Of course, sometimes the communication goes further than this; as the illustrations above demonstrate, some of these connections do result in intimate contact, often in the form of casual public sex.

Yet for every illustration that ended in ejaculation, there was one that didn't move past 'first base'. The lack of stability, shallowness of content and ephemeral nature of digital cruising means that these fleeting communications often resulted in nothing more than the equivalent of a wink, a smile or a (knowing) look.

Malinowski (1923: 314–316) coined the term 'phatic communion' to describe forms of speech that served no informational purpose but which were, nevertheless, central to all cultures:

> There is in all human beings the well-known tendency to congregate, to be together, to enjoy each other's company. ... speech is the intimate correlate of this tendency ... 'phatic communion' ... serves to establish bonds of personal union between people brought together by the mere need of companionship and does not serve any purpose of communicating ideas.

Malinowski's term has been used across a range of disciplines, most notably within the field of linguistics (see Zegarac and Clark, 1999; McCarthy, 2003, Herring, 2007). Within the study of mobile digital communication, Donner (2007: np) citing Ling (2004) has suggested that text messages and beeping offer a 'a second class' of communication 'whose function is "grooming," rather than coordination'. This, he considers a 'form of 'phatic' communication', the messages serving to nurture or reinforce relationships rather than to convey information. Daliot-Bul (2007: 956) similarly suggests that Keitai use by Japanese youth is less about the informational than it is about the relational:

> Mobile texting is based on short, phatic communication used for maintaining social contact and conveying feelings rather than exchanging information or ideas. It creates a playful and emotional connectedness among friends. It is about *feeling* and *reaffirming* the connection.

More recently, Miller (2009) has referred to the 'phatic' in his analysis of online social networking practices, taking as his departure point the types of communication afforded by services such as Twitter, Facebook and blogging sites, which often provide users with the means to remain connected to digital networks. His concept of 'phatic culture' provides a critical framework for understanding both the types of 'networked sociality' (Wittel, 2001) occurring via mobile interfaces and the type of communication orchestrated and transmitted through such networks. Miller appears roundly critical of phatic culture's focus on the network rather than the transmission, a focus, which, he argues, is the result of a flattening out of social bonds and communication practice:

> In the drift from blogging, to social networking, to microblogging we see a shift from dialogue and communication between actors in a network, where the point

> of the network was to facilitate an exchange of substantive content, to a situation where the maintenance of a network itself has become the primary focus. Here communication has been subordinated to the role of the simple maintenance of ever expanding networks and the notion of connected presence. (398)

Recognising that a culture of 'phatic media' has a purpose – namely the commodification of personal information for marketing purposes – Miller displays a strong ambivalence towards phatic culture. In his discussion of the microblogging service Twitter, for example, he regards the 'stripped down' nature of the 'tweet' (a message sent via the service, and containing no more than 140 characters) as creating an 'almost ghostly series of brief texts, conveying random thoughts, current activities, or brief greetings' (396). This culture of short, content-less (or at least content-lite) communicative acts are, he posits, the result of an 'individualisation' of society and he sees the rise of phatic media reflecting 'a process in which communities and personal relationships, social forms and commitments are less bound by history, place and tradition' (338). This builds on Bauman's (2001: 151) assertion that 'identity sprouts on the graveyard of communities, but flourishes thanks to its promise to resurrect the dead', and Miller reveals his attitude towards 'individualisation' when he considers how some people might well be 'forced to actively construct their own biographies and social bonds' (ibid).

Following the Bauman/Miller line of argument through, 'individualisation', which can be linked to an increasing 'disembeddedness' within 'consumer society' (Bauman, ibid), has resulted in a situation whereby individuals (nodes) seek constant connection to networks in order to satisfy 'the demand for intimacy' (Miller, 2009: 389) and remain 'present'. This, in turn, 'creates tenuous, individually-oriented self-defined communities or networks, which revolve around shared interests and dialogic exchange related to those interests' (ibid).

I am inclined to concur with Miller's definition of phatic culture (and by extension, elements of Bauman's analysis of 'individualisation') but remain reluctant to agree fully with his criticism of it. The argument certainly captures the movement in digital culture towards shorter communicative acts, an increase in connection and a decrease in content. Miller's brief discussion of how this movement serves the needs of the market echoes Campbell's (2005) work on 'Janus-faced' Internet portals, and his examples of tweets and updates underline claims that such practices focus on connection rather than content.

However, where Miller frames phatic culture as ultimately negative – feeding us to the capitalist machine in order that it may sell commodities back to us – I believe that its identification may provide a method for understanding what is being communicated through acts of digital cruising. Herring (2007) suggests a 'faceted classification scheme' through which we might organise and understand computer-mediated discourse (CMD). This scheme allows us to recognise how both the medium and situation of digital communication impacts on the meaning and importance of the types of phatic communication established in digital cruising.

Herring understands phatic elements of CMD as being an issue of 'tone', which 'refers to the manner or spirit in which discursive acts are performed' (np). But she also recognises how the 'the behavioural standards that normatively apply in the computer-mediated context' influences phatic communicative acts and shapes their relative importance within any given context. This fits in with Walther *et al.*'s (2005: 38) claim that 'CMC users adapt to the medium in order to express social messages'. The acknowledgement that phatic communication is not 'flat' but in fact varies in importance, meaning and resonance according to context provides an interesting response to Miller's criticism. Taking this on board, I am perhaps more ambivalent about the motivations behind and outcomes of phatic culture than Miller is.

For instance, I struggle to subscribe wholesale to the opinion that 'individualisation' is entirely bad, or at least that it means the same for everyone and that its consequences are all negative. Doubtless there are those who find themselves forced into this new mode of being, just as there are those who will mourn the death of communities, traditions, village life and family ties. 'Individualisation' means that 'not just the individual *placements* in society, but the *places* to which the individuals may gain access and in which they may wish to settle are melting fast and can hardly serve as targets for 'life projects' (Bauman, ibid: 146).

Yet for those who have never fitted into conventional conceptions of 'community', those who have never had *places* to access nor valid *placements* within which to exist, 'individualisation' has also provided avenues for constructing, experimenting and moulding meaningful lives according to other systems of belief, ideology and desire. In response to Bauman's claim, that the current state of identity means that we lack 'the confidence of being in control of one's destiny' (149), I would argue that sexually dissident folk have rarely felt in control of their destiny – it has been something thrust upon them. I say this and am, of course, aware of D'Emilio's (1992) discussion regarding the relationship between capitalism and gay identity. Morton's (1995) caution regarding desire (discussed in Chapter 5) similarly rings in my ears and I am not celebrating 'individualisation' as some form of queer revolution, nor am I wholly disagreeing with Bauman's thesis. Indeed, his discussion of how 'substitute pastimes' (150) obscure more important matters, would, if anything, only strengthen the claims I make in Chapter 3, concerning the current obsession within urban gay culture for self-regulating and self-moulding the body.

Rather, in responding to criticisms of 'individualisation', I want to consider the possibility that this movement away from traditional understandings of the self – and therefore, other(s) – comes with both costs *and* benefits. These costs and benefits are neither evenly distributed, nor equally powerful. 'Individualisation' leaves an illegal immigrant like Ernesto vulnerable to market forces, which serve to drive down his wages – wages that help him cling on to the margins of Madrid's society. But arguably, the *phatic culture* of 'individualisation' allows him to use his mobile phone to connect with men in spaces outside of the conventional gay scene – a scene that both rejects him, and costs more than he can afford. To repeat, the costs and benefits are neither evenly distributed, nor equally powerful, but they do both exist, in different registers and across different contexts.[7]

And while 'individualisation' does indeed atomise, segregate and force new boundaries of identification to be drawn, some of its effects, such as its 'liberalising' of movement, might offer conflicting results. If 'freedom of manoeuvre rises to the rank of topmost value' (Bauman, ibid: 148), for instance, might not this freedom offer opportunities for sexually dissident people to cleave new spaces within public life and, in doing so, make such spaces more 'liquid'? Berlant and Warner (1998: 558) describe the queer world as 'a space of entrances, exits, unsystematised lines of acquaintance, projected horizons, typifying examples, alternate routes, blockages, incommensurate geographies'. In comparison to heterosexual culture, queer cultures appear to be far more 'transitory' and mobile.

Digital cruising operates at an intersection where physical space encounters freedom of manoeuvrability as it is rendered through digital communications. This intersection is not only a site for pleasurable exploration; it is also fragile and contested. In his ethnographic study of American cruising sites Hollister (2002: 134) remarks that 'men who cruise a rest area experience a very different place, albeit with the same buildings, pavement, and foliage, than those who just stop to rest, use the facilities, and move on'. These different experiences of space are rarely equally weighted and this inequality reflects the fact that public spaces (whether physical or digital) are more often than not coded as heterosexual. Gove (2000: 141–142) talks of the 'sneering surveillance' of an 'overwhelmingly heterosexualised sphere of 'public' space' and Campbell (2004: 99) asserts that 'the physical world remains a hostile space for many queer-identified individuals'. Meanwhile, Hillis (2009: 234) notes that:

> With respect to gay/queer experiences of material public space, belief or desire that the Web might constitute not only mobility but also some form of actual space grows in tandem with the reality that it remains taboo, for example, to hold hands with one's same-sex partner at the mall.

The hybrid spaces of digital cruising bring together and hold the 'belief' and 'reality' Hillis identifies, in tension, causing physical space to be subjected to acts of queer digitalisation and re-coding. As de Souza e Silva (ibid: 270) notes, '[i]n the hybrid-spaces logic, cell phones do not take users out of physical space' as perhaps the static web might be seen to do, but rather, 'strengthen users' connections to the space they inhabit, because the connection to other users depends on their

---

7 Hollister (2002) notes that physical cruising sites not only provide opportunities for anonymous casual sex, but also offer an alternative site for queer men to congregate. Within the context of a city where gay culture revolves around a circuit of bars, he talks of recovering alcoholics who, feeling disenfranchised, congregate at a rest-stop to chat, catch-up, and be among other gay men.

relative position in space'. Considering the relatively small amount of information often transmitted via these techno-practices, it would seem that, like other forms of phatic 'speech', 'social contacts are often maintained through the mere act of communicating' (Provine *et al.*, 2007: 305). This notion of strengthening connections within physical space is arguably most keenly felt by those who are regularly perceived as existing (to paraphrase Hillis) somewhere 'over there' rather than ever fully 'here' (Hillis, ibid: 234).

Conclusion: Congregation and/or carnality?

We need to consider digital cruising within the wider contexts of gay male subculture, and specifically the tense and fractious relationship that continues to exist between non-normative identities and heteronormative public space. As Donner (2007: np) notes, phatic practices of mobile communication are 'undoubtedly influenced by the varied contexts and cultures of [their] adherents' and are 'example[s] of an ongoing interaction between social practices and technological factors'. Digital cruising is negotiated through these 'varied contexts' and illustrates how gay men 'have created a set of distinct social practices around the technology, rather than altering the technology itself' (ibid). This negotiation echoes De Certeau's (1984: xix) 'tactical' reading of public space, which I discussed in Chapter 5, whereby users re-imagine and appropriate space – often momentarily – for purposes that contrast their intended use. We might go so far as to say that hybrid spaces are in fact always tactical in that they remap the spaces of the city according to the connections of the users who pass through them, and the logic of the mobile phone.

Sex is undoubtedly one of the potential outcomes of digital cruising, but this practice also appears to be about *queer congregation*, reflecting both Malinowski's original use of the phrase 'phatic communion' and the work of linguists such as Herring (2007) who see computer-mediated phatic discourse as strengthening social bonds in highly mediated contexts of sociality. In other words, digital cruising might be best understood as a networked sociality that allows gay men to 'look' at (and thereby recognise and acknowledge) one another as they move through otherwise non-queer spaces. This is parallel to the kind of 'break[ing] out of the world' that Bilandzic *et al.* (2009: 1518) identify in other (non-queer) mobile-locative applications and in this sense, digital cruising is part of an array of social practices that provide for the 'testing, exploring, and experimenting with alternative ways of being' (Knopp, 2004: 123). While Knopp remains aware that such experimentation does not always work out, he argues that it continues to hold an allure for many gay men:

> it is clear that many gay men find the quest itself to be a source of considerable pleasure … and eventually, for many, it becomes a source of ontological and emotional security as well. … The fact is that being simultaneously in and out of

> place, and seeking comfort as well as pleasure in movement, displacement and place*less*ness, are commonly sought after experiences for many people. (124)

Digital cruising may well be a form of communion but arguably it is not a conscious act of social grooming. There is no evidence of a cohesive group identity amongst users of Grindr, and looking at the transcripts of the interviews I conducted I am far from convinced that carriage two of the 8:15 to London Paddington (for instance) has become a site of gay communality. Indeed, the idea of such communality is arguably impossible in spaces that are publicly coded as heterosexual. Berlant and Warner (1998: 551) suggest that one of the central projects of gay male subculture has been 'to construct the architecture of queer space in a homophobic environment' and I would argue that this project continues today. In nearly all the interviews conducted, digital media were seen as providing valuable resources for locating gay spaces – of any kind – when travelling and moving through spaces of all kinds. When asked why such spaces were sought, respondents identified a feeling of 'communality' and of 'comfort' – of 'being around one's own people' and of 'coming home'. Such comments were often made in contrast to 'straight space' or 'the rest of the world', which was seen as 'uncomfortable' and engendering a sense that one 'didn't quite fit in'. The world outside, it appears, continues to be one in which gay/queer men experience a sense of 'otherness' and non-belonging.

Miller's identification of a 'connected presence' identifies the methods by which phatic practices become embedded into the rhythms of everyday life. We need to understand this, while recognising that such techno-practices can serve to support and reinforce a sense of shared identity and shared culture. Indeed such practices 'reinforce perceptions of popularity, intimacy, and acceptance' and can 'serve to remind the sender and receiver of their common bond – their secret, specific, 'restricted' code … that they share with one another' (Donner, 2007: np). As the quotations from my interviewees demonstrate, the communicative acts that are invoked through digital cruising suggest a focus on connection rather than communication. The 'chat, chat chat' (as one respondent put it) that occurs during digital cruising often results in little more than brief flirtations and greeting notes. Such chatter may seem unimportant, but given the fact that sexually dissident subcultures are 'especially dependent on ephemeral elaborations in urban space' (Berlant and Warner, 1998: 553) it may offer opportunities for queer connection and a sense that, within the heterosexual culture of the public world, you can still be 'around one's own people'.

As such we might consider digital cruising as 'identity quests', these being the movement of gay people through space as they negotiate and new understandings of the self:

> Identity quests are, after all, very much about discovering and disclosing the self in and through place, and about changing place in such a way as to facilitate this process. They are inherently reflexive and relational practices. As we travel

> through places in these quests we internalize all manner of meanings even as we create new ones and leave legacies of our own' (Knopp, 2004: 127).

As I mentioned in the introduction to this chapter, the practices explored here are still in their relative infancy, and it will be interesting to see how, along with a raft of other mobile ICTs and practices now being adopted in wider culture, gay men compose and weave practices of digital cruising into their everyday lives in a similar fashion to how the user profile has become a ubiquitous form in gay male subculture. As these technological practices develop, indeed, as any set of technologies converge, transform and otherwise morph into seemingly new platforms, we would do well to remember the ongoing friction caused by queer people in heteronormative space, just as we should remember that queer men and women have been negotiating such spaces and finding 'work-arounds' that suit their needs long before digital mobile phones or PDAs. Digital cruising offers one iteration, or perhaps updates an older iteration, of this negotiation work and, in doing so, strengthens the queer worlds that are brought into existence within the public spaces of the city, as we move through it.

At the same time, however, and invoking the discourse of cybercarnality once more, we must recognise how digital cruising is part of a much larger framework of queer digital communication. While the technologies and techno-practices being adopted by gay men today may seem new, many of the strategies of (self)representation and (self)surveillance that are invoked through these new trends have an established history in gay male subculture.

For example, digital cruising relies on the corporeal just as much as the other forms of communication discussed in this book. While the level of communication is often remarkable low, and while phatic culture appears to offer little more than a sense of connected presence, the gay male body, and the representation of the gay male body, continues to be an important trope within this emerging practice. Whether it be the images of himself in states of undress, which Ernesto sends to potential sex partners via Bluetooth, or the profile pictures that Craig or Philip or Daniel flick through as they kill time on Grindr, the representation of an eroticised body is fundamental to digital cruising. Surpassing the 'knowing look' of the conventional cruising gaze, digital cruising offers users the opportunity to represent themselves and each other in ways that have hitherto been impossible while in public space.

As Frank described in his recounting of his hook-up with Ernesto, the public space of the carriage was transgressed through their communication. Without speaking, indeed without being next to one another, Ernesto remediated his body and Bluetoothed his desiring self to Frank's mobile phone. Frank's reflection on this was that it was that it 'was quite odd' and that within the time and space of a subway journey, a 'total random stranger', had revealed 'the intimate side of him[self]' without any physical interaction. If we understand cybercarnality as identifying the relationship between digital and non-digital aspects of gay culture, and acknowledge the central role gay men's bodies play in bridging the supposed divide between the two, then the (re)mediated body found within digital cruising provides a queer re-articulation of the body within public space. As with other forms of cybercarnal representation, the body of digital cruising is most commonly represented through pornographic discourse. The profiles on mobile Apps such as Purpll and BoyAhoy! operate in similar ways to those found on Gaydar and similar modes of representation are employed by users. Similar codes of legibility are found in digital cruising as can be found on dating/cruising sites and while this phenomenon is still in its infancy, I would argue that the issues of visibility, aesthetics and authenticity will pervade digital cruising practices.

But digital cruising is also heavily invested in other elements of cybercarnal discourse, most notably, the theme of surveillance. Like cruising, surveillance has become reconfigured and 'mobilised' via new technologies of mobile communication. As Best (2010: 14) writes 'surveillance is … freed from spaces, and found instead at mobile, ever-present sites'. The quotation from Craig above illustrates how a great deal of the appeal of digital cruising lies in the element of pursuit. From his train seat Craig would send and receive messages via Bluetooth while all the time surveying the carriage to ascertain who was sending what. The standard term for making one's Bluetooth-enabled device visible is 'discoverable' and it is uncanny how well this fits in with the practices of digital cruising. Just like a mobile phone or PDA, gay subculture exists, it is 'out there' and 'discoverable'. Echoing Shaw's (1997) statement regarding the parallels between gay bars and gay IRC channels, one just needs to have the sub-cultural knowledge to understand how to look for it, where to find it and how to engage with it.

The surveillance aspect of digital cruising should, however, not be written off simple as an erotic thrill, as nothing more than a mediated game of cat and mouse. We must not underestimate the complex relationship that mobile-locative practices have formed with surveillance. In some respects digital cruising echoes the types of surveillance seen in the cybercottage. Software such as Grindr similarly relies on users watching one another, in physical and digital spaces, and part of the experience is indeed seeing who else nearby is gay, and potentially interested in sex at that moment in time. However, digital cruising, through its reliance on and prioritising of physical space goes further than the cybercottage in terms of its surveillance practices. Users of services such as those designed for mobile Internet devices subject themselves to a process of continual tracking via GPS technology and one's success in digital cruising relies in part on forfeiting aspects of one's privacy. Best (2010: 12) identifies the fact that the research participants in her study were 'clearly aware of the profitable nature of data trade in contemporary culture' and understood, *in the abstract*, that digital technologies allowed for myriad forms of surveillance. However, many of the cohort failed to recognise how their 'clean' (ibid) digital profile could ever cause them harm. Likewise, digital cruising may engender a sense of 'breaking out' of the heterosexual world to momentarily make queer connections, but it must be remembered that the technologies that provide for such connections remain firmly embedded within heteronormative contexts.

Let me put this another way. Cruising culture is in a sense always public; one cannot cruise in private. But while traditional narratives of cruising (and I include those found within the cybercottage) often speak of men operating under the radar and eluding detection, within the digital cruising experience users are required to become 'discoverable' via a global technological apparatus who's origins lie within the military-industrial complex and government-backed surveillance projects of the United States during the Cold War. While it is not my intention to suggest that British or other Western Governments are using the specific technologies I am talking about in this chapter to spy on gay men, one does not need to look too far to see how the surveillance possibilities afforded by digital media technologies have recently been used to track, hunt and oppress (in violent ways) gay men who have used such technologies to locate and meet one another.

The rise in violence against gay and queer men in Iraq, for example, was documented by the Western press in the autumn of 2009. *The Observer* newspaper ran a story entitled 'How Islamists track and kill Iraq's gays' (Sarhan and Burke, 2009) in which it revealed that gay chatrooms and websites (a popular way for Iraqi gay men to meet one another) were being monitored by Islamist groups. These groups arranged meetings with gay men in order to then kidnap, torture and murder them. Putting aside (as difficult as this may be) the horrific nature of the crimes committed against these men, stories such as this one reflect the precarious relationship that minority groups often have with digital media technologies.

Other stories include fundamentalist militia using mobile phones to track gay men and find evidence of homosexual activity. A harrowing report in *The New York Magazine* (McAllester, 2009), for instance, revealed how mobile phone address books were used during the torture of Iraqi gay men in an attempt to get victims to name other gay men that they knew. Meanwhile the 'social filtering' of Internet content was reportedly on the rise in the Middle East during 2009, with the *Washington Internet Daily* (Cantu, 2009: np) reporting that 'Jordan installed cameras in Internet cafes in 2008 and began requiring cafe owners to report users' personal data, time of use and sites visited'. The report went on to state that LGBT content on sites such as Facebook and YouTube was being targeted as part of these censorship practices. Furthermore, such censorship or 'filtering' was being both acknowledged and approved of at a governmental level. While one must remember the specific cultural, political and social contexts in which such activities are taking place, the fact remains that technologies of communication are being used by gay men *and* against gay men, often simultaneously. My aim here is not to instil a sense of paranoia in users of digital cruising, nor do I wish to give birth to a new conspiracy theory; digital media technologies have been subjected to enough of these already. Rather, through recognising the cybercarnal dimensions of digital cruising, we can see how the questions of surveillance that I highlighted in Chapter 3 continue to be written into the architecture of gay men's digital culture.

The practices that I have explored here allow gay men to identify, recognise and communicate with one another in public space to an extent that has rarely been seen before. In doing so, they break through the wall of invisibility that heteronormative culture builds around queer individuals and provides discontinuous moments of congregation and communication. At the same time, however, the technologies through which such breaking through is achieved remain firmly ensconced within systems of control and governance, rendering gay men visible not only to other gay men but to anyone who has the power or knowledge to 'tune in' and watch them as they connect with one another in their everyday lives. Earlier in this book I wrote that practices of looking, and of being looked at, are intrinsic to gay male subculture. They are embodied in the technologies and discourses of State surveillance (medical, legal, psychological) that gay men have been (and continue to be) exposed to, and they are evident in the sexualised practices of looking that occurs in both gay spaces and non-gay space. Digital cruising collapses these two 'poles' of surveillance and renders gay men visible to one another *via* technologies that were originally designed to survey, track and monitor individuals on behalf of the State. As such, we might conclude that while the technologies, trends and habits of gay men's digital culture continue to change and adapt, this tension between visibility and invisibility remains central to gay male subculture. It is within this tension that issues of power continue to be articulated, and it is across the digital platforms gay men employ in their daily lives and through the diverse digital practices that they engage in, that such power continues to be mobilised today.

Chapter 8

Conclusion: Some Final Thoughts on Gay Men's Digital Culture

British gay male subculture has only recently become mediated through digital technologies, but in a sense the lives of gay men have always been virtual. As I have demonstrated throughout much of this book, and while a 'homonormative' gay male subculture has flourished and become more tolerated over the last twenty years, British society continues to normalise and privilege heterosexual forms of being. Improvements in civil rights, legal protection and equalities legislation have successfully granted LGBT people living in Britain, a 'place at the table' (Bawer, 1993). But legal and cultural recognition are rarely the same thing. Equality in law does not evacuate a society of its systems of privilege and prejudice.

So when I claim that gay men have always lived 'virtual' lives I am not so much referring to their use of communicative technologies, but rather am alluding to the myriad of ways in which non-heterosexual people have forged existences and constructed identities in contexts that render them inferior, invisible, invalid or impossible. This might seem like an over inflated-claim, not least at a time when the public visibility of gay men is at an all time high. However, echoing Kappeler's claim regarding women in culture, I would argue that it matters little whether more and more self-identifying gay men are becoming visible within the public sphere. Or, rather, the public visibility and public achievements of singular gay men (arguably a triumph on one level) should not be understood as illustrating the wholesale acceptance of male homosexuality within British (or any other) society. Nor should it obfuscate the genuine struggles that LGBT people continue to face, living as they do in a society that rewards heterosexual identities and relations, and which continues to place non-heterosexual people as 'outsiders' who have only recently been invited 'in'.

To anyone who disagrees with this argument, to anyone who is tired of hearing about inequality and believes that this is no longer an issue for gay men, allow me one final anecdote by way of justification. I recently attended a workshop on LGB (no T?) representation, organised by the BBC. Tasked with the job of identifying where the broadcaster had 'got it wrong' for LGB people, the participants immediately honed in on a recent incident (December, 2009) in which a discussion thread on the *World Service* 'Have Your Say' website (regarding Uganda's proposed anti-gay laws) began with the title 'Should homosexuals face execution?' The facilitators of the workshop no doubt anticipated that this would be one of the first failures to be identified and were sympathetic to our anger, agreeing that the question had been a terrible mistake and offensive in the extreme. Having previously read the BBC's retraction and witnessed the corporation's public handwringing in the press over this matter, I was unsurprised to hear such agreement from within the institution. The question that followed, however, was perhaps more insightful than the recognition of our dismay. The facilitator charged with listening to the group's responses asked us why we thought such a thing had happened. How had such a mistake occured and what did we think went wrong for this 'unfortunate' question to crop up on the online discussion site?

The answer to this cannot, of course, be separated from what I am discussing here, and what I have been discussing in much of this book. Warner coined the term 'heteronormativity' in 1991 as a means of identifying how one set of sexual relations was understood as the default in Western societies, and operates as the benchmark against which all other sexual identities and practices are measured (and found wanting). Twenty years on from *Fear of a Queer Planet*, my fellow queers and I carefully explained what Warner's term meant in order to answer what was, to our facilitator's mind, a perfectly reasonable question, and what was, to us, another painful reminder of just how uneven the cultural playing field is in Britain, especially for those who don't think, act, look, feel or identify as 'straight'.

The examples of gay male digital culture I have explored in this book can all be understood as responses to the invisibility and cultural marginalisation many gay men living in British and other Western societies either feel of have felt at some point in their lives. Whether through the establishment of a user profile on sites such as Gaydar, or the queering of gendered spaces via Uni_cock, or the mobilising of communication practices for transitory connections via Grindr, issues of seeing and of being seen are intimately tied up with gay men's digital practice. We might even think of the barebacking websites, especially BarebackJack.com, as wrestling with the theme of visibility, as a once taboo sexual practice is brought 'into the light' and explored, contested and acknowledged via digital ICTs.

In the introduction to this book I remarked upon a question that I regularly got asked when people learned of my research interests. 'Is it doing us any good?' meaning, are new technologies of communication helping or hindering gay men? For those who have read this book looking specifically for an answer to this question, I apologise. I have been unable to provide a succinct 'yes' or 'no' in response to this query and I don't think I – or anyone else – will ever be able to do so. In my defence, I would of course argue that such a question is not only impossible to answer, but also obscures more interesting, complex and productive questions – questions that I hope I have answered in some small way over the course of the preceding chapters.

These questions have framed the spaces and practices I have interrogated and can be loosely summarised as follows:

i) Why is gay male subculture so invested in digital media? What does it offer and how does it respond to the situation gay men find themselves in today?
ii) How are the integration of new media forms developing, extending and problematising contemporary articulations of that subculture? What are the political implications of this digital immersion and how do they fit with wider issues pervading gay subculture today?

Of course, these questions are also incredibly large and I have only been able to offer partial answers to them via the analyses I have carried out here. But through my examination of Gaydar (for example), I have been able to identify the methods by which the user profile – an increasingly ubiquitous form of self representation – provides avenues for identification and visibility that have historically been denied to queer people. At the same time, through an analysis of such representations, and the discourses of pornography and surveillance that often get invoked through the profile, I have demonstrated not only the relationship between new and older forms of gay male representation, but also how digital media provide for an ever more intense codification of gay male identity according to taxonomies established within other arenas of gay life.

Likewise, in my examination of the cybercottage, which we might regard as the antithesis of sites such as Gaydar, I have been able to explore some of the reasons behind why this 'outmoded' and politically 'incorrect' form of homosexual practice is flourishing online. Juxtaposing Uni_cock against both the recent history of gay male subculture and the identity-driven culture of gay dating sites, I have highlighted how these digital environments offer an opportunity to queer nearby physical locales and engage in 'nostalgic' fantasies that revisit and re-vision the history of male homosexuality. This re-visioning fits in with the queer project of the mid-90s, whereby the link between sexual identity and sexual activity came under intense scrutiny and was found, by many, to be failing to adequately capture the diverse forms of sexuality it claimed to speak on behalf of. Similarly, my discussion of online bareback subculture has drawn on recent gay male history, most notably the impact of HIV/AIDS on understandings of sexual practice, in order to explain why some men are choosing to depart from conventional strategies of harm reduction in spite of the risks invovled. Acknowledging this history and giving it a voice within the analysis has allowed me to identify the reasons why bareback subculture is embedded in digital ICTs and the ways in which these new forms of communication are providing platforms for counter-discourses to be formed, and alternative practices to be produced.

Finally in Chapter 7, and further underscoring the need to dismantle the digital/physical binary (identified in Chapter 1), in order to better understand gay male subculture, I have examined some of the most recent responses gay men have been forming to the overwhelming heteronormativity of everyday life. Digital cruising invokes older narratives of gay male subculture and its relationship to public life, and scaffolds these to new mobile technologies of communication in order to form loose, ephemeral connections between men as they move through spaces that are otherwise coded as heterosexual. The political potential of such connections may not be fully realised by users of Grindr or Purpll or by those who Bluejack one another during the daily commute, but through their engagement with such technologies and practices, these men are identifying and challenging prevailing hegemonies encountered in public space.

As I hope has become clear through the course of my discussions, being able to adequately answer the question of why gay male subculture has developed such a deep infatuation with the digital, becomes only remotely possible when we have a comprehensive understanding of the recent history of that subculture. In Chapter 2, I outlined some of the key themes and issues gay subculture has been witness to since the early 1980s. In doing so, I aimed to demonstrate how these issues served to structure and shape that subculture, and its subsequent involvement with digital media. In focusing on the history of gay political action in the UK, I wanted to chart the shift from radicalism to assimilation, which has taken place over the last forty years. Recognising this shift, I believe, helps us to understand websites as diverse as Gaydar and Uni_cock. I am not suggesting that these two spaces fall neatly in line with a particular political trend: neither appears to be consciously invested in a specific political dialogue and there is no sense of collective political identity within the 'official' discourse of either space. However, my reading of both sites does demonstrate how tensions between 'older' radical interventions and more contemporary discourses of assimilation (which might also be read as supporting homonormative understandings of queer sexuality) resonate with the practices and identities that operate in these two spaces. Arguably, in the case of Uni_cock, both may in fact be present, simultaneously.

Similarly, understanding the cultural impact that HIV/AIDS has had on British gay male subculture helps us to understand the kinds of discourses that are being deployed and subscribed to within online bareback subculture. I have argued for the continuing need to recognise the specificity of HIV/AIDS narratives, and demonstrated how the virus affected British gay men in ways that went beyond the level of viral transmission. Seeing HIV as more than 'just' a virus is key here and my discussion demonstrated how HIV/AIDS has become a discourse and a set of power relations, a mechanism for shaping gay male sexuality and a means of pushing forward a particular form of gay male identity. This recognition allows us to better understand how responses and reactions to regimes of safer sex are formulated and maintained within the bareback websites analysed. The fact that the websites under discussion are American in origin may be seen as complicating my discussion, serving to contradict my earlier demands for cultural specificity and thus, undermining the analysis. However, in truth, I do not see such a contradiction operating here. Both websites not only have an international audience, but function using discourses that further underline the need to understand HIV/AIDS as something which is experienced and engaged with differently according to any one individual's context. Finally, in my brief consideration of the gay press I demonstrated just how integral media forms such as newspapers and magazines have been to both the formation and representation of a gay community in Britain. Mapping the terrain of gay print media, as it moved from citizen's 'mouthpiece' to consumer's 'marketplace' provides a more critically informed context in which to discuss the digital spaces encountered in the ensuing case study chapters.

I have been conscious throughout this project not to claim to be speaking for, on behalf of, or about all LGBT people, or indeed for all queer identified men. Any such aim, to capture the experiences of all non-heterosexual people in some kind of a totalising narrative, is surely doomed from the start. As stated in the introductory chapter, the phrases 'LGBT community' and 'gay community' must be used carefully, not least because they run the risk of collapsing otherwise distinct identities into one seemingly homogenous grouping. Furthermore, such terms can hide the material, political, social and cultural tensions that operate between and across the categories 'lesbian', 'gay', 'bisexual' and 'trans' – categories which are themselves neither uncontested nor clearly defined. In focusing on the digital practices and spaces of gay men then, I have been conscious of locating my research within one iteration of male homosexuality, that being contemporary metropolitan gay male subculture; the urban-centric, lifestyle-oriented articulation of male-male desire so often critiqued for marginalising other queer identities, and which I outlined in detail in Chapter 2.

The choice behind this focus is in part due to my own cultural positioning within (or perhaps just to one side of) that subculture, but it can also be seen as a response to previous work on queer digital culture, which has so often focussed not on the centre but on the margins of queer life. As identified in Chapter 1, much 'cyberqueer' work positions itself outside of – and in reaction to – what some feel is an increasingly visible and powerful gay hegemony. Such work is important not least because LGBT people who find themselves marginalised in (and/or by) the gay print media, and who struggle to find themselves within metropolitan gay subculture, have used digital media as a means to challenge such marginalisation. Digital media provides the means for the marginalised to form new, meaningful discourses of the self and to forge alternative queer experiences in which their own sexual and gender dissidence is validated and celebrated. By locating my sphere of research within the dominant mode of gay male identification, however, I have been able to comment on, and critique, a subculture which, for all its ostensible dominance amongst sexual minorities, has hitherto been somewhat under-represented in queer-oriented literature on digital media.

Of course not all of the spaces I have analysed in this book might initially be thought of as metropolitan. The cybercottage, for one, ostensibly eschews the identities and lifestyles bundled up in the term 'gay' and I have shown how members of this clandestine group appear to 'withhold' or temporarily evacuate the stable gay identities that they subscribe to elsewhere online. Likewise, one can see the online bareback scene as being formed in *reaction* to the rhetoric of safe sex that has pervaded urban gay culture since the mid-80s. As Scarce (1999) notes, barebacking subculture has grown up through a network of private homes and parties but also via the Internet. The latter has proven to be a valuable resource for those who choose to have sex without condoms precisely because such a choice lies outside of the dominant frameworks of sexual health promotion found within metropolitan gay subculture. Yet while neither cybercottaging nor barebacking can be thought of as metropolitan, the spaces that support these practices, and which have been analysed in this book, do in fact have a relationship with metropolitan gay male subculture and, as fractious as this might be, this relationship to the 'centre' is key to understanding how they function, why they exist and what purpose they are trying to serve. I have endeavoured in Chapters 5 and 6 to highlight this relationship, and hope that readers are able to see how, in seeming to offer an alternative to that subculture, these spaces form complex dialogues with it and might in fact be used by men who move between the centre and the margin, according to their sexual desires and practices.

I have also tried to avoid suggesting that everyone 'plugged in' to a metropolitan scene is using Gaydar. Nor have I argued that dating/sex websites are *only* used by urban gay men. As I mentioned, during my discussion of Sex Factor in Chapter 4, bodies and identities (represented via profiles) that do not 'fit', can and do exist on such sites. But it remains the case that such subjects inevitably exist, and are read, in relation to taxonomies of idealised 'types', which find validation in metropolitan gay subculture. The individual sat behind the computer screen may not consider himself to a part of that subculture, but on sites such as Gaydar he is invariably rendered legible and understood through the prevailing discourses that structure metropolitan gay life.

These prevailing discourses have underpinned my discussions and throughout this book I have (hopefully) demonstrated how we can plot a course through seemingly disparate spaces, in order to identify the ongoing investment in two key tropes within gay male subculture. Cybercarnality, providing both a discourse and a critical tool for investigating that subculture, allows us to understanding digital forms at a granular level while also providing the means for building a meta-narrative, which ties otherwise disparate sites and practices together. This meta-narrative is slippery and malleable enough to take in, and respond to, the contradictions found between divergent spaces, but should not be thought of as a 'grand theory' for gay cyberspace. Rather, we might think of cybercarnality as a way of looking at gay men's digital experiences; one that foregrounds the processes of (self)representation and (self)surveillance in operation both on and offline. It is through cybercarnality that I hope to have drawn attention to two specific themes, which I believe not only pervade both digital and physical aspects of gay male subculture, but which increasingly structure gay men's digital interactions and understandings of the self online. These two themes can be summarised as i) the manifestation of the gay male body in digital culture via discourses of pornography and ii) the ongoing investment in mechanisms of (self)surveillance through which gay men render themselves both visible and intelligible. I have deployed a cybercarnal reading of each case study by way of concluding each investigation and have identified how similar themes operate across different digital platforms. In each case, I have demonstrated how these two themes – of pornographic representation and (self)surveillance – are woven into the space or practice under investigation. In doing so, I hope to have provided a deeper understanding of gay men's digital culture, one that operates beyond the four iterations explored in this book, and which touches upon a range of other spaces, practices, identities and technologies that gay men are invoking, experiencing and inhabiting today.

As such, and this is where I shall conclude my discussion, I hope that what I have explored, discussed and written about here resonates with the experiences of gay men who increasingly find significant parts of their lives mediated through digital forms of communication. It was through the witnessing of such experiences that this book first took shape and I am extremely grateful to all those men who have taken the time to share their anecdotes and stories of digital media use with me. I began this brief concluding chapter claiming that the lives of gay men have always been, in some sense, virtual. I am reminded of an advert, which ran in Britain in 2001, for the Orange mobile phone network. In it, the model proclaimed that through the phone service 'I make my world and take it with me'. Arguably, gay men have been 'making' their worlds for a long time and this is unlikely to change any time soon.

Like other queer folk, gay men have, for the most part, grown up in heterosexual contexts, with heterosexual families and friends. When they are born, most gay men are presumed to be heterosexual. When they go to school, those schools invariably re-inscribe heterosexuality as normalised, whether through sex education in the classroom or peer observation in the playground. The 'real world' is a heterosexual world, or at least it has been, and it continues to be dominated by the norms of heterosexual thinking and being.

Gay male identities and lives have thus been 'virtual' to the extent that they have had to be constructed, maintained and mapped *alongside* the world of 'normal' life. Gay life has not had the opportunity to exist 'here' and has, for too long, been something located 'out there', elsewhere, somewhere (over the rainbow). This situation is changing, and this is undoubtedly a positive step for many, but there remains a lot of work to be done. Faced with living a 'virtual' life then, it is perhaps unsurprising that gay men have so eagerly gravitated towards the digital and embraced the possibilities for interaction and connection that contemporary media technologies offer. How these technologies shape the identities, practices, politics and cultures that they simultaneously represent remains an ongoing discussion. I hope that this book has contributed to that discussion. I also hope that it aids our understanding of why gay male subculture, (in Britain, and elsewhere), has developed complex and sustained relationships with digital forms and practices, and what some of the consequences and implications of these relationships might be.

Bibliography

Adam, D. 2005. 'Constructing the Neoliberal Sexual Actor: Responsibility and Care of the Self in the Discourse of Barebackers'. *Culture, Health and Sexuality*, 7(4), 333–346.

Altman, D. 1994. *Power and Community: Organizational and Cultural Responses to AIDS*. London: Taylor & Francis.

Amico, S. 2001. '"I Want Muscles": House Music, Homosexuality and Masculine Signification'. *Popular Music*, 20(3), 359–378.

Anon. 1981. 'Gay Man Dies of US Disease'. *Capital Gay*, 4 December, 1.

Anon. 1983. 'A.I.D.S. Gay Death-Plot Panic – Fact or Science Fiction?' *Him Monthly,* issue 58, June, 1–35.

Anon. 1987. 'Challenge of the Century'. *Capital Gay*, 11 December, 1.

Anon. 1988. 'Out and Proud'. *Pink Paper*, 5 May, 1.

Anon. 2000. 'Why We Must Publish this BAREBACK.COM Mans Shocking Gay Confession'. *The Mail On Sunday*, 19 March, 15.

Anon. 2006. 'Blue are So Sexy'. *News of The World*, 16 April, np.

Anon. 2006. 'Pulling by Tooth: In the Beginning it was a Joke, but now 'Toothing' has Moved from Techno Myth to Full-on Reality'. *Townsville Bulletin* (Australia), 21 April, np.

Anon. 2009. 'World Aids Day'. *The Metro*, 1 December, 14.

Armstrong, J. 2004, 'Web Grrrls, Guerrilla Tactics: Young Feminisms on the Web' in *Web. Studies* (2nd ed.) edited by D. Gauntlett and R. Horsley. London: Arnold, 92–102.

Attitude Magazine, April, 1997.

Babuscio, J. 1988. *We Speak for Ourselves: The Experience of Gay Men and Lesbians*. London: SPCK.

Baker, R. 1985. 'Exploding the Myth'. *Gay Times*, April 1985, 17.

Barthes, R. 1980 [2000]. *Camera Lucida* (trans. Howard, R.). London: Vintage.

Barton, B.J. 2009. 'iPhone City'. *Architectural Design*, 79(4), 90–97.

Bassett, C. 1994. *Treachery, Performance, Visibility and Defence: Gender and Identity in On-Line Worlds*. (unpublished) Sussex University Thesis.

Bassett, C. 1995 [1997]. 'Virtually Embodied: Life in an On-Line Community' in *The Sub-cultures Reader* edited by K. Gelder, and S. Thornton. London: Routledge, 537–551.

Bassett, C. 2009. 'Up the Garden Path: Or, How to Get Smart in Public'. *Second Nature: International Journal of Creative Media*, 1(2), 42–63. [Online]. Available at: http://secondnature.rmit.edu.au/index.php/2ndnature/article/view/111/36 [accessed 12 February 2010].

Bauman, Z. 2001. *The Individualized Society*. Cambridge: Polity.
Bawer, B. 1993. *A Place at the Table: The Gay Individual in American Society*. London, Simon & Schuster.
Berg, R.C. 2008. 'Barebacking Among MSM Internet Users'. *AIDS Behaviour*, 12, 822–833.
Berger, J. *About Looking*. London: Pantheon Books.
Bell, D. 1997. 'One-Handed Geographies: An Archaeology of Public Sex' in *Queers in Space: Communities, Public Spaces, Sites of Resistance* edited by G.B. Ingram, A. Bouthilette and Y. Retter. Washington: Bay Press, 81–90.
Bell, D. 2006. 'Bodies, Technologies, Spaces: On 'Dogging'. *Sexualities*, 9(4), 387–407.
Berlant, L. and Warner, M. 1998. 'Sex in Public'. *Critical Inquiry*, 24(2), 547–566.
Berry, C. and Martin, F. 2003. 'Queer 'n' Asian Cyberspace in 1990s Taiwan and Korea' in *Mobile Cultures: New Media in Queer Asia* edited by C. Berry, F. Martin and A. Yue. London: Duke University Press, 87–114.
Berry, D.M. 2004. 'Internet Research: Privacy, Ethics and Alienation: An Open Source Approach'. *Internet Research*, 14(4), 323–332.
Bersani, L. 1995. *Homos*. London: Harvard University Press.
Best, K. 2010. 'Living In the Control Society: Surveillance, Users and Digital Screen Technologies'. *International Journal of Cultural Studies*, 3(13), 5–24.
Beswick, T. 2000. 'Bareback 'Outings' Spark Debate over Well-known Secret'. *The Bay Area Reporter* [Online]. Available at: http://www.aegis.com/news/bar/2000/BR000705.html [accessed 7 July 2005].
Bielski, Z. 2009. 'Radar Love; GPS isn't just for Clueless Drivers. Now it's Helping Singles to Navigate the Dating Scene'. *The Globe and Mail* (Canada), 18 September, L1.
Bilandzic, M., Filonik, D., Gross, M., Hackel, A., Mangesius, H. and Krcmar, H. 2009. 'A Mobile Application to Support Phatic Communication in the Hybrid Space'. *Proceedings of the 2009 Sixth International Conference on Information Technology: New Generations*, 1517–1521.
Bittman, M., Browne, J.E. and Wajcman, J. 2009. 'The Mobile Phone, Perpetual Contact and Time Pressure'. *Work, Employment and Society*, 23(4), 673–691.
Bowcott, O. 1989. 'Gays Accuse Police over Big Increase in Arrests'. *The Guardian*, 29 December, np.
Branston, G. 2000. *Cinema and Cultural Modernity*. Buckingham, UK: Open University Press.
Bronski, M. 1984. *Culture Clash: The Making of a Gay Sensibility*. Boston, MA: South End Press.
Bronski, M. 1997. 'Why Gay Men Still Have Unsafe Sex: Beauty, Self-esteem and the Myth of HIV Negativity' in *Acting on AIDS: Sex, Drugs & Politics* edited by J. Barrett, J. Oppenhiemer and H. Reckitt. London: Serpent's Tail, 118–127.

Browne, K. (with Count Me In Too Action Group, Church, A. and Law, A.) 2007. *Count Me In Too: LGBT Lives in Brighton & Hove Initial Findings: Academic Report* [Online]. Available at: http://www.spectrum-lgbt.org/cmiToo/downloads/CMIT_AcademicReport_final_June07.pdf [accessed 19 November 2009].

Bruckman, A. 2001. 'Studying the Amateur Artist: A Perspective on Disguising Data Collected in Human Subjects Research on the Internet' [Online]. Available at: www.nyu.edu/projects/nissenbaum/ethics_bru_full.html [accessed 27 April 2003].

Bruckman, A.S. 1993. *Gender Swapping on the Internet* [Online]. Available at: www.ccgatech.edu/elc/papers/bruckman [accessed 15 July 2005].

Buckingham, C. 2009. 'Kvetching for some Cruising' (Online). Available at: http://homopop.com/taxonomy/term/106 [accessed 11 October 2009].

Bukatman, S. 2000. 'Terminal Penetration', in *The Cybercultures Reader* edited by D. Bell and B.M. Kennedy. London: Routledge, 149–174.

Bull, M. 2004. 'Automobility and the Power of Sound'. *Theory, Culture and Society*, 21(4/5), 243–259.

Bull, M. 2007. *Sound Moves: iPod Culture and Urban Experience*. London: Routledge.

Burger, J.R. 1995. *One-Handed Histories: The Eroto-Politics of Gay Male Video Pornography*. New York: Harrington Park Press.

Burrell, I. 2002. 'Social Revolution: Blunkett Plans Major Change to "Archaic" Sex Laws'. *The Independent*, 20 November, 6.

Burston, P. 1995. *What Are You Looking At? Queer Sex, Style and Cinema*. London: Cassell.

Burton, P. 1985. 'The Cottaging Taboo'. *Gay Times*, February, 38.

Butler, J. 1990. *Gender Trouble: Feminism and the Subversion of Identity*. London: Routledge.

Califia, P. 2000. *Public Sex: The Culture of Radical Sex*. San Francisco: Cleis Press.

Campbell, J.E. 2004. *Getting It On Online: Cyberspace, Gay Male Sexuality and Embodied Identity*. London: Harrington Park Press.

Cantu, L. 2009. 'Government Filtering on the Rise in Middle East, Report Finds'. *Washington Internet Post*, 13 August, 10, np.

Campbell, J.E. 2005. 'Outing PlanetOut: Surveillance, Gay Marketing and Internet Affinity Portals'. *New Media & Society*, 7(5), 663–683.

Castells, M. 1999. 'An Introduction to the Information Age' in *The Media Reader: Continuity and Transformation* edited by H. Mackay and T. O'Sullivan. London: Sage, 398–410.

Caronia, L. 2005. 'Mobile Culture: An Ethnography of Cellular Phone Use in Teenagers' Everyday Life'. *Convergence: The Journal of Research into New Media Technologies,* 11(5), 960–1003.

Carter, A. 1978. *The Sadeian Woman: And the Ideology of Pornography*. London: Pantheon.

Carter, M. 2002. 'AIDS Industry Meltdown?' *Positive Nation*, issue 77 [Online]. Available at: www.positivenation.co.uk/issue77/feature6/feature6_4htm [accessed 15 July 2005].

Castells, M. 1996 [2000]. *The Rise Of The Network Society*. Oxford, Blackwells.

Champagne, J. 1997. '"Stop Reading Films!": Film Studies, Close Analysis, and Gay Pornography'. *Cinema Journal*, 36(4), 76–97.

Chauncey, G. 2002. 'Trade, Wolves, and the Boundaries of Normal Manhood' in *Sexualities in History: A Reader* edited by K.M. Phillips and B. Reay, London: Routledge, 293–326.

Chauncey, G. 1994. *Gay New York: Gender, Urban Culture, and the Making of the Gay Male World, 1890–1940*. New York: Basic Books.

Clark, C. 1991. 'Pornography Without Power?' in *Men Confront Pornography* edited by M.S. Kimmel. New York: Meridian, 281–284.

Clarke, M. 2002. 'Blunkett to Scrap Gay Sex Laws in Shake-up'. *The Daily Mail*, 2 October, 6–7.

Cole, O. and Allen, W. 1994. 'The Black Perspective' in *Stonewall 25: The Making of the Lesbian and Gay Community in Britain* edited by E. Healey, and A. Mason. London: Virago Press, 122–136.

Cooper, D. 1994. *Sexing The City: Lesbian and Gay Politics in the Activist State*. London: Rivers Oram Press.

Corber, R.J. 1999. 'Queer Regionalism'. *American Literary History*, 11(2), 391–402.

Coté, M. and Pybus, J. 2007. 'Learning to Immaterial Labour 2.0'. *Ephemera*, 7(1), 88–106.

Coupland, J. 1996. 'Dating Advertisements: Discourses of the Commodified Self'. *Discourse & Society*, 7(2), 187–287.

Coxon, A.P.M. 1996. *Between the Sheets: Sexual Diaries of Gay Men's Sex in The Era of AIDS*. London: Cassell.

Crewe, B. 2003. 'Class, Masculinity and Editorial Identity in the Reformation of the UK Men's Press' in *Masculinity and Men's Lifestyle Magazines* edited by B. Benwell. Oxford: Blackwell, 91–111.

Crisp, Q. 1985. *The Naked Civil Servant*. London: Fontana.

Cull, M., Platzer, H. and Balloch, S. 2006. *Out On My Own: Understanding the Experiences and Needs of Homeless Lesbian, Gay, Bisexual and Transgender Youth – Executive Summary*. [Online] Available at: www.spectrum-lgbt.org/downloads/.../Out_On_My_Own___summary.pdf [accessed 15 November 2009].

Daliot-Bull, M. 2007. 'Japan's Mobile Technoculture: The Production of a Cellular Playscape and its Cultural Implications'. *Media, Culture and Society*, 29(6), 954–971.

De Certeau, M. 1984. *The Practice of Everyday Life* (trans. Rendall, S.). Berkeley: University of California Press.

D'Emilio, J. 1992. *Making Trouble: Essays on Gay History, Politics and The University*. New York: Routledge.

De Jongh, N. 1988. 'Thousands Join Protest on Section 28 Curb on Gay Rights'. *The Guardian*, May 2, np.

De Souza e Silva, A. 2006. 'From Cyber to Hybrid: Mobile Technologies as Interfaces of Hybrid Spaces'. *Space and Culture*, 9(3), 261–278.

Dean, T. 2009. *Unlimited Intimacy: Reflections on the Subculture of Barebacking*. Chicago: University of Chicago Press.

Deleuze, G. 1992. 'Postscript on the Societies of Control'. *October* 59 (Winter), 3–7.

Derne, S. and Jadwin, L. 2000. 'Male Hindi Filmgoers' Gaze: An Ethnographic Interpretation'. *Contributions to Indian Sociology*, 34(2), 243–269.

Dishman, D.J. 1995. *Digital Divas: Defining Queer Space on the Information Superhighway* [Online]. Available at: www.usc.edu/isd/archives/queerfrontiers/queer/papers/dishman.html [accessed 15 July 2002].

Donner, J. 2007. 'The Rules of Beeping: Exchanging Messages via Intentional "Missed Calls" on Mobile Phones'. *Journal of Computer-Mediated Communication*, 13(1), [Online]. Available at: http://jcmc.indiana.edu/vol13/issue1/donner.html [accessed 12 November 2009].

Dowsett, G.W., Williams, H., Ventuneac, A. and Carballo-Dieguez, A. 2008. "Taking It Like a Man': Masculinity and Barebacking Online'. *Sexualities*, 11(2). 121–141.

Drummond, K.G. 2003. 'The Queering of Swan Lake'. *Journal of Homosexuality*, 45(2), 235–255.

Duberman, M. 1994. *Stonewall*. London: Penguin.

Duggan, L. 2003. *The Twilight of Equality?: Neoliberalism, Cultural Politics, and the Attack on Democracy*. Boston, Mass: Beacon Press.

Dworkin, A. 2000. 'Pornography and Grief' in *Feminism and Pornography* edited by D. Cornell. Oxford: Oxford University Press, 39–44.

Dyer, R. 1989. 'A Conversation About Pornography' in *Coming On Strong: Gay Politics and Culture* edited by S. Shepherd and M. Wallis. London: Unwin Hyman, 198–212.

Dyer, R. 1992. *Only Entertainment*. London: Routledge.

Edwards, T. 1994. *Erotics & Politics: Gay Male Sexuality, Masculinity and Feminism*. London: Routledge.

Elford, J. 2006. 'Changing Patterns of Sexual Behaviour in the Era of Highly Active Antiretroviral Therapy'. *Current Opinion in Infectious Diseases*, 19, 26–32.

Elford, J., Bolding, G., Davis, M., Sherr, L. and Hart, G. 2007. 'Barebacking Among HIV-Positive Men in London'. *Journal of Sexually Transmitted Diseases*, 34(2), 93–98.

Engel, S.M. 2001. *The Unfinished Revolution: Social Movement Theory and the Lesbian and Gay Movement*. Cambridge: Cambridge University Press.

Fall, J. date unknown. *Gay Men and Unsafe Sex* [Online]. Available at: http://www.users.dircon.co.uk/~eking/features/gayunsafe.htm [accessed 7 July 2005].

Firestone, S. 1970. *The Dialectic of Sex: The Case For Feminist Revolution*. New York: Morrow.

Flowers, P., Marriott, C. and Hart, G. 2000. 'The Bars, The Bogs and the Bushes': The Impact of Locale on Sexual Cultures'. *Culture, Health and Sexuality*, 2(1), 69–86.

Flowers, P. and Church, S. 2002. 'To Test or Not? HIV Antibody Testing amongst Gay Men'. *Culture, Health and Society*, 4(1), 43–56.

Flynn, P. 2003. 'Wired World: A New Cottaging Industry'. *The Guardian*, 2 December, 4.

Foster, T. 2001. 'Trapped by the Body? Telepresence Technologies and Transgendered Performance in Feminist and Lesbian Rewriting of Cyberpunk Fiction' in *The Cybercultures Reader* edited by D. Bell and B.M. Kennedy. London: Routledge, 539–459.

Foucault, M. 1976 [1990]. *The History of Sexuality: Volume 1 – An Introduction* (trans. Hurley, R.). London: Penguin.

Foucault, M. 1977a [1995]. *Discipline & Punish: The Birth of The Prison* (trans. Sheridan, A.). New York: Vintage.

Foucault, M. 1977b [1982]. *The Archaeology of Knowledge* (trans. Sheridan-Smith, A.M.). London: Tavistock.

Fraser, S. 2008. 'Getting Out in the "Real World": Young Men, Queer and Theorics of Gay Community'. *Journal of Homosexuality*, 55(2), 245–264.

Freud, S. 1905 [1991]. On Sexuality: Three Essays on the Theory of Sexuality and Other Works (trans. Strachey, J.). London: Penguin.

Garcia-Montes, J.M., Caballero-Muñoz, D. and Pérez-Álvarez, M. 2006. 'Changes in the Self Resulting from the Use of Mobile Phones'. *Media, Culture and Society*, 28(1), 67–82.

Garfield, S. 1994. *The End of Innocence: Britain in the Time of AIDS*. London: Faber & Faber.

Gay Times, issue 73, September 1984.

Gay Times, issue 92, April 1986.

Gay Times, issue 198, February, 1995.

Gendin, S. 1997a. 'Riding Bareback: Skin-on-Skin Sex: Been There, Done That, Want More'. *Poz Magazine Online* [Online]. Available at: www.poz.com/pozgibin/page?p=HOME&f=content&a=24/myturn&x=1 [accessed 12 January 2001].

Gendin, S. 1997b. 'Generation X Gay Men Speak Out'. *San Diego Sex Panic Summit*, 13–15 November, San Diego, CA. (transcript) [Online]. Available at: www.managingdesire.org/sexpanic/sexpanicpressrelease.html [accessed 12 February 2010].

Giddens, A. 1991. *Modernity and Self-Identity: Self and Society in the Late Modern Age*. Stanford: Stanford University Press.

GLC 1985. *Changing The World: A London Charter for Gay and Lesbian Rights*. London, Greater London Council.

Glover, S. 2003. 'Rulers are Odder than the Ruled' in *The Daily Mail*, 2 December, 13.

Goggin, G. 2009. 'Adapting the Mobile Phone: The iPhone and its Consumption'. *Continuum – Journal of Media and Cultural Studies*, 23(2), 231–244.

Goldsmith, N.M. 1998. *The Worst of Crimes: Homosexuality and The Law in Eighteenth Century London*. Aldershot UK: Ashgate.

Goldstein, R. 2001. *The Attack Queers: Liberal Society And The Gay Right*. London: Verso.

Gove, B. 2000. *Cruising Culture: Promiscuity, Desire and American Gay Literature*. Edinburgh: Edinburgh University Press.

Gray, M.L. 2009. *Out in the Country: Youth, Media and Queer Visibility in Rural America*. London: New York University Press.

Greer, G. 1970. *The Female Eunuch*. London: MacGibbon and Kee.

Grey, A. 1992. *Quest For Justice: Towards Homosexual Emancipation*. London: Sinclair-Stevenson.

Grey, A. 1997. *Speaking Out: Writing on Sex, Law, Politics and Society 1954–95*. London: Cassell.

Griffiths, K. 1998. 'New Research Dispels the Myths, Confirms Reality About Men Who Cruise for Sex'. *The Queer Resources Directory* [Online]. Available at: www.qrd.org/qrd/world/wockner/assorted/1998/report.finds.park.cruisers.are.not.closet.cases-07.28.98. [accessed 20 April 2003].

Gross, L. 2002. *Up from Invisibility: Lesbians, Gay Men and the Media in America*. New York: Columbia University Press.

Gross, L. 2003. 'The Gay Global Village in Cyberspace' in *Contesting Media Power: Alternative Media in a Networked World* edited by N. Couldry and J. Curran. Oxford: Rowman and Littlefield, 259–272.

Grov, C. 2006. 'Barebacking Websites: Electronic Environments for Reducing or Inducing HIV Risk'. *AIDS Care*, 18(8), 990–997.

Grov, C., DeBusk, J.A., Bimbi, D.S., Golub, S.A., Nanin, J.E. and Parsons, J.T. 2007. Barebacking, the Internet, and Harm Reduction: An Intercept Survey with Gay and Bisexual Men in Los Angeles and New York City'. *AIDS Behaviour*, 11, 527–536.

Gye, L. 2007. 'Picture This: the Impact of Mobile Camera Phones on Personal Photographic Practices'. *Continuum: Journal of Media & Cultural Studies*, 21(2), 279–288.

Haggerty, K.D. and Ericson, R.V. 2007. The Surveillant Assemblage. *British Journal of Sociology*, 51(4), 605–622.

Halkitis, P.M., Parsons, J.T. and Wilton, L. 2003. 'Barebacking Among Gay and Bisexual Men in New York City: Explanations for the Emergence of Intentional Unsafe Behaviour'. *Archives of Sexual Behaviour*, 32(4), 351–357.

Hall-Carpenter Archives and Gay Men's Oral History Group.1989. *Walking After Midnight: Gay Men's Life Stories*. London: Routledge.

Hampton, K.N., Livio, O. and Sessions, L. 2009. 'The Social Life of Wireless Urban Spaces: Internet Use, Social Networks, and the Public Realm' [Online].

Available at: http://www.mysocialnetwork.net/index2.php?p=118&c=1 [accessed 30 September 2009].

Harraway, D. 2000. 'A Cyborg Manifesto: Science, Technology and Socialist-Feminism in the Late Twentieth Century' in *The Cybercultures Reader* edited by D. Bell and B.M. Kennedy. London: Routledge, 291–324.

Healy, M. 1996. *Gay Skins: Class, Masculinity and Queer Appropriation*. London: Continuum.

Hearn, K. 1991. 'Disabled Lesbians and Gays Are Here To Stay!' in *High Risk Lives: Lesbian and Gay Politics After The Clause* edited by T. Kauffman and P. Lincoln. Bridport, Dorset: Prism Press, 29–39.

Hearn, J. 2008. 'Sexualities Future, Present, Past ... Towards Transsectionalities'. *Sexualities*, 11(10), 37–46.

Hennessy, R. 1995. 'Queer Visibility in Commodity Culture' in *Social Postmodernism: Beyond Identity Politics* edited by L. Nicholson and S. Seidman. Cambridge: Cambridge University Press, 142–186.

Herring, S.C. 2004. 'Slouching Toward the Ordinary: Current Trends in Computer-Mediated Communication'. *New Media and Society*, 6(1), 26–36.

Herring, S. 2007. 'A Faceted Classification Scheme for Computer-Mediated Discourse'. *Language@Internet* [Online]. Available at: http://www.languageatinternet.de/articles/2007/761 [accessed 12 February 2010].

Hewitt, C. 1995. 'The Socioeconomic Position of Gay Men: A Review of the Evidence'. *The American Journal of Economics and Sociology*, 54(4), 461–479.

Hickson, F., Davies, P., Wych, G. and Project SIGMA. 1993. 'Brief Encounters: Characteristics and Sources of Casual Sex Partners Among Gay and Bisexual Men' in *AIDS: Facing The Second Decade* edited by P. Aggleton, P. Davies and G. Hart. London: Falmer Press, 83–98.

Hiel, B. 2007. 'Modern Times, Islamic Rules in Saudi Arabia'. *Pittsburgh Tribune Review*, 28 May, np.

Hillis, K. 2009. *Online a Lot of the Time: Ritual, Sign, Fetish*. Durham: Duke University Press.

Hoffman, W. 1996. 'Skipping the Life Fantastic: Coming of Age in the Sexual Devolution' in *Policing Public Sex: Queer Politics and the Future of Aids Activism* edited by Dangerous Bedfellows. Boston, MA: South End Press, 337–354.

Holland, S. 1996. 'Descartes Goes to Hollywood: Mind, Body and Gender in Contemporary Hollywood Cinema' in *Cyberspace, Cyberbodies, Cyberpunk: Cultures of Technological Embodiment* edited by M. Featherstone, and R. Burrows. London: Sage, 157–174.

Hollister, J.W. 2002. *Reconstructing Social Theory at a Cruising Site*. Unpublished Dissertation, State U New York, Binghamton.

Holt, M. and Griffin, C. 2003. 'Being Gay, Being Straight and Being Yourself: Local and Global Reflections on Identity, Authenticity and the Lesbian and Gay Scene'. *European Journal of Cultural Studies*, 6(3), 404–425.

Horne, P. and Lewis, R. 1997. 'Visual Culture' in *Lesbian and Gay Studies: A Critical Introduction* edited by A. Medhurst and S. Munt. London: Cassell, 99–112.

Hossfeld, K. 1995. 'Why aren't High-tech Workers Organized? Lessons in Gender, Race, and Nationality from Silicon Valley' in *Working People of California* edited by D. Cornfield. Berkeley: University of California Press, 406–432.

Houlbrook, M. 2005. *Queer London: Perils and Pleasures in the Sexual Metropolis, 1918–57*. Chicago: University of Chicago Press.

Hugh, D. 1997. *On Queer Street: A Social History of British Homosexuality 1895–1995*. London: HarperCollins.

Humphrey, J.C. 2000. 'Cracks in the Feminist Mirror? Research and Reflections on Lesbians and Gay Men Working Together'. *Feminist Review*, 66 (Political Currents), 95–130.

Humphries, L. 1970. *Tearoom Trade: A Study of Homosexual Encounters in Public Places*. London: Duckworth.

Ito, M., Okabe, D. and Anderson, K. 2008. 'Portable Objects in Three Global Cities' in *The Reconstruction of Space and Time* edited by R. Ling and S.W. Campbell. Edison, NJ: Transaction, 67–88.

Jackson, E. 1995. *Strategies of Deviance: Studies in Gay Male Representation*. Bloomington: Indiana University Press.

Jeffrey-Poulter, S. 1991. *Peers, Queers & Commons: The Struggle for Gay Law Reform from 1950 to the Present*. London: Routledge.

Johnson, P. 2007. 'Ordinary Folk, and Cottaging: Law, Morality and Public Sex'. *Journal of Law and Society*, 34(4), 520–543.

Jones, A. 2002. 'The "Eternal Return": Self-Portrait Photography as a Technology of Embodiment'. *Signs: Journal of Women in Culture and Society,* 27(4), 947–948.

Jones, S.G. 1995. *Cybersociety: Computer-Mediated Communication and Community*. London: Sage.

LeVay, S. and Nonas, E. 1995. *City of Friends: A Portrait of the Gay and Lesbian Community in America*. Cambridge, MA: MIT Press.

Kappeler, S. 1986. *The Pornography of Representation*. Cambridge: Polity Press.

Kaye, K. 2004. 'Male Prostitution in the Twentieth Century'. *Journal of Homosexuality*, 46(1), 1–77.

Kendall, L. 2002. *Hanging Out in the Virtual Pub: Masculinities and Relationships Online*. London: University of California Press.

Kibby, M. and Costello, B. 1999. 'Displaying the Phallus: Masculinity and the Performance of Sexuality on the Internet'. *Men and Masculinities*, 1(4), 352–364.

Kimmel, M.S. 1991. 'Introduction: Guilty Pleasures – Pornography in Men's Lives' in *Men Confront Pornography* edited by M.S. Kimmel. New York: Meridian, 1–22.

Kindberg, T. and Jones, T. 2007. '"Merolyn the Phone": A Study of Bluetooth Naming Practices' [Online]. Available at: http://citeseerx.ist.psu.edu/viewdoc/summary?doi=10.1.1.84.9010 [accessed 19 November 2009].

King, E. 1993. *Safety in Numbers: Safer Sex and Gay Men*. London: Cassell.

Kinsey, A.C. 1948 [1998]. *Sexual Behaviour in the Human Male*. Bloomington: Indiana University Press.

Kitchin, R. 1998. *Cyberspace: The World in Wires*. Chichester: Wiley and Sons.

Knight, B.A. 2000. 'Watch Me! Webcams and the Public Exposure of Private Lives'. *Art Journal*, 59(4) 21–25.

Knopp, L. 2004. 'Ontologies of Place, Placeless and Movement: Queer Quests for Identity and their Impacts on Contemporary Geographic Thought'. *Gender, Place and Culture*, 11(1), 121–34.

Kramer, L. 1983. '1112 and Counting'. *New York Native*, 14–27 March 1983, 21–27.

Kramer, L. 1990. *Reports from the Holocaust: The Making of an AIDS Activist*. London: Penguin.

Kramer, L. 2004. *Cooper Union Address* [Online]. Available at: http://towleroad.typepad.com/towleroad/2004/11/larry_kramer_sp.html [accessed 31 May 2005].

Kuntsman, A. 2007. 'Belonging Through Violence: Flaming, Erasure and Performativity in Queer Migrant Community' in *Queer Online: Media, Technology and Sexuality* edited by K. O'Riordan and D.J. Phillips. Oxford: Peter Lang, 101–120.

Lacan, J. 1999. *Ecrits: A Selection* (trans. Sheridan, A.). London: Routledge.

Lawson, H.M. and Leck, K. 2006. 'Dynamics of Internet Dating'. *Social Science Computer Review*, 24(2), 189–208.

Leap, W.L. 1996. *Words Out: Gay Men's English*. Minneapolis: University of Minnesota Press.

Lent, A. 2003. 'The Transformation of Gay and Lesbian Politics in Britain'. *The British Journal of Politics and International Relations*, 5(1), 24–49.

Lin, D.C. 2006. 'Sissies Online: Taiwanese Male Queers Performing Sissinesses in Cyberspaces'. *Inter-Asia Cultural Studies*, 7(2), 270–288.

Ling, R. 2004. *The Mobile Connection: The Cell Phone's Impact on Society*. San Francisco: Morgan Kaufmann.

Lumsden, A. 1988. 'Parrot Cries' in *Radical Records: Thirty Years of Lesbian and Gay History* edited by B. Cant and S. Hemmings. London: Routledge, 195–205.

MacKinnon, C. 2000. 'The Roar on the Other Side of Silence' in *Feminism and Pornography* edited by D. Cornell. Oxford: Oxford University Press, 130–144.

Macnair, B. 1996. *Mediated Sex: Pornography and Postmodern Culture*. London: Arnold.

Macrae, S. 1997. 'Flesh Made Word: Sex Text and the Virtual Body' in *Internet Culture* edited by D. Porter. London: Routledge, 73–86.

Malinger, M.S. (1998) *About Anal Sex, Barebacking: Slogans Aren't Enough* [Online]. Available at: http://gaytoday.badpuppy.com/garchive/viewpoint/040698vi.htm [accessed 12 February 2010].

Malinowski, B. 1923. 'The Problem of Meaning in Primitive Languages' in *The Meaning of Meaning* edited by C.K. Ogden and I.A. Richards. London: Routledge, 146–152.

McAllester, M. 2009. 'The Hunted'. *New York Magazine*, 12 October, np.

McCarthy, M. 2003. 'Talking Back: "Small" Interactional Response Tokens in Everyday Conversation'. *Research on Language and Social Interaction*, 36(1), 33–63.

McIntosh, M. 1993. 'Queer Theory and the War of the Sexes' in *Activating Theory: Lesbian, Gay, Bisexual Politics* edited by J. Bristow and A. Wilson. London: Lawrence & Wishart, 30–52.

McLelland, M. 2000. *Male Homosexuality in Modern Japan: Cultural Myths and Social Realities*. Surrey: Curzon Press.

McLelland, M. 2001. *Out on the Global Stage: Authenticity, Interpretation and Orientalism in Japanese Coming Out Narratives* [Online]. Available at: www.japanesestudies.org.uk/articles/Mclelland.htm [accessed 11 October 2002].

Medhurst, A. 1998. 'Tracing Desires: Sexuality in Media Texts' in *The Media: A Critical Introduction* edited by A. Briggs and P. Cobley. Harlow: Pearson Education, 283–294.

Medhurst, A. 2000. 'If Anywhere: Class Identifications and Cultural Studies Academics' in *Cultural Studies and the Working Class – Subject to Change* edited by S. Munt. London: Cassell, 19–35.

Meiring, J. 2006. 'Gaydar Love'. *The Sunday Times* (South Africa), 11 June, 12.

Mercer, K. 1993. 'Looking For Trouble' in *The Lesbian and Gay Studies Reader* edited by H. Abelove, M.A. Barale and D.M. Halperin. London: Routledge, 350–359.

Metz, C. 1985. 'Photography and Fetish'. *October*, 34 (Fall), 81–90.

Miller, V. 2009. 'New Media, Networking and Phatic Culture'. *Convergence: The International Journal of Research into New Media Technologies*, 14(4), 387–400.

Mitra, R. and Gajjala, R. 2008. 'Queer Blogging in Indian Digital Diasporas: A Dialogic Encounter'. *Journal of Communication Inquiry*, 32(4), 400–423.

Moon, D. 1995. 'Insult and Inclusion: The Term *Fag Hag* and Gay "Community"'. *Social Forces*, 74(2), 487–510.

Morgan, R. 1980. 'Theory and Practice: Pornography and Rape' in *Take Back The Night: Women on Pornography* edited by L. Lederer. New York: William Morrow and Co., 134–140.

Mort, F. 1996. *Cultures of Consumption: Masculinities and Social Space in Late Twentieth Century Britain*. London: Routledge.

Morton, D. 1995. 'Queerity and Ludic Sado-Masochism: Compulsory Consumption and the Emerging 'Post-al' Queer'' *in Post-Ality: Marxism and Postmodernism*

(Transformation 1) edited by M. Zavarzadeh, D. Zavarzadeh and D. Morton. Washington DC: Maisonneuve Press, 185–215.

Morton, D. 1996. 'Changing The Terms: (Virtual) Desire and (Actual) Reality' in *The Material Queer: LesBiGay Cultural Studies Reader,* edited by D, Morton. Colorado: Westview Oxford, 1–34.

Morton, D. 1999. 'Birth of the Cyberqueer' in *Cybersexualities: A Reader in Feminist Theory, Cyborgs and Cyberspace* edited by J. Wolmark. Edinburgh: Edinburgh University Press, 295–313.

Mowlabocus, S. 2009. 'Porn 2.0? Technology, Social Practice and the New Online Porn Industry' in *Porn.com: Making Sense of Online Pornography* edited by F. Attwood. New York: Peter Lang, 69–87.

Mukerji, C. and Simon, B. 1998. 'Out of the Limelight: Discredited Communities and Informal Communication on the Internet'. *Sociological Inquiry*, 68(2), 258–273.

Mulvey, L. 1975. 'Visual Pleasure and Narrative Cinema'. *Screen*, 16(3), 6–18.

Neale, S. 1983. 'Masculinity as Spectacle: Reflections on Men and Mainstream Cinema'. *Screen*, 24(6), 2–17.

Nevins, P. 1991. 'The Making of a Radical Blackgay Man' in *High Risk Lives: Lesbian and Gay Politics After The Clause* edited by T. Kauffman, and P. Lincoln. Bridport, Dorset: Prism Press, 93–108.

Nip, J. 2004. 'The Queer Sisters and its Electronic Bulletin Board: A Study of the Internet for Social Movement Mobilization'. *Information, Communication and Society*, 7(1), 23–49.

Norton, R. 1992. *Mother Clap's Molly House: The Gay Subculture in England, 1700–1830.* London: Gay Men's Press.

OfCom 2004. *The OfCom Internet and Broadband Update – April 2004*. Available at: www.ofcom.org.uk/research/telecoms/reports/bbresearch/int_bband_updt/may2004 [accessed 14 April 2009].

Offord, B. 2003. 'Singaporean Queering of the Internet: Toward a New Form of Cultural Transmission of Rights Discourse', in *Mobile Cultures: New Media in Queer Asia*, edited by C. Berry, F. Martin and A. Yue. London: Duke University Press, 133–157.

O'Hara, S. (1998). *Rarely Pure and Never Simple: Selected Essays of Scott O'Hara*. London: Haworth Press.

O'Riordan, K. 2007. 'Queer Theories and Cybersubjects: Intersecting Figures' in *Queer Online: Media, Technology and Sexuality* edited by K. O'Riordan and D.J. Phillips. Oxford: Peter Lang, 13–30.

O'Toole, L. 1999. *Pornocopia: Porn, Sex, Technology and Desire*. London: Serpents Tail.

Palmer, A. 1995. 'Lesbian and Gay Rights Campaigning: A Report from the Coalface' in *A Simple Matter of Justice? Theorizing Lesbian and Gay Politics* edited by A.R. Wilson. London: Cassell, 32–50.

Patton, C. 1991. 'Safe Sex and the Pornographic Vernacular' in *How Do I Look? Queer Film and Video* edited by Bad Object Choices. Seattle: Bay Press, 31–64.

Patton, C. 1996. *Fatal Advice: How Safe Sex Education Went Wrong*. Durham: Duke University Press.

Peacock, B., Eyre, S. L., Quinn, S.C. and Kegeles, S. 2001. 'Delineating Differences: Sub-communities in the San Francisco Gay Community'. *Culture, Health and Sexuality*, 3(2), 183–201.

Plant, S. 1997. *Zeroes and Ones: Digital Women and the New Technoculture*. New York: Doubleday.

Power, L. 1995. *No Bath But Plenty of Bubbles: An Oral History of the Gay Liberation Front 1970–73*. London: Cassell.

Pringle, K., Kaufmann, T. and Lincoln, P. 1991. 'Clause 28 in Practice' in *High Risk Lives: Lesbian and Gay Politics After The Clause* edited by T. Kauffman, and P. Lincoln. Bridport, Dorset: Prism Press, 4–12.

Provine, R.R., Spencer, R.J. and Mandell, D.L. 2007. 'Emotional Expression Online: Emoticons Punctuate Website Text Messages'. *Journal of Language and Social Psychology*, 26(3), 299–307.

Puar, J.K. 2006. 'Mapping US Homonormativities'. *Gender, Place & Culture*, 13(1), 67–88.

Pullen, C. 2004. 'The Household, The Basement and The Real World: Gay Identity in the Constructed Reality Environment' in *Understanding Reality Television* edited by S. Holmes and D. Jermyn. London: Routledge, 211–232.

QX International – GMFA advert. Issue 365, November 2001, 36.

QX International – Westminster Primary Care Group NHS advert. Issue 368, February 2002, np.

QX International Issue 373, March 2002.

QX Magazine Issue 461, December 2003.

Radel, N.F. 2001. 'The Transnational Ga(y)ze: Constructing the East European Object of Desire in Gay Film and Pornography after the Fall of the Wall'. *Cinema Journal*, 41(1) 40–62.

Rahman, M. 2001. *Sexuality and Democracy: Identities and Strategies in Lesbian and Gay Politics*. Edinburgh: Edinburgh University Press.

Rayside, D. 1998. *On The Fringe: Gays & Lesbians In Politics*. London: Cornell University Press.

Reaney, D. 2000. 'What's Behind Barebacking' in *MetroM8 F***sheet*, August 2000, Issue 57 [Online]. Available at: www.metromate.org.uk/fsheet/57/wbb.phtml [accessed 15 August 2004].

Rechy, J. 1978 [1984]. *The Sexual Outlaw: A Documentary*. London: W.H. Allen.

Reddick, A. 2006. 'Dangerous Practices: Ideological Uses of the "Second Wave"' in *Policing Public Sex: Queer Politics and the Future of Aids Activism* edited by Dangerous Bedfellows. Boston, MA: South End Press, 91–104.

Rheingold, H. 1993. *Virtual Community: Finding Connection in a Computerized World*. London: Minerva Press.

Ridge, D., Hee, A. and Minichiello, V. 1999. '"Asian" Men on the Scene'. *Journal of Homosexuality*, 36(3), 43–68.

Rimmerman, C.A. 2000. 'Beyond Political Mainstreaming: Reflections on Lesbian and Gay Organizations and the Grassroots', in *The Politics of Gay Rights* edited by C.A. Rimmerman, K.D. Wald and C. Wilcox. Chicago: University of Chicago Press, 54–78.

Rofes, E. 1998. *Dry Bones Breathe: Gay Men Creating Post-AIDS Identities and Cultures*. New York: Harrington Park Press.

Rotello, G. 1997. *Sexual Ecology: AIDS and the Destiny of Gay Men*. New York: Dutton.

Russell, J. 2005. 'Bio-Power and Biohazards: A Projective System Reading of Gay Men's Community-Based HIV Prevention'. *Journal of Culture, Health and Sexuality*, 7(2), 145–158.

Russo, V. 1987. *The Celluloid Closet: Homosexuality in the Movies*. New York: Harper & Row.

Sadar, Z. 1995. 'alt.civilizations.faq: Cyberspace as the Darker Side of the West'. *Futures*, 27(7), 717–794.

Sandell, J. 1996. 'Reinventing Masculinity: The Spectacle of Male Intimacy in the Films of John Woo'. *Film Quarterly*, 49(4), 23–34.

Sarhan, A. and Burke, J. 2009. 'How Islamists Track and Kill Iraq's Gays'. *The Observer*, 13 September, 34.

Scarce, M. 1999. 'A Ride on the Wild Side'. *Poz Magazine* [Online]. Available at: www.poz.com/articles/february1999/inside/rideonthewildeside.html#safer [accessed 9 July 2002].

Schwartz, M.F. and Southern, S. 2000. 'Compulsive Cybersex: The New Tea Room'. *Cybersex: The Dark Side of the Force – A Special Issue of the Journal Sexual Addiction & Compulsivity*, 7(1 and 2), 127–144.

Schwartzberg, S. 1996. *A Crisis of Meaning: How Gay Men Are Making Sense of AIDS*. New York: Open University Press.

Scott, P., Coxon, A., Kirk, M. and Pinson, D. 1998. *Cottaging and Cruising in Barnet, Brent and Harrow: Final Project Report* [Online]. Available at: http://www.racoon.dircon.co.uk/bbh/f3.htm [accessed 23 May 2003].

Sedgwick, E.K. 1991. *Epistemology of the Closet*. Herts: Harvester Wheatsheaf.

Sharratt, T. 1987. 'Home Office may Gag Anderton: Prophet Police Chief is Ordered to London for Urgent Talks'. *The Guardian*, 21 January, np.

Shaw, D.F. 1997. 'Gay Men and Computer Communication: A Discourse of Sex and Identity in Cyberspace' in *Virtual Culture: Identity and Communication in Cyberspace* edited by S.G. Jones. London: Sage, 133–145.

Sheller, M. and Urry, J. 2003. 'Mobile Transformations of 'Public' and 'Private' Life'. *Theory, Culture and Society*, 20(3), 107–125.

Sheon, N. and Plant, A. 1997. *Protease Dis-inhibitors? The Gay Bareback Phenomenon* [Online]. Available at: http://www.managingdesire.org/TheorizingDesire.html [accessed 12 February 2010].

Sherwood, J. 2001. 'Now the Fear Has Gone a Red Ribbon Means You're Available'. *The Independent*, 26 January 2001, 3.
Shilts, R. 1987. *And The Band Played On*. New York: Stonewall Inn Editions.
Sibalis, M. 2004. 'Urban Space and Homosexuality: The Example of the Marais, Paris' "gayghetto"'. *Urban Studies*, 41, 1739–1758.
Signorile, M. 1995. 'Taking Responsibility and Seeing Why We Should'. *Reproductive Health Matters*, 3(5), 121–123.
Signorile, M. 1997. *Life Outside; The Signorile Report on Gay Men: Sex, Drugs, Muscles, and the Passages of Life*. New York: HarperCollins.
Signorile, M. 2002. *The "Bareback" Lie*. [Online]. Available at: www.signorile.com/articles/nyp37.html [accessed 3 June 2003].
Simpson, M. 1999. 'Gay Dream Believer: Inside the Gay Underwear Cult' in *Anti-Gay* edited by M. Simpson. London: Cassell, 1–12.
Simpson, M. 2003. 'Confessions of a Gaydar Junkie'. *The Independent on Sunday*, 7 December, 17.
Sinfield, A. 1997. 'Identity and Subculture' in *Lesbian and Gay Studies: A Critical Introduction* edited by A. Medhurst and S. Munt. London: Cassell, 201–214.
Sinfield, A. 1998. *Gay and After*. London: Serpent's Tail.
Skeggs, B., Moran, L., Tyrer, P. and Binnie, J. 2004. 'Queer as Folk: Producing the Real of Urban Space'. *Urban Studies*, 41, 1839–1856.
Slater, D. 1998. 'Trading Sex-pics on IRC: Embodiment and Authenticity on the Internet'. *Body and Society*, 4(4), 91–117.
Smith, D. 2008. 'Sex Uncovered; Cybersex'. *The Observer*, 26 October, 49.
Stallabrass, J. 1996. *Garguantua: Manufactured Mass Culture*. London: Verso.
Stoltenberg, J. 1991. 'Gays and the Pro-pornography Movement: Having the Hots for Sex Discrimination' in *Men Confront Pornography* edited by M.S. Kimmel. New York: Meridian, 248–262.
Stone, A.R. 1998. *The War of Desire and Technology at the Close of the Mechanical Age*. Cambridge, Mass: MIT Press.
Stone, A.R. 2000. 'Will the Real Body Please Stand Up? Boundary Stories about Virtual Cultures' in *The Cybercultures Reader* edited by D.Bell and B. Kennedy. London: Routledge, 504–528.
Strossen, N. 1995. *Defending Pornography: Free Speech, Sex and the Fight For Women's Rights*. New York: Scribner.
Strub, S.O. 1999. '"Safer Barebacking" is in the Grassroots, Take-Charge-of-Your-Own-Life Tradition Pioneered by Michael Callen'. *Poz Magazine* [Online]. Available at: http://www.poz.com/articles/211_7124.shtml [accessed 12 February 2010].
Strudwick, P. 2009. 'Under the Gaydar'. *The Observer*, 28 June, 24.
Suffredini, K. 2001. 'Pride and Prejudice: The Homosexual Panic Defense'. *Boston College Third World Law Journal*, 21, 279–314.
Sullivan, A. 1998. *Love Undetectable*. London: Vintage.
Sullivan, D. 2006. 'Saudi Youth Use Cellphone Savvy to Outwit the Sentries of Romance'. *Washington Post*, 6 August, np.

Tatchell, P. 1999. 'Its Just a Phase: Why Homosexuality is Doomed' in *Anti-Gay* edited by M. Simpson. London: Cassell, 35–54.

Tattelman, I. 1999. 'Speaking to the Gay Bathhouse: Communicating in Sexually Charged Spaces' in *Public Sex/Gay Space* edited by W.L. Leap. New York: Columbia University Press, 71–94.

Taylor, M. 1999. 'Give It To Me Raw Big Boy'. *Outcast Magazine* [Online]. Available at: http://www.outcastmagazine.co.uk/13004htm [accessed 13 August 2003].

Tomsen, S. 2006. 'Homophobic Violence, Cultural Essentialism and Shifting Sexual Identities'. *Social and Legal Studies*, 15(3), 389–407.

Treichler, P.A. 1997. 'How to Use a Condom: Lessons from the AIDS Epidemic' in *Acting On AIDS: Sex, Drugs & Politics* edited by J. Barrett, J. Oppenhiemer and H. Reckitt. London: Serpent's Tail, 34–57.

Tsang, D.C. 1996. 'Notes on Queer 'n' Asian Virtual Sex' in *The Material Queer: LesBiGay Cultural Studies Reader*, edited by D. Morton. Colorado: Westview Press, 310–316.

Tucker, S. 1991. 'Radical Feminism and Gay Male Porn' in *Men Confront Pornography* edited by M.S. Kimmel. New York: Meridian, 263–276.

Turkle, S. 1995 [1998]. *Life On The Screen: Identity in the Age of the Internet*. Cambridge, Mass: Simon and Schuster.

Urbach, H. 1996. 'Closets, Clothes, Disclosure'. *Assemblage*, 30, 62–73.

Valenzuela, T. 1999. *Barebacking is a Cherished Act* [Online]. Available at: http://www.xtra.ca/site/toronto2/arch/body166.shtm [accessed 7 June 2003].

Valocchi, S. 1999. 'The Class-Inflected Nature of Gay Identity'. *Social Problems*, 46(2), 207–224.

Wakeford, N. 1997. 'Cyberqueer' in *Lesbian and Gay Studies: A Critical Introduction* edited by A. Medhurst and S. Munt. London: Cassell, 20–38.

Wakeford, N. 2001. 'Cyberqueer' in *The Cybercultures Reader* edited by D. Bell and B.M. Kennedy. London: Routledge, 350–359.

Walters, A. 1980. *Come Together: The Years of Gay Liberation 1970–73*. London: Gay Men's Press.

Walther, J.B., Lo, T. and Granka, L. 2005. 'Let Me Count the Ways: The Interchange of Verbal and Nonverbal Cues in Computer-Mediated and Face-to-Face Affinity'. *Journal of Language and Social Psychology*, 24(1), 36–65.

Warner, M. 1991. 'Introduction: Fear of a Queer Planet'. *Social Text*, 29, 3–17.

Watney, S. 1994. *Practices of Freedom: Selected Writings on HIV/AIDS*. London: Rivers Oram Press.

Watney, S. 1996. *Policing Desire: Pornography, AIDS and the Media*. Minneapolis: University of Minnesota Press.

Watney, S. 2000. *Imagine Hope: AIDS and Gay Identity*. London: Routledge.

Weeks, J. 1990. *Coming Out: Homosexual Politics in Britain from the Nineteenth Century to the Present*. London: Quartet Books.

Weeks, J. 1991. *Against Nature: Essays on History, Sexuality and Identity*. London: Rivers Oram Press.

Weinstein, D. and Weinstein, M.A. 2000. 'Net Game Cameo' in *The Cybercultures Reader* edited by D. Bell and B.M. Kennedy. London: Routledge, 210–215.

Wells, M. 2000. 'Sex On The Edge'. *The Guardian*, 14 March, 2.

Whisnant, C.J. 2003. 'Masculinity and Desire in the Works of J.R. Ackerley'. *Journal of Homosexuality*, 43(2), 127–142.

Wilbur, S.P. 1997. 'An Archaeology of Cyberspaces: Virtuality, Community, Identity' in *Internet Culture* edited by D. Porter. London: Routledge, 5–22.

Williams, L. 1992. 'Pornography on/scene or Diff'rent Strokes for Diff'rent Folks' in *Sex Exposed: Sexuality and the Pornography Debate* edited by L. Segal and M. McIntosh. London: Virago, 233–265.

Wilson, E. 1992. 'Feminist Fundamentalism' in *Sex Exposed: Sexuality and the Pornography Debate* edited by L. Segal and M. McIntosh. London: Virago, 15–28.

Winner, L. 1986. *The Whale and the Reactor: A Search For Limits in an Age of High Technology*. Chicago: University of Chicago Press.

Wittel, A. 2001. 'Toward a Network Sociality'. *Theory, Culture and Society*, 18(6), 51–76.

Woodland, R. 2001. 'Queer Spaces, Modem Boys and Pagan Statues' in *The Cybercultures Reader* edited by D. Bell and B.M. Kennedy. London: Routledge, 416–431.

Zegarac, V. and Clark, B. 1999. 'Phatic Interpretations and Phatic Communication'. *Journal of Linguistics*, 35(2), 321–346.

Websites

Act-Up New York – transcript of Vito Russo speech. Available at: www.actupny.org/documents/whfight.html [accessed 16 November 2004].

AEGIS – The AIDS Education Global Information Service. Available at: www.aegis.com/topics/timeline/default.asp [accessed 16 November 2004].

Avert – AIDS Statistics – UK. Available at: www.avert.org.uk/statsyr.htm. [accessed 16 November 2004].

Bareback.com – Ask Mike. Available at: http://www.bareback.com/askmike/kb.asp?list=36 [accessed 25 January 2004].

Bareback.com – Mission Statement. Available at: http://www.bareback.com [accessed 2 February 2004].

BarebackJack.com. Available at: http://www.barebackjack.com [accessed 15 January 2004].

BarebackJack.com – Health. Available at: http://www.barebackjack.com/health.html [accessed 15 January 2004].

BarebackJack.com – Jack's Perspective. Available at: http://www.barebackjack.com/perspective.html [accessed 15 January 2004].

BarebackJack.com – Letters. Available at: http://www.barebackjack.com/dearjackmain.html [accessed 15 January 2004].

BarebackJack.com – Headline News. Available at: http://www.barebackjack.com [accessed 29 July 2005].

BarebackUK.com. Available at: http://www.barebackuk.com [accessed 15 January 2004].

Bluejackq.com – The Worlds First and Most Authoritative Website dedicated to Bluejacking. Available at: www.bluejackq.com/what-is-bluejacking.shtml [accessed 15 November 2009].

Channel 4's Gay-O-Meter. Available at: www.channel4.com/life/microsites/G/gayometer/gayometer.html.html [accessed 9 February 2010].

Coming Out Stories. Available at: www.comingoutstories.com [accessed 17 January 2003].

Gay Cottaging GB. Available at: www.gaycottaginguk.co.uk [accessed 10 November 2005].

Gay DVD Sex Videos Online – Store and Reviews. Available at: www.gaydvdsexvideos.com/dvd-genres.html [accessed 12 February 2005].

Gay History Today. Available at: www.gayhistory.com/rev2/factfiles/ff1948.htm. [accessed 26 March 2005].

Gaydar. Available at: www.Gaydar.co.uk [accessed 9 February 2005].

George House Trust. Available at: www.ght.org.uk [accessed 18 July 2004].

Grindr. Available at: http://tinyurl.com/ydjx263 [accessed 12 September 2009].

Knitting Circle Lesbian and Gay History – A Timetable of Lesbian and Gay History. Available at: myweb.lsbu.ac.uk/~stafflag/timetable.html [accessed 28 November 2004].

Life or Meth.com. Available at: www.lifeormeth.com [accessed 5 December 2009].

Macword – Boy Ahoy app review. Available at: http://www.macworld.com/appguide/app.html?id=92165&expand=false [accessed 12 September 2009].

Mad.bear.org – Madrid's Gay Bear website. Available at: http://tinyurl.com/y8gchac [accessed 15 November 2009].

*MetroM8 F*ctsheet* (2000) *Watchdog to Probe GMFA Bareback Ads*. Available at: www.metromate.org.uk/fsheet/57/wtpgb.phtml [accessed 13 January 2002].

Mind – The Mental Health Charity. Available at: www.mind.org.uk/Mind/Templates/Content [accessed 31 May 2005].

National AIDS Manual. Available at: http://www.aidsmap.com/cms1038153.aspx [accessed 8 February 2010].

OutRage! Available at: www.outrage.org.uk. [accessed 20 November 2004].

Pink Paper – remit. Available at: www.pinkpaper.com/JD04/tmPgs/office/index.lasso [accessed 6 November 2004].

Purpll. Available at: http://www.rippll.com/purpll/ [accessed 12 September 2009].

QSoft Consulting. Available at: www.qsoft.co.uk [accessed 22 June 2005].

QSoft Consulting – Awards. Available at: www.qsoft.co.uk/content/about_awards.aspx [accessed 19 January 2009].

Squirt. Available at: www.squirt.org [accessed 16 October 2008].

Stonewall – Civil Partnership Bill. Available at: www.stonewall.org.uk/stonewall/information_bank/partnership/civil_partnership_bill/#2 [accessed 29 November 2004].

Stonewall – Organisational Information and Remit. Available at: www.stonewall.org.uk/stonewall/about_us/brief_overview_of_stonewall/ [accessed 29 November 2004].

Straightacting.com – Your Masculine Gay Guy Hangout. Available at: www.straightacting.com [accessed 9 February 2010].

The Tatchell Rights Fund. Available at: www.tatchellrightsfund.org/aboutpeter.htm [accessed 2 November 2004].

Tatchell Website. Available at: www.tatchell.net [accessed 2 November 2004].

The Terrence Higgins Trust – Gay Men's Health. Available at: http://www.tht.org.uk/informationresources/professionals/chaps/ [accessed 12 February 2010].

The Terrence Higgins Trust – History of Organisation. Available at: www.tht.org.uk/about_us/history.htm [accessed 9 November 2004].

The Terrence Higgins Trust – Statistics. Available at: www.tht.org.uk/hiv_info/stats.htm [accessed 15 November 2010].

Vidshop.com – The Very Best in Adult Entertainment. Available at: www.vidshop.com/main.php [accessed 12 February 2005].

Film and Television

Bad Lad's Army [Television] (ITV Productions, 2004).

Cruising (dir. W. Friedkin, 1980).

Lads Army [Television] (ITV Productions, 2002).

Queer As Folk, Series 1 [Television] (Channel 4 Productions, 1999).

Philadelphia (dir. J. Demme, 1993).

Priest (dir. A. Bird, 1994).

Sex and the City, Season II [DVD] (dir. D. Star, 1999).

The Likely Lads [Television] (Clement and Le Frenais, 1964).

Index

Figures are indicated by **bold** page numbers, tables by *italic* numbers.